PROPERTY LADDER

THE DEVELOPER'S BIBLE

PROPERTY LADDER

THE DEVELOPER'S BIBLE

SARAH BEENY

WITH BARTY PHILLIPS

CASSELL
ILLUSTRATED

TO THE PERFECT BILLY

First published in Great Britain in 2004 by
Cassell Illustrated
a division of Octopus Publishing Group Limited
2–4 Heron Quays, London E14 4JP

Text copyright © 2004 Talkback (UK) Productions
part of the FremantleMedia Group
Design copyright © 2004 Octopus Publishing
Group Limited

Text by Sarah Beeny with Barty Phillips
Editorial, design and layout by Essential Works

A CIP catalogue record for this book is available
from the British Library.

ISBN 1 84403 279 5
EAN 9781844032792
Printed in Italy by Printer Trento S.r.l.

CONTENTS

INTRODUCTION

Every time I have a question about just about anything in life I ring my father – who in the last 32 years I have discovered generally either knows the answer or has an amazing ability to just happen to have a book to hand with an answer within. The great thing about this telephonic encyclopedia is that the answer is pretty concise and easy to understand and if not you can always ask for a more understandable explanation. For those of you not fortunate enough to have my father's phone number, you have this book! Within its pages I hope you will find clear, easy to understand and comprehensive information covering just about all your building questions, starting with getting onto the property ladder or dabbling in your first development and your next purchases after that.

It is clear that up-to-date information is what is desperately needed to have an accurate picture of the market. Here we have provided as much information as we can and guided you in the right direction as to how to get more specific details together about your particular property. I personally believe that you can never know everything about anything so there will always be more to learn.

It is now about four years since *Property Ladder* the series first started and so much has changed in that time. The property market itself has fluctuated, though actually so far remained relatively stable, but our television screens are now quite literally full of variations on the theme with some more entertaining and/or informative than others, but just about all containing the odd nugget of useful information to take away. Watching them all would be such a full-time job that you would have no time to put the knowledge you have gained into practice, so hopefully

now you can watch those that entertain you and delve into this book for any information you require.

During these last years, though, there has clearly been no decline in the nation's interest in buildings – how and why we live the way we do has been pondered on endlessly. Since thousands of years ago, when we all lived in caves, we have wanted our surroundings to be not only comfortable but also aesthetically pleasing and so it is not surprising that there is a demand for our homes to evolve in both ways.

The design of a house is therefore about both these important issues. A perfect home must not only be lovely to look at but also lovely to live in and with such a rich and diverse population there are many different variations on what these ideals involve. What I am endlessly impressed with, is people's willingness to 'have a go' and stamp their own very personal mark on their home. Varying from the monastically minimalist to the wild and wacky, the personal expression not to mention time and effort devoted is something it is impossible not to admire.

Does all this home-creating make us happier? That I'm not sure about – although most psychologists agree that

During these last years, though, there has clearly been no decline in the nation's interest in buildings

one's surroundings play an important part in personal contentment. As long as it's not to the detriment of interest in the general community, being inwardly content with the walls around you can only be a good thing. If we can be depressed by lack of light, I believe we can also be depressed by lack of design.

So developing is not only a business but can be a therapy! However, when you are developing you need to walk the fence of creating the perfect home without making it your own statement of personal expression. First, houses must be practical; but what was practical years ago may no longer be, as the galley kitchen shows. The days when whoever was cooking would disappear and busy themselves are pretty much defunct. We now have convenience foods requiring just the ping of the microwave and what spare time we do have we want to spend socialising with the whole family, so the kitchen/breakfast/living room is now well established as a number one design favourite. No doubt in 50 years' time things will have moved on again but for now big, flexible space is the order of the day.

Fashions in decoration move on more quickly as they do not require our actual lifestyles to evolve in order to change. In many ways it is here that most people can indulge themselves with a bit of creative flair in their own homes. My only piece of advice is stick with it – don't chicken out of a decorative concept halfway through or it will be unlikely to work. Once you have the initial idea, go ahead, dare yourself to really carry it off – unless, of course, the house is a development project, in which case make the house work for your market and let the new purchaser of the building turn it into their home.

I
THE MARKET

THE MARKET

Whether you are just looking for a new home to live in and develop, buying to sell, or buying to let, getting to grips with the housing market is your first important task. This involves the general market conditions – which govern the type and price of property, supply and demand, interest rates and the scale of your profit – as well as correctly targeting the market for your property through informed development. To familiarise yourself with the market, you are going to need to do some research. Get to know which areas are on the up, the different periods and styles of architecture and different building techniques, so that you can plan development that's in keeping with the local building style and attractive to your market. Research areas thoroughly so you can really target the sort of people who will want to live there, and keep your target market well in mind as you start to draw up your plans.

If you are buying a home I have only two pieces of advice: don't overstretch yourself financially and don't be tempted to buy anything other than a type of house you want to live in, in an area you want to be in. You can invest all the money you can afford and make the place as personal as you like. You can indulge your creative talents and passions and stamp your own style right across it.

However, things are different when you are buying to sell or let. Then it becomes a business and to succeed you must be very businesslike about it. The safest development is one that will appeal to as wide a section of the population as possible. More specifically, it should appeal to the sorts of people who want and are able to live in the area. There's no point in refurbishing a property suited to well-off young high-flyers if there are no suitable jobs locally and no transport. Tumbledown old chapels, chocolate-box thatched cottages and disused mills may have the qualities that make up your own romantic dream, but tread carefully as romance is a very personal notion and you need to ensure there is a market for your product.

To appeal to the widest possible market, look at the location, size, layout and facilities the property offers and the local amenities. This is where any research you do about the area you've chosen pays off. You can find out whether there is actually a market for the property you want to develop. And remember, this is not a home for you but for your potential buyer/renter.

Property development works on the basis of supply and demand. Your task is to create a desirable product for an existing market. The better the picture you have of your potential market, the more able you will be to design for their needs.

The first thing to do is identify this market. Much will depend on where you want to do your developing.

WHERE TO BUY

Choosing where to buy your property is a very important consideration. Don't rely on chance. Consider the people who will want to live there and what factors might put them off; a desirable property situated in the wrong street or the wrong area may spell disaster. Time spent on research at this stage will pay dividends.

DECIDING ON AN AREA

The age-old adage location, location, location is as valid now as it has ever been. But along with location you need to consider the situation of any development. Where you buy your property will have an important bearing on who you will sell it to. Properties vary enormously in style, cost and potential in different parts of the country. In some areas, particularly those where there is widespread unemployment, property may be easy and cheap to buy but difficult to sell. In other areas that are more affluent, houses are much more difficult and more expensive to buy.

It is partly this lack of supply that forces owner-occupiers to buy unmodernised homes for premium prices, leaving no space for any profit to be made by the company or individual for actually doing the work.

A site near you

Especially if you are relatively inexperienced, it is best to choose somewhere near to where you live. You can then properly get to know the area and will be able to get a feel for the market. If you are brave enough to choose somewhere far afield, you might follow the example of Kim in Series 3, who drove her car down the motorway until she came to an area she could afford. Even then, she booked herself into a B&B there and got to know the area well before committing herself to buying a property.

Do the research

As in any business, it is important that you get every aspect right from the beginning, so do the research. Find out what sort of properties have recently sold and for what price in the area you've chosen. You need to know all about an area in order to make a wise investment of your money and be confident you can succeed there.

WHAT YOU NEED TO FIND OUT

Background knowledge is the key to many successful businesses and local knowledge gives valuable insights into the sort of people who live in the area and therefore what sort of properties it is most logical to buy. The following are all important to know:

Transport

- How good is the local bus system? Do the buses have low platforms to take buggies and wheelchairs?
- Is there a train system? How frequent and reliable is the service? Do the trains run to the nearest big cities?
- Is there an underground transport system and are there suitable properties near to an underground station?
- How convenient/expensive are local parking facilities?

Education

- Are there plenty of good nursery schools and other pre-school facilities?
- Are there plenty of primary and secondary schools and what is their reputation?
- Are there further education colleges or language schools locally? Is there a university?

Amenities

- Are there good leisure facilities such as an arts centre, museums, art galleries and libraries?
- Are there good sports facilities such as fitness centres, football pitches, children's play areas and tennis courts?
- Are there open green spaces such as public parks and gardens? Green and open spaces are highly desirable, but there could be plans to develop them into something less attractive like a shopping centre. Check with the local council whether they are protected areas.
- Are there shopping facilities such as local grocery shops and supermarkets?
- Are there restaurants? Are they take-aways and burger bars or upmarket, expensive designer restaurants?

Health

- Is the area well supplied with doctors and dentists?
- Is there a convenient general hospital?

A checklist will give you something realistic to refer back to when it comes to making decisions about who you are hoping to sell to and how to do your renovation.

THINGS TO BEWARE OF

Whilst you can make a profit developing any property if you buy it at the right price, there are a number of things that may affect the desirability of a property when you come to sell it. You will have to be realistic about the price and be prepared to not necessarily achieve a premium. Factors to watch for include:

- Areas with poorly rated, problem schools.
- Proximity to electricity pylons and mobile phone masts.
- Signs of poor council services such as abandoned cars, graffiti and litter in the streets.
- Homes near industrial areas, main roads, railway tracks, low flight paths and areas that suffer from congestion.

SOURCES OF INFORMATION

Research is the key to successful developing and that's as true when sounding out a suitable area to buy in as when planning the actual work to the property. Sound out as many people and organisations as possible, using your phone, your computer and local libraries. Always make notes so that you can readily refer back to them.

USE YOUR COMPUTER

Surfing the Internet is a quick way to access a great deal of information about areas all over the country. The following are some of the websites that can give you information on various aspects of an area.

For example Hometrack (www.hometrack.co.uk) produces an independent property database by assessing the sale results of 3,500 estate agency offices covering 2,200 postcode districts in England and Wales. Similarly, Alliance & Leicester's 'movingimproving' online index (www.movingimproving.com) is a quarterly survey that pinpoints where in the UK people are currently buying homes, or areas to which people want to relocate.

To find out about local schools and colleges the Department for Education and Skills website (www.dfes.gov.uk) gives information and performance tables; the Office for Standards in Education (OFSTED), (www.ofsted.gov.uk) has reports on local schools.

For environmental issues The Environment Agency (www.environment-agency.gov.uk) will tell you about anything from local air quality to the likelihood of flooding.

The Up My Street website (www.upmystreet.com) is a treasure trove of information on property prices, local events and affairs, crime statistics, plus neighbourhood profiles on matters like average earnings, employment levels and preferred TV channels. Simply type in the postcode of the area that interests you. It also has information on local estate agents and letting agents, advice on personal loans, lists of local tradesmen and DIY stores.

For information on transport links and train timetables the Travel Line (www.traveline.org.uk) gives impartial information on train times and destinations, bus, train and ferry companies and park and ride schemes.

WHO WILL YOU SELL TO?

Recognising the sort of person who will want to buy the particular property you develop in any area is essential if you want to end up with a profit. There's no point in developing a property suitable for a single, affluent young businessperson if the area is more suited to a young family of modest means. Look at the various categories of possible buyers before deciding who your purchasers are likely to be.

VISIT THE AREA

When you have gained some knowledge about the property market in an area, make a trip there to see it for yourself. Spending a morning or afternoon in your chosen location is definitely the best way to discover all the information you need first-hand. And when you are there, be proactive – make a checklist of the area's positive and negative features so that you use your time efficiently.

Having considered the market in general terms, begin to focus on the actual people for whom you are developing – those most likely to be looking for somewhere to live in the area. It is often helpful to home in on a particular group. As always, try to put yourself in their shoes. There's no point in purchasing a warehouse apartment up five flights of stairs with no garden and developing it for an elderly couple with a love of gardening.

Forget your own ideas of home and remember your product must be appealing to those wanting to buy in the area.

CATEGORIES TO CONSIDER

- Students (perhaps with parental help) will want something good value, generally large enough and arranged conveniently for sharing. Gardens are not an important factor, but good transport links and a supermarket are.

- First-time buyers will want something at the cheaper end of the market, possibly with a small garden, good transport links, shops and a supermarket.
- Business professionals are likely to be able to afford to spend more and so will demand more. They will be looking for three- to four-bedroom homes with at least one ensuite, well-planned interiors, parking, a garden, leisure facilities, convenient restaurants and shops.
- Most families will require three to four bedrooms, two bathrooms, storage space, a garden and parking. Ideally, the property should not open directly onto a busy road or street.
- Retired people will probably want a smaller home with either a lift or a ground floor property, or a bungalow with two or three bedrooms. They will also be attracted to an easy walk to the shops and amenities, good public transport, near the library and possibly a home incorporating a small, easily maintained garden.

RECOGNISING AN UP-AND-COMING AREA

Every property developer strives to buy in an area fast going upmarket, and to sell a few months later at a profit. Unfortunately, this seldom happens in real life. Areas thought to be up-and-coming have a way of taking much longer to mature than predicted. So do your research and look for the signs of new affluence in the area.

Riding the market upward within an area that is currently less popular but becoming more so is every property developer's dream, but it is not as easy as it sounds. The reality is nobody actually knows for certain where the next profitable area is going to be. Even if you get it right, an area like this may take some time to mature and property prices don't always rise as quickly as predicted, if at all. Always play it safe and look out for businesses, groups and organisations that have already done the research and have already invested. But remember that extensive

commercial or large-scale housing developments can also affect the atmosphere of an area and are not necessarily seen as desirable by home-hunters.

It is really worth taking time to do this initial research. Keep a notebook with you when visiting the area and note down relevant facts that might come in handy. Contact local newspapers and the property press for information on crime, local services (like refuse collection) and parking facilities. Make a habit of looking in estate agents' windows to get an idea of what is selling and has recently been sold and for how much. This will help you spot up-and-coming areas as well as good deals yourself rather than relying on estate agents to tell you.

Use professional indexes and surveys to chart trends in the marketplace. Visit your local council's planning office to view planning histories – all planning applications must be lodged there before they are approved or refused. Local groups such as Neighbourhood Watch may be able to tell you about any local issues that your estate agent has not mentioned. The vendor is legally obliged to disclose to your solicitor whether there have been any official complaints lodged about noise from any neighbourhood disputes.

There are a number of possible indicators that an area may be up-and-coming in a town or region with a quantity of unmodernised housing. These areas may be popular with mid-income home-hunters, especially if they are close to an already established area in which they aspire to live. Handy indicators of up-and-coming areas are:

■ Supermarket chains and off-licences springing up.
■ Estate agents, especially those with a chain of offices,

moving in to new premises – this is a sign of a healthy or recently increased turnover of domestic property.
■ Major banks located on the high street.
■ An increasing number of specialist businesses moving into the area, including delis, cafés and art galleries.
■ The presence of new large-scale developments such as apartments and lofts.
■ Major companies locating head offices, production plants or new divisions to an area. The increased employment will mean a greater demand for housing.
■ Planned improvements in transport links, evidence of council or government regeneration, plans for large-scale buildings or other such initiatives.
■ Properties in good condition with well-presented façades and well looked-after gardens.
■ The look of the locals – residents comprising young businesspeople and families.
■ 'Fashion' renaming of an area by estate agents (like 'Brackenbury Village' instead of just 'Hammersmith'), may make some people think more highly of an area.

COMPARING AREAS
The following pages look at towns that are ostensibly similar, but in reality quite different. This shows the necessity of researching your area thoroughly, the type of data you need to collect, as well as the importance of learning how to read the results of your research.

Launceston and Kings Lynn, for example, are market towns of a similar size but in very different parts of the country. Purchasers in both towns seem to be young couples with low incomes, but Kings Lynn also has a high student population, so offers more scope for developing on a buy-to-let basis. In Launceston the chances of appealing to the retired market are good but one disadvantage is the distance to the nearest hospital.

Scarborough and Hastings attract summer visitors. Scarborough has a large retirement and holiday home market so relies more on the summer influx, whereas Hastings needs homes for professionals who work in the university and hospitals. It also has opportunities for the student letting market. Hastings may be an up-and-coming area, but it may take some time to achieve its potential.

Leicester and Liverpool are two cities which seem to have a lot in common. Both attract a mixed group of buyers and have many students who will want to rent. The most popular houses in both cities are terraced and semi-detached two- to three-bedroom homes. In both, property prices have also been escalating recently, so they may not offer opportunities for maximum returns on development.

TWO MARKET TOWNS

Launceston (North Cornwall)

DESCRIPTION

Inland, fairly congested market town with medieval castle just off the A30 – good for access to other parts of Cornwall. Good tourist area. Plenty of pay-and-display car parks. Nearest big town: Plymouth (64km/40 miles) or Exeter (80km/50 miles), both 40–45 minutes in a car. Light industry factories in industrial estate. Two supermarkets just outside town. One sports centre with swimming, gym and squash; two 18-hole golf courses. Not many pubs – surrounding villages provide picturesque pubs.

WHO WANTS TO BUY/RENT IN THE AREA?

Generally people who want a good quality of life and enjoy the countryside that north Cornwall offers. Young couples who cannot get on the property ladder rent; outsiders moving into town for buy-to-let investments; people working from home or retiring.

AVAILABLE PROPERTIES

Not enough detached homes to satisfy need. Extensive building of two- to three-bedroom semis since the end of the 1990s. For a sought-after two- to three-bedroom semi prices range from £120,000 to £225,000. Areas vary enormously.

PUBLIC TRANSPORT

Reasonable bus service. Very good local taxi services. No train station; nearest is Liskeard or Bodmin (27km/17 miles away).

SCHOOLS

Three infant schools with good reputations. Highly sought-after private school, St Josephs.

HOSPITALS

Own hospital with small A&E unit. Nearest main hospitals are in Plymouth or Truro.

Kings Lynn (Norfolk)

DESCRIPTION

Market town and port on the River Ouse just south of the Wash. Ample parking facilities. Nearest big town is Norwich. Industrial estate with Campbell Soup Co. and Masterfoods, both major employers in the area. Williams and Foster, refrigeration companies, also have factories. There are supermarkets in town and in the Hardwick Industrial estate but there is lack of choice at the top end of the market. The town centre has been redeveloped to provide a wider variety of shops, a new medical centre and homes, but most people go by car to Norwich or Peterborough to shop. There are two main leisure centres, numerous pubs and a cinema. Few intimate restaurants, mainly chain eateries available. There is a high student population from West Anglia College.

WHO WANTS TO BUY/RENT IN THE AREA?

Many first-time buyers who are renting until they are able to buy their first home, which usually falls in the under-£100,000 bracket. Many buys-to-let for students, workers from overseas and single working people.

AVAILABLE PROPERTIES

Usually three-bedroom semis on estates, around the £130,000–160,000 mark. The cost of the average four-bedroom detached home is around £200,000. At the lower end of the market are two-bedroom mid-terrace family starter homes at £75,000. All snapped up very quickly.

PUBLIC TRANSPORT

Buses frequent to and from the main towns. Good direct train service to London (1 hour 40 mins) and Cambridge – change at Ely for Peterborough.

SCHOOLS

Three high schools all with good reputations.

HOSPITALS

The Queen Elizabeth Hospital has its own A&E and has a good reputation.

TWO SEASIDE TOWNS

Scarborough (North Yorkshire)

DESCRIPTION

Britain's first seaside town, now a bustling town catering for the whole family, with an ancient castle and Victorian esplanade and spa, fishing harbour and award-winning beaches. Good tourist area. Population of 40,000 quadruples in summer months. Problems with road congestion in the area, especially in the summer. Parking facilities are not good with only one park-and-ride scheme, though there are plans to tackle this problem. Nearest big towns: York, Hull and Teesside (all about 64km/40 miles away). McCain Foods (potato chip manufacturers) is the main employer in the area. There is a good range of shops.

WHO WANTS TO BUY/RENT IN THE AREA?

First-time buyers plus a moving population of families stepping up from terraces to semi-detached properties. Also a retirement and holiday home market. As elsewhere in the country, investment buy-to-lets are becoming increasingly popular. Town areas are less expensive than outskirts,

AVAILABLE PROPERTIES

Fairly limited. Many converted flats in Victorian/Georgian esplanades. Many available semis and detached houses. Prices start from £80,000 for a two-bedroom terrace; £120,000 for a semi; £160,000 upwards for a detached house. The largest housing stock is a two- to three-bedroom semi.

PUBLIC TRANSPORT

Direct rail links to York. From there the East Coast Mainline gives links to London/Edinburgh. Many people choose to commute to York for work but to live in Scarborough, which is cheaper.

SCHOOLS

One sixth form college and two private, four secondary and ten primary schools of mixed reputations.

HOSPITALS

Scarborough main hospital was once dubbed a failing hospital but has been improved with added investment. Dentists in short supply; people go as far as Bridlington to find an NHS dentist.

Hastings (East Sussex)

DESCRIPTION

Resort town with a long history. Good example of a town that may be up-and-coming. Had a reputation for being run down but has long-term plans for revitalisation. Streets not congested, with plenty of parking in multi-storey car parks; no park-and-ride. Large pedestrian area. Handy for Brighton (30 minutes by car) and London (70 minutes by car). There are three main factory sites and many retail supermarkets, leisure facilities including gyms and a swimming pool, and watersports by the sea. There is a lively nightlife with many new clubs and bars recently opened. In the Old Town the pubs are quieter and there are the beginnings of a live music scene.

WHO WANTS TO BUY/RENT IN THE AREA?

Many people from outside the area are looking for cheaper properties. Many professionals, particularly hospital employees, are also looking for homes. A new university, opened in 2003, means there are students looking for places to rent. There is a mixture of local people wanting to buy and outside investors.

AVAILABLE PROPERTIES

Semi-detached three-bedroom properties sell for around £145,000; many sea-front converted Victorian flats. Prices are rising fairly fast. There is an ongoing need for affordable housing in town and the St Leonards area is the core of many of the regeneration projects. The council, working closely with the community, also has various regeneration schemes in the area.

PUBLIC TRANSPORT

There are three mainline stations: Hastings in the town centre and St Leonards and West St Leonards nearby. There's a good local bus service.

SCHOOLS

There are five senior schools, three special schools and 19 primary schools, all with reasonable reputations.

HOSPITALS

The main hospital replaced several old Victorian ones demolished ten years ago. It has a good reputation. There are plenty of doctors and dentists.

TWO SUBSTANTIAL CITIES

Leicester (Midlands)

DESCRIPTION

Leicester was founded as a Roman settlement and has a 14th-century cathedral. Noted as a hosiery, textile and engineering city. Home of De Montfort University (formerly Leicester Polytechnic). Can be congested, but plenty of car parking spaces available. Good park-and-ride scheme. Good motorway links to Coventry (M69), Birmingham (M42) and London (M1); M42 links to South West. Many factories and workshops because of big rag-trade industry. Great variety of shops in the Fosse Park shopping centre. Surprisingly sparse sports facilities: no swimming pool and only two sports centres. Huge boom in pubs and bars over recent years, attracting larger numbers of young people into the area. Leicester Regeneration Company is planning waterside developments.

WHO WANTS TO BUY/RENT IN THE AREA?

A very mixed group: mainly buyers to invest, first-time buyers, families and large student population renting (12%). There is a current trend for first-time buyers to move into the city centre.

AVAILABLE PROPERTIES

Many houses have been being converted into flats. Most in demand are terraced and semi detached two- to three-bedroom houses, with the average price £90,000–100,000 for a two-bedroom. Prices have escalated by 300% in the past five years and are still going up. Barratt Homes is currently building 900 new homes. Smaller Victorian terraced houses are most popular to buy.

PUBLIC TRANSPORT

Direct train service to all nearest cities including Nottingham, Birmingham and London. There are bus services throughout the city.

SCHOOLS

Near to good schools, property prices can shoot up by £20,000. Popular schools include Montrose and Granby.

HOSPITALS

There are three major hospitals: Leicester Royal Infirmary, Leicester General and Glenfield. All have good reputations. As in many major cities, there is a shortage of NHS dentists.

Liverpool (Merseyside)

DESCRIPTION

Liverpool's port trade developed in the 17th century when it became a centre of the slave trade. Later imported cotton from the USA and exported textiles produced in Yorkshire and Lancashire. Its traditional industries of shipbuilding and engineering have declined but it remains one of the chief Atlantic ports in Europe. There are a number of car parks. Factories are situated in the outskirts. Two cathedrals, two universities. many sports centres and cinemas, and enormous numbers of pubs, clubs, bars and restaurants. There are many supermarkets for all budgets. Liverpool has been designated European City of Culture 2008 and this is already having a dramatic effect. Development and regeneration has started across the city, with old buildings being demolished and run-down areas renovated.

WHO WANTS TO BUY/RENT IN THE AREA?

All walks of life. Possibly the main groups are investors from Ireland and the South of England buying to let. Many students rent but some with affluent parents may buy the property as an investment.

AVAILABLE PROPERTIES

Most sought-after and most available are three-bedroom terraced houses. Many pockets of more deprived areas are under regeneration and property prices are rising very quickly.

PUBLIC TRANSPORT

Excellent with regular, cheap buses to all outskirts, and tramlines being laid to link outer areas to the city centre. Trains run directly from Liverpool Lime Street and Liverpool Central to all major cities.

SCHOOLS

A huge variety of choice from poor performance to the best.

HOSPITALS

Liverpool is well endowed with hospitals which include The Royal, Walton, Alder Hey and Liverpool Women's Hospital. There is no shortage of doctors or dentists.

EARL'S COURT: QUANTITY AS WELL AS QUALITY

Martin Sutherland was running his own import business when he bought a three-bedroom maisonette and decided to turn it into a top-spec luxury apartment with five bedrooms and rent it out as a long-term investment. He saw his market as young professionals who would pay that little bit extra for luxuries. There are plenty of cafés, restaurants and bars in the area and transport is good. He used up all his savings and borrowed the rest of the money to buy the property.

THE PLAN

Martin planned to project manage the development himself. His plan was to cut the kitchen in half and put a larger shower room in. The old shower room would become a tiny fourth bedroom. Upstairs there would be a new ensuite bathroom in the largest bedroom. This meant that four out of the five bedrooms would all be very small. He intended to spend on luxury fixtures and fittings to try to attract the kind of person who would not be at home that much, spending most of the time out, but when they come home wanted luxury.

This is how he broke down his budget for the work:

PROJECT COSTS	
COST OF PROPERTY	£312,000
RENOVATION BUDGET (MAX)	£45,000
TOTAL COSTS	£357,000
TARGET RENTAL (PER MONTH)	£2,500

PROPOSED RENOVATION COSTS	
BUILDING WORK	£27,800
THREE BATHROOMS	£6,000
KITCHEN	£2,500
DECORATION AND FURNITURE	£3,700
CONTINGENCIES	£5,000
TOTAL	£45,000

At £2,500 rental a month, Martin would get £140 a week – an annual 8% rental return – not at all bad for the financial climate at the time. He was taking a long-term view, though, and it would mean a lot of work for long-term gain. 'I think of it as my pension,' he said.

When Martin bought the property it was spread over the top two floors of a four-storey terrace, with three bedrooms and a bathroom upstairs. Downstairs there was a large sitting room, a decent-sized kitchen and tiny shower room.

SARAH'S ADVICE

I felt the bedrooms in Martin's plan would be tiny, the kitchen would be cramped and so would the internal bathroom. Squeezing the shower room into the kitchen would make them both seem small. The size of the renovated kitchen would be too small for the five bedrooms and the successful young professionals that Martin had in mind as his market would be unlikely to want to share a five-bedroom flat. I thought it would be better to keep the sitting room and kitchen as a spacious living area. I'd have three good bedrooms, two bathrooms and a generous living space. To create a greater sense of space it would also be best to have an open-plan living area, which is popular with the young professional market. However, Martin was sure he could earn more by squeezing more tenants in and felt it was worth compromising a big sitting room for an extra small bedroom. This may be true in the short term, but the maintenance long term would be considerable. Martin was not keen on open-plan living himself and was convinced others wouldn't be either.

If you are uncertain as to what to do it really is worth talking to local agents before committing to a plan. Martin spoke to an agent who advised him to aim for an open, airy living room. Martin eventually decided to take this advice and the kitchen and sitting room were knocked together. The results were great and he did agree this had been a real improvement.

Martin also wanted to get rid of the existing original sash windows. 'I'm getting a much better design, these are obsolete,' he said. This would be a considerable expense that could even down-value the property. Sash windows are correct for this period of property and in the area period features are a selling point. Whilst they would be less maintenance, original sash windows would be more popular.

Martin was already running his own import business and didn't realise how tough it would be project manage the development on top of that whilst also aiming at the top end of the professional market. The proposed renovation budget would certainly not be enough. I was worried Martin's top-end finish would not come cheap, but he was confident that he wouldn't go more than 10% over budget.

This bedroom was well finished and looked quite good but it was tiny; there was no room for storage and you had to clamber onto the bed in order to open the window.

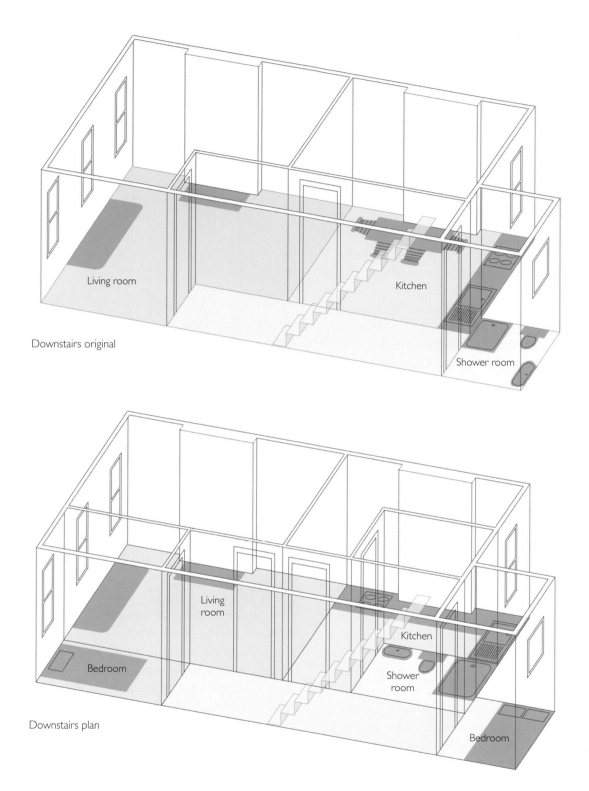

Downstairs original

Living room

Kitchen

Shower room

Downstairs plan

Living room

Bedroom

Kitchen

Shower room

Bedroom

Martin wanted to fit in as many bedrooms as possible, so he divided the living room to create one bedroom with a balcony and converted the original shower room downstairs into a bedroom with ensuite shower room. This made the kitchen much smaller and gave it a very awkward shape.

HOW THE JOB PROGRESSED

Work began on the project straight away. Martin ordered custom-built windows from the Continent which he considered were much better designed than the original sash windows. Importing can save money if you do your research first. Things can be cheaper when bought directly from their country of origin. Italian door handles, for example, cost half as much as they would here and Martin saved hundreds of pounds on German bathroom fittings. However, you must add in costs like transport, shipping and import duties before deciding. These do add up quickly and you must also check that the items are interchangeable with UK fittings. Double check that you have ordered enough – it's very expensive to run out and have to order more.

Martin would have to charge a lot in rent if he was going to spend so much. A more appropriate finish for five sharers would be a simpler, more basic interior, as students are more likely to want to share such a big flat with no outside space.

But Martin got spending. The parquet flooring he chose cost £2,000 just for materials – £5,000 in all including fitting. The flat was beginning to look gorgeous but he'd spent nearly £4,000 over his budget just on the flooring, not including the carpet that still had to be laid. He now conceded that the work would cost well over the £45,000 he had budgeted – 'I've earmarked £57,000 for the worst-case scenario.'

At this stage he had to take out an extra bridging loan costing £300 a month in interest alone and this development still had a long way to go. The small kitchen had to be carefully designed, but on a tight budget. Kitchens can be affordable if you hunt around, though Martin had fallen for a designer number.

Considering his rental market, Martin would have been better installing a cheaper kitchen which he could

Martin did agree eventually to create an open-plan living space and it did make the whole room feel more spacious. The room was well finished and good-looking but still small for the five people he hoped would be living in the property.

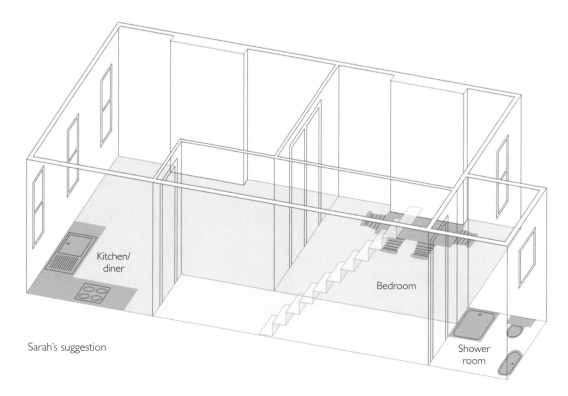

Kitchen/
diner

Bedroom

Sarah's suggestion

Shower
room

I thought Martin would have done better to create a spacious, open-plan kitchen/dining area with double doors leading from the dining area to the kitchen. This would suit his target market of young professionals.

Because rental kitchens take a beating, choose durable, practical worktops and avoid wood as it requires tlc and tenants may not look after it

replace regularly. Choosing a kitchen for the rental market is different to selling. You should make sure the units are standard sizes and that you can get replacement units when necessary. Because rental kitchens take a beating, choose durable, practical worktops and avoid wood as it requires tlc and tenants may not look after it. Granite is hard wearing and looks classy, but is very expensive. Commendably Martin showed restraint and managed to keep to his £2,500 budget, ending up with a kitchen that looked great.

When developing it is crucial to keep an eye on the market. There was a property on the rental market just round the corner for £2,200 a month, £300 less than Martin wanted to make, with three big bedrooms, a kitchen/diner and decent sized living area. For the same rent as Martin was hoping for, there was a luxury apartment with a huge sitting room, four large bedrooms and three ensuites — all with balconies overlooking the Thames — as well as free membership of the gym. He needed to offer the same standard and I was worried that with this sort of choice these young professionals just wouldn't rent his property.

The bedrooms were going to be very small and there were five bedrooms sharing one small kitchen and no outside space. He would certainly be able to rent these rooms but perhaps not long term to the people he wanted for the price he wanted.

The solution would be to spend less on specifications and make the property appeal to the student market. But Martin was adamant that he didn't want students in his flat. He intended to rent out the rooms individually, hoping that this way he might make more than renting the property as a whole. I thought he would be making a lot of work for himself and in the long run be unlikely to get that much more rent.

THE OUTCOME

After four months' hard work and a lot of stress Martin had created a five-bedroom high-spec apartment. The main bedroom with ensuite bathroom was a great success. The other bedrooms were very small with practically no storage. However, although he did end up spending £74,350, no one could deny the finish of the flat was fantastic. The open-plan living space made the whole room feel bigger.

So four of the five bedrooms were very small; in one you had to crawl across the bed to reach the window. The new downstairs shower and the kitchen, although

Martin saved hundreds of pounds on German bathroom fittings and the bathroom did look good, but it was ensuite with the largest bedroom and not only very small but would have to be shared by all four upstairs bedrooms.

The kitchen, which had originally been a sizeable room with space for a small table and chairs, became a tiny L-shaped space. It was beautifully finished but hardly satisfactory for five people to share.

beautifully finished, were really quite small for five sharers. Martin seemed certain of who his potential tenants were – he wanted professional people with plenty of money who were well-groomed and were non-smokers. I felt that he would be very unlikely to find five such people who would all want to share the property on a long-term basis. It certainly is possible to rent that way, but it might not be sustainable in the long term.

The other option would have been to go and let the flat as one whole unit through a letting agent. This would cost 10 to 15% of the letting price. If you want to do the letting yourself, make sure you have a proper contract drawn up and a complete inventory list. Remember that you will have to collect the rent, keep the place in order and deal with any problems that may arise in the property.

SUMMARY OF ACTUAL RENOVATION COSTS

	ORIGINAL BUDGET	FINAL SUMS
LABOUR AND MATERIALS	£27,800	£47,000
BATHROOMS	£6,000	£6,300
KITCHEN	£2,500	£2,650
FLOORING	£1,200	£5,250
FURNISHING	£2,500	£8,650
WINDOWS	£0	£4,500
CONTINGENCIES	£5,000	£0
TOTAL	£45,000	£74,350

LESSONS LEARNED

1 *Think of your target market.* Whether you are buying to sell or buying to let, it is vital that you keep in mind your target market. Martin had in mind people like himself who would appreciate good quality, luxurious finish but he wanted to fit in as many people as possible and the two things don't necessarily go together. Martin thought he could earn more money by squeezing more tenants in so he compromised a big sitting room for very small bedrooms.

2 *Curb your spending.* In his enthusiasm Martin spent nearly £30,000 over his budget which would make it very difficult to be able to extract enough rent for the return he had in mind.

3 *Design for your market, not for yourself.* Martin was very much against the idea of open plan but in the end took the advice of a local agent that the young professional market would in this instance prefer open plan. In the end he was delighted with the result.

HISTORY OF HOUSING

It would be difficult to get involved with property and buildings without becoming interested in the different styles and building methods used at different times in our history. Not only does such knowledge make the whole project more interesting, it can help enormously when deciding how to approach the renovation.

It can help with your decision on what sort of property to buy if you know a little about the architecture, building techniques and materials you may come across. Very old houses are rare. Hardly any houses survive from before Elizabeth I's reign and any that do are almost certainly of historic interest and will come under the protection of a body such as English Heritage. The houses most likely to come up for sale that are suitable for the first-time developer are those produced from the end of the 18th century onwards.

RECOGNISING STYLES

Houses from different periods have their own very recognisable styles. Within a particular style there may be many variations and over time, styles have altered to take in new ideas. Styles may vary slightly in different parts of the country so it is impossible to be too precise, but in general you can recognise a house's probable date of construction within a few decades by its architectural features. Knowing the style and date will tell you other things about it such as its probable method of construction and what will be suitable ways of developing it.

GEORGIAN

Houses described as 'Georgian' are roughly equivalent to the 18th-century period, particularly from 1730–1800 when Kings George I, II and III were on the throne. Few Georgian houses may be within the price range of most first-time buyer these days, but it is useful to be able to recognise them and to compare them with later Victorian houses. Georgian architecture was based on the Classical styles of Ancient Greece and Rome, favouring elegant proportions, refined sash windows and a simple exterior. Georgian houses range from the large and stately to the tiny and terraced. Walls between the houses were thick to prevent the spread of fire. The front doors are sometimes reached by a flight of steps, leaving space for a serving floor below. The front entrance may have a semi-circular fanlight above the door (not as part of the door).

VICTORIAN AND EDWARDIAN

By the end of the 18th century the idea of a single source of style had gone. The Victorians turned with enthusiasm to a huge range of influences largely based on historic British architecture, such as the Tudor or Gothic styles, which featured pointed church-like windows and asymmetrical silhouettes embellished with fairy-story towers. Towards the end of the 19th century, designs became less flamboyant. By the time Queen Victoria died

> It is possible to recognise a house's date of construction within a few decades by its architectural features

GEORGIAN

VICTORIAN

EDWARDIAN

1930s

POST-WAR HIGH-RISE

MODERN DOCKLANDS-STYLE FLAT

A small gas explosion at Ronan Point contributed to high-rise building falling out of favour

and Edward VII came to the throne, people were anxious for something new and fresh and the Edwardian style evolved as an antidote to the previous years of heaviness and clutter. This often drew on Italianate influences, with tall, elegant houses harking back again to Classical features with symmetrical structure, and big windows with large panes of glass and delicate glazing bars. At the same time a move to revert to something simpler and more hand-made produced the Arts and Crafts style. These homes used a more basic, barn-like look with red brick, and incorporated tall chimneys and well-made wooden features with careful detailing. Following this the Art Nouveau movement was born.

TWENTIETH CENTURY

In the region of four million homes were constructed during the 1930s, more than have been built in any decade since. The feminine and organic feel of Art Nouveau was replaced by the more masculine lines of Art Deco. Many of these adopted new architectural styles, which varied from starkly simple modernist villas with rounded corners and 'Crital' metal-framed windows with a horizontal silhouette, to the ubiquitous 'between-the-wars semis', which were more traditional-looking with gabled roofs and often with rounded arches over the front door. Many houses of this period blended traditional design with modern features, as epitomised by 1930s mock Tudor.

By the 1960s high-rise concrete blocks had become the fashionable means of housing a great number of people in the smallest possible space. High rises consisted of up to 20 storeys of dwelling units. For various reasons this did not work well in Britain and a small gas explosion at Ronan Point which caused five floors to collapse contributed to high-rise building falling out of favour.

During the 1970s high-rise accommodation was replaced by modern low-rise houses built individually or as part of housing estates and complexes. They varied from concrete to brick and from comparatively spacious family houses to small living units within an area devoted solely to housing.

RECOGNISING BUILDING TECHNIQUES

Learning to recognise different building techniques and materials can save a lot of time and hassle when planning any conversion. Buildings that may look similar on the outside, with similar bricks and roof construction, may actually have been built using substantially different techniques depending on when the house was built.

Building methods have changed progressively over the years. Until the 1930s most walls were built in solid brickwork. Cavity walls were introduced in about 1930 but were not used for all pre-war housing. Foundation details were not specified in by-laws until about 1914, although many houses prior to that did have brick footings.

In terms of development and building, the most likely properties to come onto the market at reasonable prices are categorised in builders' terms in the following way:

OLDER TRADITIONAL

This describes housing stock built from the late-19th century until the end of World War II. It includes small, brick two-storey terraced houses and Arts and Crafts and Edwardian houses from the 19th century to larger semi-detached homes, terraced houses with two to five floors and a basement or cellar, and mansion or tenement blocks of flats from four- to eight-storeys high. All these would be built of regionally produced bricks with a consistent local colour. Many were given stucco or cement rendering to cover unsightly or faulty brickwork. The roofs are usually of slates or tiles. In 1975 half of the national housing stock had been built before the end of World War II. Most housing association stock is therefore older traditional. There may be no damp-proof course in the buildings.

MODERN TRADITIONAL

This describes properties built since World War II and includes terraced and semi-detached houses as well as blocks of flats. They usually don't have basements, except in larger blocks, to house heating or electrical plant. Tiles and bricks are not necessarily made from local materials. Some blocks of flats have flat timber or concrete roofs covered with asphalt or layers of roofing felt. Houses are usually two-storeys high and flats up to six storeys. The windows are usually side- or top-hung casements, with frames of timber, aluminium or steel. Post-war properties generally have cavity walls on concrete foundations with a damp-proof course. Post-war new-build stock is mainly modern traditional to rationalised traditional.

RATIONALISED TRADITIONAL

This covers a range of construction methods which used traditional materials and building techniques, but in a way that improved the efficiency of the construction process. It includes cross-wall construction, which describes masonry load-bearing gable and separating walls with infill panels for front and rear elevations. Major structural defects require very different methods of treatment to previous houses but minor repairs and day-to-day maintenance is substantially similar.

INDUSTRIALISED BUILDING

A range of systems was developed in the 1960s for low-, medium- and high-rise housing. These were built mainly by local authorities. There were many different structural styles including timber-framed panels, steel frames with infill panels and precast concrete panels.

LISTED BUILDINGS

Older houses may be listed and require permission for any building work. Understanding the way such houses were built makes it easier to design a solution that will be acceptable to the authorities. Listed buildings are usually rewarding to tackle, but check carefully what your responsibilities are or you may hold up the project.

Are you thinking of buying an old building for the first time? The chances are you may fall in love with the romantic appeal of the property, the pleasure of possessing something with a historic and special character, but take care – your building may be listed. Your solicitor should tell you while you are buying whether it is listed and it should be on the estate agent's particulars, but may not, in fact, be mentioned. If it is listed you will need listed building consent for any work to the inside if it affects the character of the building.

WHAT IS A LISTED BUILDING?

The listing scheme was created in 1950 to give protection to buildings of special architectural or historic interest in England and Wales. Listing covers all features within the boundaries of the property besides the buildings themselves. Historic association with people and events of national importance, construction methods and rarity

Your solicitor should tell you while you are buying whether it is listed and it should be on the estate agent's particulars

value can also feature as listing criteria. There are three grades for listing: Grade I; Grade II* and Grade II, with a total of about 500,000 listed buildings in the UK.

Buildings of high quality and character, or designed by nationally recognised architects from 1840–1914, are listed, as are high-quality buildings from the period 1914–1939. Outstanding buildings built post-1939 may also be listed but they have to be at least 30 years old. The same situation now exists in Wales, Scotland and Northern Ireland.

YOUR RESPONSIBILITY

If the building is listed, whatever its Grade, you will need to get listed building consent from your local council if you want to demolish it or any part of it, or make any alterations that would affect its character inside or out. Repairs that match exactly may not need consent, but your local council will advise you on this as other minor repairs may need consent. Contact your local planning department as soon as possible to discuss whether an application is required. Listing does not automatically stop you from making changes. It ensures that what you propose will be given consideration. Obtaining consent takes time, so don't leave it until the last minute.

Work that will need consent includes changing windows and doors, painting over brickwork or removing external surfaces, putting in dormer windows or roof lights, putting up aerials, satellite dishes and burglar alarms, changing roofing materials, moving or removing internal walls, making new doorways and removing or altering fireplaces, panelling or staircases.

Remember, if you go ahead and do the work without any consent, you could be prosecuted and have to pay for expensive remedial works. Carrying out unauthorised work to a listed building is a criminal offence punishable by a fine or a prison sentence or both. Not only that but the local council can require you to put the building back as it was. Ultimately if you do not have the money to reinstate/repair the listed building English Heritage/the local council have the right to carry out essential repair works on your behalf and bill you for it – this becomes a debt that must be paid much like any debt and normal debt collecting procedures will be taken.

MARKET CHECKLIST

1 Decide on an area, preferably a site near you.
2 Research the area. This should include getting information on transport, education, amenities, health facilities, and spotting an up-and-coming area.
3 Use as many information sources as possible including local estate agents, local newspaper and property publications, the local council, local groups and online sources.
4 Target your market: students and first-time buyers, business professionals, families and retired people will all want different things.
5 Run your business efficiently. Be organised, do your sums, get professional advice and be realistic.
6 Recognise types of building and house styles.
7 Understand what's involved if you buy a listed building or a building in a Conservation Area.

2
YOU, THE
DEVELOPER

2 YOU, THE DEVELOPER

Developing a property means altering it from the state it's in to a more marketable state and, for your efforts and time, making a profit in the process. This may sound simple but over the whole project, from initial purchase to final sale, a whole range of skills will be necessary. Even experienced property developers find that development can be stressful, expensive, time-consuming and fraught with crises. For the beginner, therefore, it is hardly surprising that taking on the first project can be a very high-risk business.

Developing property to make a profit is as much a business as any other money-earning venture, so every aspect of the project must be run in an efficient way. This includes organising the work and workers, collecting and filing information, keeping accounts and employing experts where needed. Being businesslike is an absolute must and something you should learn to enjoy if you really wish to make a living from property development.

A BUSINESSLIKE APPROACH FOR SUCCESS

Firstly, start thinking like a developer. It is important to bear in mind that what you are doing is running a business, not buying a home for yourself. Don't think of the property as 'yours' – it's not a dolls' house or a toy. It's a business proposition and, as with any business, if you do not make a profit then there will be no money to develop another property and therefore you have no business. Get personal and it may fail.

One thing is for certain, though. If you don't actually enjoy the process of buying, developing and selling, you are unlikely to succeed. However, you must also get each part of that process right if you want to stand any chance of making a profit.

Your property is simply a product. Develop it for a particular market and be objective – it's not going to be

yours in the long run. Keep in mind your end product. Create a realistic budget and stick to it. Don't be tempted to make expensive, unnecessary changes that won't add to its final value.

Be organised
Buy a filing system, a concertina pocket system or a system of box files. Keep records of everything you have researched, everyone you have contacted and the quotes they have given. These records can be invaluable to refer to later on for further developments. Make sure you keep a good, clear set of accounts for your own records and for your accountant.

Do your sums
Do your research and find out whether the property you are interested in can actually make you money. You should be realistic about the costs of all the works involved and then also set aside a contingency sum. Modernising an older building is an uncertain business and problems will always come up along the way. Do not delude yourself into thinking that just because a property requires modernisation there is profit in modernising it.

Get professional advice
Don't be too proud to ask the experts. They have training and experience and their advice can prevent you from making expensive and time-consuming mistakes. From the initial purchase to the planning and developing, professional advice can be invaluable.

Be realistic
Be realistic about what you can take on. Unless you are very experienced in general building work, it may end up being more expensive to try and do the work yourself than to pay an experienced workforce to do it for you.

> If you don't actually enjoy the process of buying, developing and selling, you are unlikely to succeed

Thinking it through

So have you thought why you are considering such a traumatic and stressful undertaking? Are you going to be able to cope? What are your strengths and what are your weaknesses? Before you make the decision to go ahead and buy a property for development, check that you are doing this for the right reasons. It is imperative that you think it through to make sure you can cope with the financial, organisational, design and labour aspects before you begin.

ARE YOU A BUDDING DEVELOPER?

Ask yourself the following searching questions and if the answers are not favourable, make sure you can afford to buy in the necessary skills.

1 Have you or can you obtain enough money for: a) the initial purchase; b) the purchase and legal fees and borrowing costs; c) specialist advice and help; d) building materials; e) the building work; f) furniture if dressing; g) contingencies (things that go wrong or for the unexpected).
2 Are you objective enough to develop the property for the most likely buyers and not as a self-indulgence to fulfil a dream of your own?
3 Are you prepared/experienced enough to do some of the work yourself?
4 Are you hoping to use friends to help with the work? If so, are you sure you are not stretching your friendship a bit far by asking them to do the work for free? (Don't forget if they are doing you a favour you have little control over either their timescale or quality of work.)
5 Are you intending to manage the project yourself? If so, have you the skills required to do such work? Can you juggle the tradesmen, ordering of materials, the order of work? Do you have a contingency plan for your contractors if you have to wait for planning permission or other delays?
6 Have you an understanding of basic building practices and interior spaces? Can you design a satisfactory workable plan, if you and the property require it, and do you know where to find a designer or an architect if you need one?
7 Have you a lot of patience, an ability to manage a workforce and a proper businesslike attitude to the whole project?
8 Have you explored the market?

BUYING TO SELL

When buying to sell, the absolute priority is to be honest with yourself and to do your sums correctly. Always calculate your figures on the pessimistic side, since unforeseen circumstances are usually negative and are bound to affect the final sums. It's also easy to overlook the day-to-day administration costs, which must also be factored in.

The most important thing when buying to sell is to keep the image of your target market foremost in your mind at all times. Be sure to work out your figures after viewing any property you are serious about. That way, you won't waste any time considering properties that are financial 'no gos'. The most simple and comprehensive way to work out the maths is to subtract the associated fees and costs, renovation and purchase costs from the potential selling price of your property. But, to get to this stage you must calculate the following:

■ The realistic resale value of the property.
■ The cost of renovation works to the property.
■ The sum total of all associated fees and costs you will incur during the project.

THE REALISTIC RESALE VALUE

Ask yourself what will your property be worth in peak condition? What are people willing to pay for newly renovated properties in your area? The answers to these questions will provide the basic information for you to go on and make sensible calculations later in the project.

Finding out the realistic resale value or 'ceiling price' of a property can tell you instantly whether you have a deal. It will guide you towards buying for the right price, reveal how much the property will be worth once it looks its best and help you work out your potential profit margin. So, before investing in a property, ensure that calculating its realistic resale value is your prime concern.

■ Build a profile of the property you are interested in. Try to be as realistic as possible and base your profile on the property's location, building type, number of rooms, features and layout.
■ Next, contact three local estate agents. Ask how much newly modernised properties of this profile have recently sold for in your area. See how the details of these properties match your profile.
■ Calculate a realistic resale value from the comparables that closely match your profile. If the sale of a comparable property was completed more than two months ago, get an up-to-date opinion of what a newly renovated property of the same calibre would fetch now. Then get two more estimates to substantiate the first.

ADMINISTRATIVE COSTS

Once you have worked out your realistic resale value, the next step is to look at the administrative costs and budget. Buying a property always costs more than the purchase price. Forget to include the following costs in your calculations and you will get a nasty shock. These include legal fees – solicitor/conveyancer's fees, which start at about £400; stamp duty – a government tax on properties over £60,000; borrowing set-up costs and interest. Your lender will want to carry out a valuation (usually around £150) on the property to check that their loan is secure.

There are also extra fees like the cost of the survey; Land Registry costs (about £80–150); site services – gas, water, electricity and council tax (see Chapter 3, The Money). Don't forget to include other administrative costs specific to your project – for example the costs of selling the property once developed, planning and building control fees.

LIVING IN YOUR DEVELOPMENT

Common sense should tell you that living in a property that you are developing is a nightmare, so only consider doing this if there is no alternative. Apart from the cramped conditions, there are problems of dust, noise and possible disconnection of gas, water and electricity for some periods. Decide whether you can cope with this sort of disruption.

If you are short of cash, have a secret penchant for rubble in your bed and are generally pretty hardy, you could certainly consider living in your development. This may sound like a simple option but it does have its pitfalls.

For example, are you really going to be able to continue to live in the property while the work is being carried out? This can be noisy, dusty, and intrusive and you may find yourself without luxurious facilities such as hot (or even cold) water, use of a loo or use of a basic kitchen while the work is in progress, and this situation could last a number of weeks.

As with all developments you also want to be very sure that the work you do is actually going to raise the value of the property. Because you are living in the house, you could be mistaken into thinking that say fitting the UPVC double-glazed windows that you have always wanted as they are low maintenance and highly insulative will also be what a purchaser would want. But if fashions in your area mean that original wooden sashes are more popular you may well find that your improvements actually down-value the house. Equally, in some areas UPVC double-glazed units are essential in a modernised house and without them your house will be more difficult to sell.

It is vital to do your research first. Don't fall into the trap of thinking that if you do what you want to the property that this will automatically increase its value. Even if you were to convert the loft or add an extension out into the garden, you might find that the costs involved in carrying out this work would exceed the amount that it adds in value to the property.

BUYING TO LET

Buying to let may sound like an ideal way to deal with property and may provide the longed-for pension in the form of rent. However, first consider the realities. Will it always be possible to find tenants? Who will manage the property? Will the cost of maintaining the property take up all the income? Can you manage if the rental price falls in the future?

Rather than sell a property, many people choose to buy one, develop it and then let it out, hoping that their capital asset will increase while they receive a stable income through the rental market over a number of years. The success of this relies heavily on the state of the rental marketplace. During the late 1990s residential property investment became increasingly popular as property prices rose, interest rates fell and specialist buy-to-let mortgages were created. These offered preferential rates to individual investors compared with the commercial investment mortgages already available. At the same time the stock market became lacklustre and other forms of long-term investment failed to recover from the unscrupulous salesmen scandals of the time.

The popularity of buying to let increased rapidly and this in itself helped to fuel the increase in property prices by an average of 15% in 2001, while the stock market fell by more than 15% in the same period. Many sectors of the general public lost confidence in investing in stocks and shares and with no other obvious place to invest, even more people were compelled to buy to let.

THE FUTURE

There are two major questions about buying to let. Firstly, will the high demand for rental properties continue in what some describe as a saturated market? Secondly, are buy to lets likely to perform as well as other forms of medium- to long-term investment?

At the time of writing growth in the rental sector is anticipated to continue because:

- There is a mood of apprehension in the property market. Some potential buyers are being cautious and choosing to rent rather than buy or sell, while they wait for both the UK's economic situation and the property market to stabilise.
- First-time buyers are finding it increasingly difficult to get on the property ladder and are waiting longer before buying property. The average age of first-time buyers is 32 in Greater London, The Midlands and the North-East,

Look closely at all other investment options available to you before you choose to invest in a buy to let

and 34 in Scotland, according to the Halifax building society. Many young people cannot afford the deposit for a home or afford mortgage repayments on their wage. Even so, many still decide to move out of their family home by their mid-twenties and the only affordable way to do this is by renting.

- Working practices have changed considerably in recent years. The increasing number of company relocations away from the South-East is creating new demand for rental properties. In addition, a higher percentage of people are working on short-term contracts and medium-term placements for several months at a time, as well as workers on contract from overseas; the majority of these workers will rent.

In short, the strength of the rental market seems set to continue. The RICS (Royal Institute of Chartered Surveyors) found that demand for rented accommodation in August 2003, for example, was at its strongest level for two years as a result of booming housing prices. However, there are great swathes of the UK where an excess of housing stock to let has driven rents downwards – most notably in major cities and especially at the cheaper end of the market.

In Scotland, for example, in April 2004, rental prices in some areas plummeted as supply outstripped demand, threatening serious financial difficulties for investors who had stretched themselves. Some landlords had already cut advertised rates by 30% or more at the request of would-be tenants just to obtain some steady income to cover their mortgages.

A buy to let is not therefore a guaranteed money-spinner. Look closely at all other investment options available to you before you choose to invest as it is possible that neither rental nor sale prices will experience a sharp rise in the near future.

TOP TEN TIPS FOR BUYING TO LET

If buying to let seems a good investment for you, bear the following things in mind before you start looking for the perfect property. As always, careful planning is the key:

1 Carry out thorough research. Check local rental conditions, analyse rental demand and determine the types of renting in your area. Look for obvious clues such as a large company relocation, the opening of trendy bars and shops (attractive to young professionals) or the existence of good schools nearby (attractive to families) and choose a property with features that will appeal to your market.

2 An appealing rental property is one that is close to transport links and/or has off-street parking.

3 If you plan to rent your property to professionals, all of the bedrooms should ideally be doubles (even if one or more are small doubles).

4 Think low maintenance. You want a property that will run itself as smoothly as possible.

5 If you are managing the property yourself, be prepared to do some hard work. A buy-to-let property is far from being a hassle-free income.

6 Choose a property close to home, which will enable you to pop over and sort out any problems easily. If you are not able to do this it can cost you more than a week's rent to get someone in.

7 Bear in mind that family rental homes require plenty of space and storage.

8 If you are the sole freeholder of the property, you will need to ensure that the common parts and the exterior of the property are well maintained. You may wish to spend a couple of hours a week vacuuming and polishing or employ a professional cleaning company to keep these areas up to scratch. If your buy to let is leasehold, however, the responsibility for the maintenance of the exterior and interior communal areas will rest with the freeholder unless your lease specifies otherwise (although this in itself is no absolute guarantee the maintenance will be done).

9 Steer clear of large gardens, especially in a town property, unless you intend adding the cost of a gardener to the weekly rental and you are aiming to market your property as a family home. As any keen gardener knows, it doesn't take long for a little neglect to show.

10 Consider whether you want to let furnished or unfurnished. Sometimes there is little difference between the rents commanded by unfurnished compared with part- or fully-furnished properties to let. It all depends on your market and the demand in your area. Before you go looking for furniture, do your research and find the best option for you.

BUY TO LET AS PENSION OR INVESTMENT

When rental returns are not booming you are likely to have to hang on to your rental property for at least ten years if you want to make money with a buy to let. Even then, after all the hard work and stress of renting a property, there is still no guarantee that your asset will increase in value, although you will have the rental stream as an income.

I would always advise you to look into the state of the market and at predicted conditions even if you are considering a buy to let as a long-term investment. Interest rates have a direct impact on property prices and any changes will affect the stability of the market.

It's also a good idea to see how buying to let compares with other forms of long-term investments. It's worth noting that if your capital appreciates in value you will have to pay tax on that appreciation.

Other options to consider:

- Pension funds have the benefit of tax relief.
- You have 100% control over your own funds in a property, but it is a high-risk investment.
- Look at the returns from savings plans, for instance by using the index published by Micropal. Compare figures over different time frames so as to take into consideration slumps and rises in the property market and savings funds.

FINANCING A BUY TO LET

The advent of specially tailored mortgages has both fuelled and been a product of the boom in the investment market. Buying a property to produce an income was until relatively recently viewed solely as a commercial undertaking. If borrowers wanted to enter this market they had to pay commercial rates of interest and their income was less important when assessing their ability to repay their mortgage.

The situation has changed quite dramatically and is now very different. Demand for an alternative form of an investment than the stock market together with low interest rates has encouraged lenders to tailor-make buy-to-let mortgages. These mortgages recognise that rental income will be used to service the loan and they offer non-commercial rates. It is worth shopping around to find the right deal for you, but the general characteristics of this type of mortgage are as follows:

- Buying-to-let mortgages are generally available for between five and 45 years and for up to 80% of the property's value.
- Your income will be taken into account by the lender and you will be able to make before-tax deductions against the rental income for various costs such as insurance, maintenance fees, agents' fees and other types of expenses.
- You are able to claim for replacing items of furniture, fittings or fixtures, although their original costs are not tax deductible. Alternatively, you may find a 'wear and tear' allowance based on 10% of your rental income is deductible.
- Insurance cover is available for the buildings and contents, as well as legal expenses in the event of court action against a defaulting tenant.
- Many lenders expect landlords to use a letting agent to manage the property and for an Assured Shorthold Tenancy Agreement to be drawn up.

Additional costs

For most investments lenders require that your gross return (the total rent received before tax) is at least between 130% and 150% of your monthly mortgage repayment. This helps budget for the additional financial commitments required when buying to let. Which many investors underestimate.

For a realistic calculation of your profit, deduct all of these additional costs from your rental income to work out how much you are likely to make. The good news is that the tenant is generally responsible for council tax, any utility bills and a TV licence.

Remember that you will then need to deduct an appropriate amount of tax depending on the tax band you are in. If this final figure leaves you struggling to meet mortgage repayments, then proceed with caution or at your peril!

CALCULATING YOUR RENTAL PROFIT

RENTAL INCOME	– MAINTENANCE FEES
	– FOUR MONTHS WITHOUT A TENANT
	– INSURANCE
	– AGENTS' FEES/COST OF YOUR OWN LABOUR
	= REALISTIC GROSS PROFIT

WATCHING THE EXTRAS

Take these seemingly small extras into account as they can add to your outlay and so reduce your gross income:

1 Maintenance fees. These include the cost of cleaning communal areas, general repairs to the property, replacing damaged furniture and redecorating rooms regularly.
2 Vacant periods. You may experience vacant periods or have to take a cut in the rental price due to market conditions. You also need to set aside money to cover your mortgage for several months should there be a break between lets.
3 Falling rents. Remember rents can fall as well as rise. The reality is that an overpriced house may sell, but an overpriced house for rent almost certainly will not.
4 Buildings insurance. This is calculated on the cost of rebuilding. The larger the property, the more it is likely to cost.
5 Agents' fees. If you choose to pay for help with the management of your property and in finding tenants, then you will also have to include agents' fees in your calculations. These vary between 8 and 15% of your rental income.
6 Tax. Remember your rental income is just that, an income. As such you will need to pay tax on it. While you can offset the cost of actually running your buy to let, your mortgage repayments must be paid net of tax. For further advice I would strongly suggest you contact an accountant or financial advisor as everyone's personal tax situation is different.

Tax and allowances

Deductions against tax on rents received may be claimed for the costs of maintenance, such as insurance, cleaning, gardening, agent's commission and other reasonable management expenses (but not improvements to the property). The initial costs of furnishings, fittings and fixtures is not allowable but the cost of subsequent replacements may be claimed.

LETTING TO BUY

Letting your own home, or even a room in your house, to pay for a second property to develop sounds like a good idea. If you can be sure that you'll always have tenants and you've done your sums correctly, this can be a satisfactory way of moving on in the development business. But do be realistic about the rental market in your area and take a long-term view of what you can afford.

In the 1990s, when interest rates were low but the housing market slowed due to oversupply, many home-owners found that they were unable to sell their properties for the amount they wanted to so decided to let to buy. Rents were high and home-owners were not able to afford to simply buy a second home. Many decided to let their homes and buy another often smaller property to reduce their outgoings.

LETTING TO BUY TODAY

In the current economic climate, letting to buy is still popular. Rather than selling a home to fund a new purchase, some home-owners are taking advantage of the low interest rates and, in theory, improving their pension prospects by renting out a property they no longer want to live in, in order to cover a second mortgage. Others are choosing to rent out a property rather than sell it due to the perceived instability of the property market.

According to the Home Sale Network, a group of 740 independent agents specialising in mid- and lower-priced homes, in the summer of 2003 it was taking typically six weeks to sell a property in the UK with an increase in people wishing to sell and a drop in numbers of buyers.

There was a demand for smaller houses including two-bedroom terraced and three-bedroom semi-detached houses – and average sale prices fell from 97% of asking prices in the spring of 2003 to 95.6% by the summer.

Much of the reason for this is that the amount people perceive their home to be worth and the actual value of their property are often two very different figures. When there was a shortage of property on the market a few years ago, vendors could be greedy, but those days are past. If you really want to sell you have to be realistic about the asking price. Letting to buy sounds like a good prospect in today's climate but think hard before you rush into anything. It works best with an average or below-average priced property; you may struggle to get enough rent to pay a mortgage on an expensive home.

MONEY FROM LODGERS

If neither buying to let nor letting to buy seems a viable option for you, you can always consider renting out a room in your own home to accrue extra income from your property. This is especially useful and least stressful if you rent for a relatively short period so as to fund your next property purchase.

NOTTINGHAM: MANAGING THE PROJECT

Alex and Vonny Shelley bought a two-up/two-down terraced house in Sherwood, Nottingham. Alex is a building surveyor for the local council and Vonny is a part-time music teacher. They bought the property for £50,450, then Vonny became pregnant so they rented it out for a year for £4,560, which was a big success as it more than covered the cost of the mortgage of £2,640. With a massive rise in the market over the year, the property's value had risen to around £75,000 which, if they had sold then and there, would have made them a gross profit of £26,470. They decided to put it on the market for almost £80,000, but when the only offer at that level fell through they decided to develop.

Sherwood is popular at the moment. It's a short hop into Nottingham city centre, it has restaurants and is popular with students and young professionals who would be their market. A massive 50% of the market is made up of landlords looking for long-term investment which makes for a huge demand for buy-to-let property.

PROJECT COSTS	
COST OF PROPERTY	£50,450
BUDGET	£5,000
TARGET RESALE	£85,000
ANTICIPATED PRE-TAX PROFIT	£29,550

THE PLAN

Alex and Vonny hoped to get the work done in 12 weeks and get the property back on the market. Their ambition was to buy a piece of land on which to build a home, with the proceeds of the sale together with the money from the sale of their own home.

Like many properties refurbished in the 1970s, almost all the original features had been replaced by a sea of Artex and woodchip wallpaper. The sash windows needed overhauling and the house needed completely modernising. It suffered from damp, the kitchen and bathroom needed replacing and it needed a new central heating system.

Downstairs there was a small sitting room at the front with a dining room behind it. The kitchen was a tiny addition at the back of the house. Homes with layouts like these are not ideal for how we now live. Upstairs there were two bedrooms and you could only get to the bathroom by going through the back bedroom. This awkward layout was a problem they would have to sort out. They planned to build a corridor with access from the front bedroom straight to the bathroom. Unfortunately this would make the back bedroom much smaller but in such a highly rented area access to the bathroom had to be independent of both bedrooms. There were other ways in which the space could have been arranged, but the corridor was the cheaper option although it made one bedroom very small.

This is how they broke down the budget for the work:

PROPOSED RENOVATION COSTS	
CENTRAL HEATING	£1,800
KITCHEN AND BATHROOM	£1,400
PLASTERING AND DAMP-PROOFING	£500
REDECORATION	£950
GARDEN AND WINDOWS	£350
TOTAL	£5,000

Although this was very little for the amount of work involved, they had a secret weapon – Alex's best friend Dave, who is a builder. He would be doing most of the work in his spare time at a special discounted rate, and a group of friends were willing to work for nothing. This might well be satisfactory at the start of the project but how long would it last? There was no contingency fee for professional labour – just in case they did need it.

SARAH'S ADVICE

Even with friends doing the work, the budget was spectacularly low. The key to good development is to spend money wisely rather than not at all. You do need to control the spending but not at any cost. It is important to do the essential work first. Alex and Vonny were thinking of replacing just some of the tiles on the roof. I was worried about how poor the condition of the roof was, though, and not replacing it I felt was a massive mistake. However, there was nothing in the budget for this work and they were reluctant to take this advice.

Because they would be unlikely to keep within their budget, it was important to make their layout appeal to the broadest possible market. Fifty per cent of buy-

Alex and Vonny decided to open up the original period fireplace and replace it with a new one, something that was not in the budget.

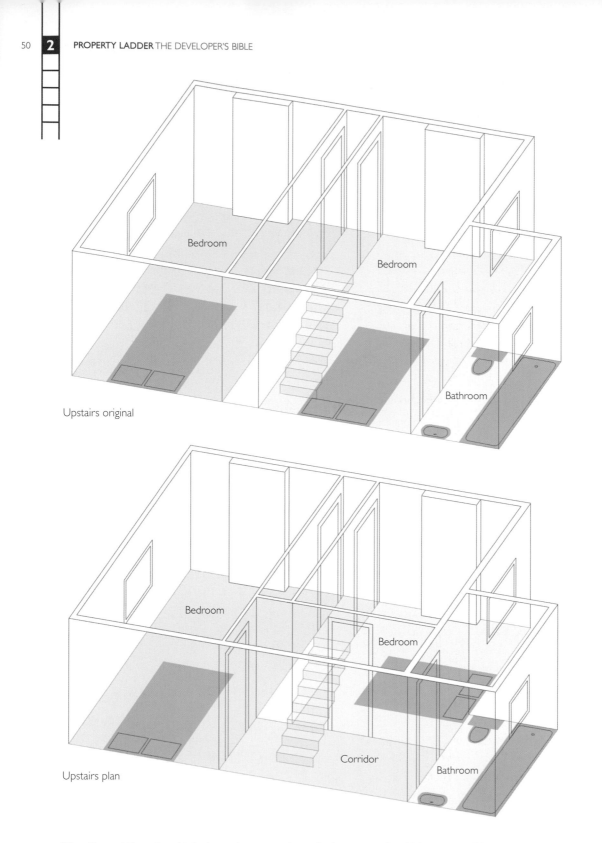

Upstairs original

Upstairs plan

When Alex and Vonny bought the house there was only one bathroom upstairs which was accessible only through one of the bedrooms. They decided to make the bedroom smaller and to create a corridor to the bathroom from the other bedroom.

to-let landlords who want this sort of house want two good-sized double bedrooms that they can rent for the maximum amount. One suitable solution for this particular house that would have worked well for the market would have been to create a kitchen/dining space downstairs in the back reception room with French doors out onto the garden. This would appeal to young starter families or the buy-to-let market. With French windows onto the garden it would have made the room feel much larger. The original kitchen space could then have become a second bathroom.

But they were determined to keep the kitchen separate. Because it was small, the kitchen needed to be perfect – difficult on a tiny budget as they had set aside only £1,000 for the entire kitchen. Cabinets on legs give the illusion of space, light colours and reflective surfaces all help to make a room seem larger. Despite the extra cost, Alex and Vonny decided to go for integrated units.

Almost every other decision made during the project was about cutting costs. To sell to the market this property needed two decent-sized bedrooms and if they had put a second bathroom in the original kitchen space, upstairs they could have kept two double bedrooms with one ensuite. Alex felt quite confident they would sell with what they were proposing and spend less money doing it. But Alex and Vonny chose the cheaper option of creating a corridor, which made the second bedroom very small.

Despite this, some of the decisions they made were not the cheapest options available to them. They wanted to put in a new bathroom suite and a skylight, both of which were not entirely necessary. The simple fact was that the budget was not realistic for all the things they wanted to do and the money they did have was not spent in the most logical places.

Alex and Vonny originally decided only to replace any damaged tiles on the roof but eventually found they had to replace the roof completely. The new skylight did let in more light but was unnecessary, and damaged the roof further while it was being installed.

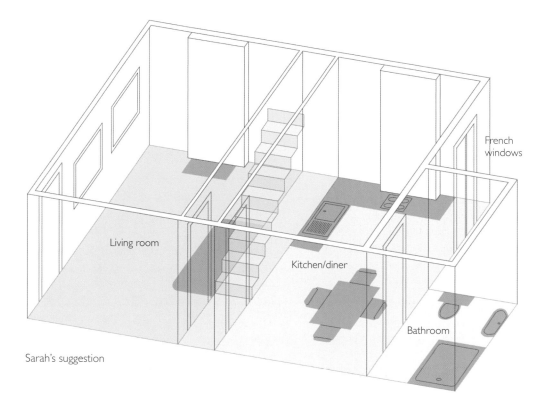

French windows

Living room

Kitchen/diner

Bathroom

Sarah's suggestion

Downstairs the small front sitting room had a dining room behind it. The kitchen was a tiny addition at the back of the house. To appeal to the market they could have created a kitchen/dining space in the rear reception room with French windows leading into the garden. This would have made the room feel larger and the original kitchen could have become a much-needed second bathroom.

HOW THE PROJECT PROGRESSED

The work started enthusiastically with the demolition, but Dave agreed with me that the roof really needed to be renewed. Even without this, it was pretty soon clear that the budget was unrealistic.

Alex and Vonny opened up the dining room fireplace, a job that was neither in the original plan or the budget. They thought the work would be minimal, but often small jobs end up becoming much larger ones. Taking out the fireplace turned out to be much more expensive than they expected and it was probably a little counter-productive.

Two weeks into the project and Alex and Vonny had smashed their house to pieces. After six weeks there was still little happening when Dave was busy elsewhere and not able to work on the job. Finishing in the allotted 12 weeks seemed less and less likely. They were over budget, over schedule and no work had been done on the property for six weeks. Every room was in chaos and Dave was busy elsewhere and had little time for them. The friends had disappeared and a week later there was nothing going on at all.

In the bathroom their £400 budget had gone entirely out of the window. The extra light created by the skylight could have been achieved with white paint and reflective surfaces. It would also actually have paid them to spend money on certain features, for example a Victorian fireplace. The people with most money to spend in this area really appreciate traditional features.

After four months they had overspent on building work, the fireplace and the roof light. They also finally realised that they had no option but to to re-tile the roof after all. Alex's builder advised using professionals but Alex decided to go ahead just with his friends. Everyone was working in their spare time which meant that things took longer than expected.

Alex had been afraid that re-tiling the roof would eat into their profit, but some costs just have to be borne, especially since adding the bathroom roof light had damaged the roof still further. Although every decision is about spending money sensibly, it would have saved money in the long run to have had the roof re-tiled as one of the first priorities.

The work had already taken much longer than expected and the stress and strain started to show. Meanwhile they still had their mortgage to pay and the house they had set their hearts on had fallen through.

Three weeks later they were close to finishing. Although a newly refurbished house should have a good finish, they'd patched the woodchip and decided to decorate in just one day by organising a painting party with friends. If the quality of finish is poor it does let down a development so it's important to watch the details. They still hoped to sell the property for £85,000 but they really needed thousands more on top of this just to break even.

Alex had been afraid that re-tiling the roof would eat into their profit, but some costs just have to be borne

The second bedroom was now so small that there was no space for a wardrobe.

THE OUTCOME

The work took nearly six months to complete from the time Alex and Vonny started on the project. Although the whole project had taken a very long time it was a massive improvement, although the house lacked any period features giving it that little extra interest, and the kitchen was so small that there was no room for a draining board. Because of the new corridor the second bedroom was barely big enough for a double bed and there was no room for a wardrobe.

ACTUAL RENOVATION COSTS		
	ORIGINAL BUDGET	FINAL SUMS
KITCHEN AND BATHROOM	£1,400	£3,900
CENTRAL HEATING	£1,800	£2,200
PLASTERING AND DAMP-PROOFING	£500	£1,250
REDECORATION	£950	£2,050
GARDEN AND WINDOWS	£350	£160
ROOF	£0	£2,318
BUILDING WORK	£0	£1,800
FEES AND EXPENSES	£0	£1,750
TOTAL	£5,000	£15,428

The kitchen was beautifully finished but very small indeed and there was no room even for a draining board. The original kitchen, a tiny extension to the back of the house, could have become a second bathroom.

LESSONS LEARNED

1 *Watch the budget.* Alex and Vonny spent three times the amount they had set aside as their budget. The roof light was unnecessary and didn't add any value to the property. From the beginning they were unrealistic and had never been in control of the budget. The only place they cut back their spending was by skimping on the garden and the windows.

2 *Get your priorities right.* It's important to have a clear plan of what work is to be done before you start. Before allocating any money on improvements that you fancy, make sure you do essential works first. Alex and Vonny started with a skylight anyway, despite needing the money elsewhere. The money would have been well spent sorting out the woodchip ceilings, putting period features back, creating a kitchen-breakfast room and replacing the roof.

3 *Keep the work moving.* You can't develop a house and make a profit by doing no work. While the builders were away they could have done some of the preparation for painting at least. Developing does take a lot of hard work.

4 *Have a clear plan before you begin.* Otherwise you won't know what the costs are going to be and when the work will be finished.

SOME STRATAGEMS THAT CAN HELP

Once you have worked out your budget, add at least 10% as a contingency. Be businesslike – make sure you have written a detailed specification of works together with all necessary drawings. If in doubt, ask for professional advice and don't be too proud to take advice from anyone who is handing it out. Ensure all extras are agreed before work is carried out and keep a written record. A wall planner is a good way of keeping a record of not only when all works are undertaken but also when tradesmen are booked in and when materials are due to be delivered. Make sure you get the proper planning consents when necessary so there's no fear of having to undo work that's already been done before your receive the permission. Keep an efficient filing system with all paperwork and receipts being properly kept.

ASSESSING YOUR SKILLS

Think your project through and assess your own skills for dealing with each stage. Where you do not possess the necessary skills, set money aside for getting the professionals in to do the job.

The purchase

Are you confident you can assess the housing in the area you've chosen? If not, get advice from local estate agents and your surveyor. Before you buy a property you will need to find out about not only the condition of the property but also the market. If you are planning on buying at auction you need to do all this research before the auction date as once you have bought the property, it will be too late.

The money

Do you know where and how you are going to borrow the money for the purchase price, legal and professional fees, loan costs, insurance costs and all the other things you will need to pay for, quite apart from the cost of the actual building work?

The budget

Underestimating the cost of the development is one of the most common errors. Plucking a sum out of the air and simply hoping it will be enough is a recipe for disaster. You need to work out an accurate total budget and work within it. There are nearly always hidden costs with second-hand buildings so make sure you have a healthy contingency fund.

Be realistic about the work required if you need a new roof or to re-wire the property and don't brush the cost under the carpet. Don't forget time delays also cost money. Simply waiting for six weeks for planning permission or delivery of materials or fittings that have not been ordered in time can add to the cost in terms of extra loan repayment. If in doubt, ensure you get professional estimates done.

The plan

Even if it's just pretty much only a question of redecorating, unless you are a confident designer it is nearly always best to get a professional architect or designer to have a look at the possibilities (and impossibilities) for the property. When it's a question of carrying out major works such as knocking down walls, building extensions, doing loft or cellar conversions, or altering or removing stairs, an inexperienced developer can come very unstuck very quickly. At least if you get initial advice from an architect or designer, you will be able to get a good idea of what you can and cannot expect to be able to do with or without official permission, and if you do need to get permission what is likely to be acceptable.

There may be by-laws and legal restrictions on the work you are allowed to undertake and it can be helpful to consult someone who knows the ropes. They will be able to advise you on the best use of space and can even approach the local authorities on your behalf in the best way. This may seem like an unnecessary extra cost, but may save you money in the long run by speeding up the process and preventing you from making expensive and time-consuming mistakes.

The work

It may be tempting to call in all favours and use friends to help with the work but it is not always wise or cost-effective in the long run. Friends may be happy to commit themselves to the odd day or so or even a week, but if they are not being paid, they would have to be truly saintly to keep an unlimited timespan open waiting for other work to be completed, permissions to come through or materials to be delivered.

DEVELOPER CHECKLIST

1 Decide whether you want to buy to sell or buy to let. Each requires a different approach and you need to be sure which one you have chosen.

2 If you decide that the only way you can get going is by letting to buy, check on the current letting situation and that you will receive enough money to cope with the mortgage and the costs of developing.

3 Make sure your budget for any renovation or conversion work is realistic and allow enough for the inevitable contingencies.

4 Assess your skills realistically and be prepared to buy in any skills you don't have.

5 Make sure the work is well finished. If you skimp on the details it will put a lot of potential purchasers off.

6 Ensure that you get your priorities right. Check that the fabric of the building is sound before embarking on expensive alterations.

3

THE
MONEY

3 THE MONEY

One of the most stressful aspects of developing a property is managing the large sums of money required. Not only must you find the money to buy the property in the first place, but you will also have to work out the amount the renovation will cost. This can be as long as a piece of string and will be an endless headache if you have not been realistic about the cost. Always allow for contingencies and for the work to take longer than estimated. And don't leave the sums to the mortgage lenders. Work out for yourself if you think an offer is realistic for you and your circumstances.

HOW TO SET UP

It's important when you are taking on a development for the first time to do things in the right order. Do some preliminary research, find a property and then arrange your finance. Part of your original planning must include how you will finance your purchase and any future building works, but mortgage companies will also need to know what property their money is going into. When you feel secure about the money, you can get a survey done and work out a budget for any renovations and make sure you stick to it through careful management.

WHERE TO START

If you are a first-time buyer finding a suitable property and financing the purchase may seem like an impossible task. Even if you have owned a property previously but are looking for another, trying to work out what all the available options are can be as stressful as doing it first time around.

The idea of legal documents, large sums of cash and all the red tape that inevitably surrounds anything to do with property ownership may seem very daunting. But take heart. If hundreds of thousands of households in England can do it, so can you. However, you must take time to understand the various steps and processes required. This chapter takes you through the main points.

THE PROCESS

The finances you have available will influence every aspect of your project, from which areas and type of housing you can consider to whether you will buy to let or buy to sell, to how you will carry out your development. Cash-flow will determine how quickly you can realise your plans and managing cash-flow successfully is part of the skill of being a successful developer. Every aspect of the process of property development relies on you being a successful property manager. The process involves:

- Conducting initial research on areas, property types and finance options.
- Finding a suitable property.
- Arranging your finance.
- Getting a survey.
- Working out your budget.
- Finding contractors/sub-contractors.
- Getting quotes.
- Finding and getting professional advice.
- Managing the project and finances.
- Managing your profit and taxes.

When you begin to get an idea of what sort of property you feel able to take on and what is available, you must then make sure you can finance the project. Use the information in this book on mortgages as a pointer, but study all the options so that you really understand what is involved. The general rule is that you can relatively easily secure a mortgage of at least up to three-and-a-half times your annual income and up to 70% of the value of the property. Don't take a lender's guide to what you can or cannot actually afford. Look carefully at your finances and do not assume that interest rates will not rise. Take advice from your accountant or bank manager if necessary.

Study all the options for yourself so that you really understand what is involved

Remember that you will have to find your percentage of the purchase price and also other costs involved in actually buying the property. These include stamp duty, lender's fees, Land Registry costs, legal fees and survey costs as well as extras such as cash for buildings insurance, moving costs and VAT.

JOINT PURCHASE POINTERS

If you are buying jointly with someone else, make sure you do the following:

- Spend time discussing how the partnership will work.
- Make sure your solicitor draws up a contract between you regardless of whether you are sure you will never fall out.
- Decide between yourselves who will be responsible for what aspects of the project and exactly what your plans are for your development.
- Don't leave anything up to chance – it's easy to assume you are both thinking along the same lines and then find out at a later date that you each have something quite different in mind for any of element of your development.
- Make sure you set aside an official time each week to discuss any issues either of you are concerned about.

INDEPENDENT FINANCIAL ADVISORS

It is wise to approach several different mortgage lenders to see what loans are available. You may find it easier to contact an independent mortgage broker or research the market yourself. You need to see how much they will be prepared to lend you and what types of mortgage are available. Once you have decided on your lender, ask for a written 'offer in principle' to confirm the terms. This will give you an indication of what you can spend and the paperwork may help when you are negotiating an offer. However, you know your cash flow requirements better than any advisor, so be realistic about what you can afford. For the sake of your beauty sleep, not to mention the success of your development, don't be tempted to stretch yourself too far.

A wise developer will buy at a price that assures them a 20% gross return of their total investment. This ensures there is a reasonable return on investment even with the uncertainty of movement in the market. Though you may start developing with a slightly lower percentage profit rate than this, you are strongly recommended to err on the side of caution.

FINDING THE MONEY

Be flexible at this stage of your project. If you cannot immediately get a loan for the property you want, perhaps you should choose a smaller property. Consider all the options, such as splitting the cost of the mortgage with somebody else. And make sure you get the most advantageous mortgage – there are many types to choose from.

While researching the area and properties you are considering developing, you should begin to look for the best ways of funding your project. House prices in the UK have reached staggering new heights, way beyond the general cost of living, which means that first-time buyers have a really hard struggle to afford their own home. However, there are three ways for even first-time buyers to get onto the property ladder without too much difficulty.

Get advice from various sources, compare them and make your own diagnosis about what you can afford

These are to find the right mortgage for the particular property you have in mind or choose a smaller property; to split the cost of the mortgage with another party – say a friend or partner or a member of your family; or to apply for a government or council scheme. There are a confusing number of mortgage options available. Don't jump at the first deal you are offered. Mortgage companies can make their offers sound much more generous than they actually are and may well imply your income can cope with higher payments than it actually can.

Get advice from various sources, compare them all and make your own realistic diagnosis about what you really can afford. Wishful thinking can be disastrous. Take time to study the whole business of mortgages and borrowing money. Make sure you understand the technical terms and are aware of the implications that each deal could have for you if interest rates rise, for example.

FINDING THE RIGHT MORTGAGE

In recent years interest rates in the UK have been at their lowest for 30 years and though they have risen slightly are still a competitive business for lenders. There are therefore plenty of options on offer. In general there are two types of mortgages: interest-only and repayment mortgages, with variants of both on the market.

Interest-only mortgages

With an interest-only mortgage your monthly payments will only cover the interest on the loan taken out with the lender. The full amount borrowed needs to be repaid by the end of the loan term. Most people with an interest-only mortgage invest additional money each month into a savings fund with the expectation that it will grow at least enough to enable them to repay the loan at the end of the term. An endowment is one of these means of saving. Your lender may also insist on life insurance to cover the repayment of the loan in the unlikely event of you dying before the mortgage is paid off.

Repayment mortgages

With a repayment mortgage your monthly repayments repay some of the capital along with the interest on the loan. No other way of repaying the mortgage is needed although, as with interest-only mortgages, your lender may also insist on life insurance in case you die.

See the following table to check on the different types of repayment mortgage available.

TYPE OF REPAYMENT MORTGAGE

Fixed-rate mortgage	Discounted mortgage

DESCRIPTION

Probably the most popular type of mortgage. You and your lender agree to fix the interest rates for a set period of time, usually between one and five years. After that period the interest rate on your loan is usually reset to the lender's variable rate.

Not too dissimilar to fixed-rate mortgages in terms of pricing. The interest rate on offer is set at a set margin below the standard variable rate. Very popular in recent years while interest rates have been falling.

ADVANTAGES

Allows you to budget and provides protection against interest rate increases. Easy to understand and generally extremely competitive.

The 'discount' may be for a number of years, but in some cases the lender offers big discounts for short periods of time, for example 6% off your home loan rate for six months.

DISADVANTAGES

There can be high set-up fees. You are tied in with a redemption penalty, making it expensive to change. However, these are relatively minor points. If the interest rate drops you may be paying more than on a variable rate, but if it rises you are not gambling your home.

These mortgages can be too good to be true. There is no rate protection. The borrower usually has to agree to stay with the lender for a certain period of time or face 'withdrawal penalties'. If rates increase and you are tied in, you are trapped.

| Capped-rate mortgage | Base rate tracker mortgage |

DESCRIPTION

Capped-rate mortgages are a compromise between fixed rate and variable mortgages. There is a fixed upper rate charged on your home loan but if the base rate remains stable or falls, the interest charged on it remains in line.

A base rate tracker mortgage tracks the Bank of England's base rate and changes in accordance with a constant differential set by the lender. Your mortgage payments go up when the base rate goes up and down when the rate goes down. The interest rate is usually set between 0.5% and 0.1% higher than the Bank of England's base rate.

ADVANTAGES

A safe option. If rates are increasing you are protected and can still budget, as with a fixed-rate mortgage. If, say, you are capped at 5% and interest rates go up to 6%, your mortgage will never go higher than 5%. If interest rates fall below 5% you can take advantage of the interest rate coming down.

The Bank of England Committee meet monthly to decide what to do with the base rate and produce the result on the first Thursday of each month. You might therefore have your interest rate cut each month with immediate effect.

DISADVANTAGES

You cannot benefit from the best rates available; better deals can be found on fixed rate and discount mortgages.

If the Committee decides to increase the rates every month and your mortgage has a redemption penalty then you could see your mortgage repayment increasing every month and you will be stuck unless you pay the redemption and get out.

TYPE OF REPAYMENT MORTGAGE

Cashback mortgage	100% mortgage

DESCRIPTION

Almost obsolete now that 100% mortgages are available. From the mid-1990s Abbey National brought out a 95% mortgage, which gave you 5% cashback and meant you didn't need a deposit to buy property.

You can borrow the complete cost of the purchase of the property. Extremely popular in today's market as more and more people stretch their incomes.

ADVANTAGES

Provides you with a cash lump sum, and enables you to buy property with no capital.

Negates the need for a deposit. With a 100% mortgage if the market goes up and your property rises in value by 10% in the first year then you have accrued some equity in the property and made some money on it. Interest rates are not prohibitively high.

DISADVANTAGES

Normally on standard variable rate (SVR); no rate protection and if you want to pay off the mortgage early you have to pay back the full cashback.

The choice of mortgage deals available is limited. You tend to pay a premium for a 100% mortgage so you won't benefit from the best rates on the market.

Australian/flexible mortgage

Offset and current accounts

DESCRIPTION

Still relatively unknown in the UK despite its introduction a few years ago. Allows people to pay their mortgage weekly and gives more flexibility. Each lender offers different types of flexible mortgages with varying combinations of all or some of a set of flexible features – including regular overpayments, lump sum withdrawals and payment holidays.

Combination of mortgage, current account, savings account, credit card and personal loans into one account with the interest set at the mortgage rate which is always higher than the savings rate. Interest is calculated daily and you can put your salary into it.

ADVANTAGES

Beneficial if you get paid weekly. Payment holidays are allowed if you have been paying off the loan for at least six months.

You pay less interest at this reduced amount and your money is working harder saving interest at the mortgage rate than it would be earning it on a lower savings rate. You are using your savings to pay off your mortgage and reduce the interest you pay. For example, if you have a £100,000 mortgage and £40,000 savings you can put that into the account. Offsetting £40,000 against the £100,000 means you pay interest on only £60,000.

DISADVANTAGES

In the British market not many people wish to pay their mortgages on a weekly basis.

If you can offset only £5,000 your payments would be cheaper through a normal fixed-rate or discounted mortgage at a lower rate.

TAUNTON: SECURING THE MONEY

Paul Dare was looking for a project to lose himself in after separating from his wife. He spent part of his divorce settlement on a brand new Mini Cooper S and put the rest, along with a loan of £110,000, into buying and renovating a three-bedroom Victorian terraced house in Taunton, Somerset. It was in a desirable area, just five minutes from the town centre with a primary school just over the road and other luxury developments being built nearby. The house was on two floors wrapping around a corner, with a huge road frontage of 17m (55ft). From outside the property seemed enormous but as it was triangular it was much smaller inside with every room being a different shape. It contained masses of period features.

Upstairs there were three reasonably-sized bedrooms, a big family bathroom and a long, thin room at the top of the stairs. Downstairs was a large dining room with a tiny kitchen squeezed into one of the property's many corners and a reasonably sized sitting room, but all that was about to change. Paul intended to turn the sitting room into a garage, take out the window, widen the opening and have electrically operated garage doors to house his new car. He was going to open up the fireplace and install an indoor barbecue to turn it into a garage-cum-games room. On the other side of the house he was going to knock down a wall to open up the inadequate kitchen area. Outside he was going to do away with the sheds and create a sort of Mediterranean courtyard complete with jacuzzi. Upstairs he intended to move the

bathroom into the smallest room at the top of the stairs complete with sauna, and turn one of the bedrooms into a sitting room.

Paul took out a loan of £110,000 but the mortgage company wouldn't release the money until he had done the structural work.

PROJECT COSTS	
COST OF PROPERTY	£110,000
BUDGET	£27,000
TARGET RESALE	£170,000

This would mean a gross profit excluding fees of £33,000 for five months' work.

This is how Paul broke down the budget for the work:

PROPOSED RENOVATION COSTS	
ROOF	£4,075
GARAGE	£5,000
KITCHEN, BATHROOM AND SAUNA	£4,000
BUILDING AND DECORATION	£7,035
PLUMBING, ELECTRICS, FIXTURES ETC.	£5,000
LEGAL AND PROFESSIONAL FEES	£1,900
TOTAL	£27,010

There was nothing in the budget for contingencies.

SARAH'S ADVICE

This was a big project for someone with so little experience because along with its period features, the property had some serious structural problems. The roof was not properly tied in and the walls were bowing under the weight.

Paul could have turned this into a straightforward, profitable development but he wanted something special. He wanted to make the house different, but it was different anyway. This was a development and was supposed to make money but in a road that already has residents parking, turning the living room into a garage seemed a waste of money. He'd have to reinforce the floors, make the entire room fireproof and with the electric doors it would cost at least £5,000 and I didn't think it would make him a penny.

I also felt very strongly that it would be unwise to move the bathroom into the tiny storeroom space and especially to install a sauna. If he'd been designing a bachelor pad it might have been fun but he wasn't, and for a small family house in Somerset the bathroom seemed very impractical.

There was certainly money to be made from this house but I felt he'd do better to create a simple, stylish family home and forget saunas, garages and indoor barbecues. House prices in Taunton are lower than in surrounding areas; a similar property in Bristol or Exeter would be £100,000 more. And there's no significant student rental market. It's a traditional market town with many buyers with more traditional tastes who won't go for jacuzzis and indoor barbecues. And he was planning to do it all for just £27,000 – it seemed to me more like at least a £50,000 job. Unusually shaped rooms have potential but it's easy to get them wrong if you are too fussy. In a house like this I would recommend putting in fitted cupboards to best utilise the space.

The original kitchen was awkwardly shaped and very narrow at one end. Paul knocked through, creating a spacious and comfortable open-plan kitchen/dining room, probably the most successful space in the conversion.

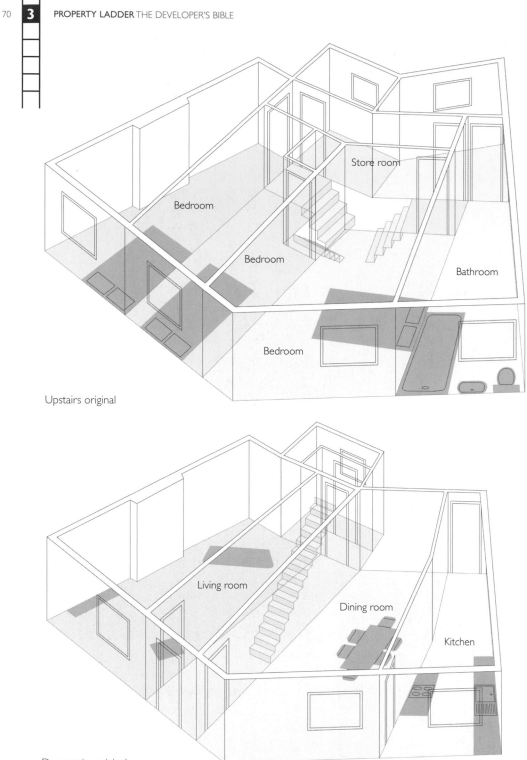

Upstairs original

Downstairs original

Paul bought an eccentric-shaped property with a huge road frontage creating awkward triangular rooms inside. He intended to install a sauna in a tiny store room at the top of the stairs and transfer the bathroom to the narrow space next to it. Downstairs he was going to turn the living room into a garage/party room with electrically operated garage doors.

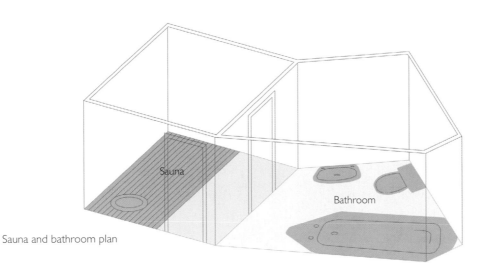

Sauna and bathroom plan

HOW THE PROJECT PROGRESSED

Paul had never done anything like this before and his job as a licensing officer with the local council hadn't prepared him for what was in store. He was working alongside a builder friend who was also helping to manage the project. Although the work got off to a flying start as they dug up the downstairs floor and demolished the lath and plaster walls upstairs, it was not long before Paul found the roof was not the only thing wrong with the house; the floor timbers were in a bad state as well. Then there were hold-ups: the scaffolding went up three days late so they couldn't take the roof off immediately. When they did they found the timbers were too small to support the roof and they would have

The living room was a reasonable size for a family house but Paul decided to turn it into something much more suitable for a bachelor pad: a garage with electronically-operated doors that doubled up as a party space with a built-in barbecue.

to build a totally new roof structure to tie the back and the front together. They had to wait for timbers to be delivered and then wait for the weather.

The work was now two weeks late and Paul couldn't afford delays because his mortgage company had told him they wouldn't release the loan until the roof was completed. He had to give notice on his rented flat and was planning to move into the property. But he now found there was an issue with the head height above the stairs which would have to be moved two feet. Meanwhile his builder, while testing the positioning of an RSJ, managed to smash a hole through the front of the house. This meant more work that had not been planned. He had earmarked £5,000 – 20% of his budget for structural work and couldn't afford any more unexpected problems – and this job had hardly started and was very behind schedule. There were major problems with the electric garage doors which had been set too far back into the opening and had to be repositioned, taking an extra half day. Paul realised that the mortgage company would not release the money until the house was actually habitable and it was a long way from that.

The upstairs bathroom was moved to make room for an extra bedroom and installed in a tiny, narrow space next to the sauna. It was reached through the sauna, and was so small that you had to get into the bath to turn the taps on.

Paul's hot tub took up most of the space in the garden. In fact, all his expensive gadgets and high-tech equipment generally ended up doubling his costs.

Twelve weeks into the project there was still not nearly enough done. Paul took a week off work to help with the building. Time and money were forcing compromises and he gave up the proposed tiles that were to have gone onto the concrete garage floor, and the sauna in the bathroom.

THE OUTCOME

Paul had created a home just right for himself with its own garage/games room, an upstairs living room, around £2,000 worth of cable so that all the rooms could be linked with sounds, computers and TV. There was only a small outside space and that was dominated by the jacuzzi. He had doubled his costs and was unlikely to make a profit, but he moved in temporarily to enjoy using his high-tech bachelor pad himself.

ACTUAL RENOVATION COSTS

	ORIGINAL BUDGET	FINAL SUMS
KITCHEN AND BATHROOM	£2,200	£9,670
GADGETS: NETWORKING AND HOT TUB	£1,900	£8,000
LABOUR	£2,700	£9,580
STRUCTURAL WORK, PLUMBING, ELECTRICITY	£6,500	£6,500
FIXTURES AND FITTINGS	£6,155	£12,750
SELLING FEES AND MORTGAGE REPAYMENTS	£0	£8,500
TOTAL	£19,455	£55,000

LESSONS LEARNED

1 *Where possible, make sure the money is available.* Paul was inexperienced and had no idea that there was so much structural work to be done on the house or that he would not get his mortgage until the roof was sound and the house habitable.

2 *Consider your target market.* Paul's house had a quirky charm which could have appealed to a wide market but Paul seemed to be creating his own bachelor pad and forgetting most of his market.

3 *Keep your market in mind throughout the project.* Paul found the developing very therapeutic and designed a house that he would enjoy but would it suit a more traditional family in Taunton? He had decided to put a jacuzzi bathtub in his very small outside courtyard. Jacuzzis, whirlpools, hot tubs and saunas don't add to the value of a property such as this. Whatever improvements you do, make sure they add more to your development than the original cost of putting them in.

BUYING JOINTLY

If you prefer not to work alone or simply cannot afford to invest in a property on your own, you might consider buying jointly with someone else. Getting a joint mortgage will increase your borrowing power. Theoretically you can apply for a joint mortgage for up to four people although most lenders base their calculations for a loan on the incomes of two people. As with a single borrower, the amount is generally based on three-and-a-half times the main income, but with a second borrower add one of the secondary incomes to the equation.

A word of warning here. A joint mortgage with one other person is quite common and can be very successful. Just remember, though, that whilst more people in your new enterprise can provide the comfort of more brains to tackle problems, not to mention more money, the more people you add to the equation the more difficult it can be to reach decisions since there are more alternative opinions to put into the boiling pot and more salaries to draw out of the project at the end. So think very hard before putting all your resources into a property that may become a cause of dissent.

If you decide against a joint or multiple joint mortgage, there are other ways of splitting the cost. A parent or family member may be willing to act as guarantor on your loan. If so, it is important that all parties fully appreciate the implications of this arrangement – that the guarantor becomes liable for the loan in its entirety should your payments fall behind. Not only is this a big responsibility for the mortgage, but ultimately it is an even bigger responsibility for the guarantor.

If you do buy with a partner (or partners) you must have an agreement drawn up by a solicitor. This should state how much each party is contributing in terms of the down-payment and who is going to be responsible for the mortgage repayments (though legally you are joint and severally liable). Most importantly it will state what percentage of the profit is to belong to each of the parties. It should also state the course of action to be taken if one owner wishes to sell the property early. (Generally one partner may have the option to buy out the other at the current market price or it may be necessary to sell the property and divide the money.) An agreement such as this will not only protect both parties in the event of a disagreement but also makes things clear from the beginning and will hopefully avoid a disagreement from occurring.

GOVERNMENT AND COUNCIL SCHEMES

If you cannot afford a mortgage and you are not looking for a development but just want to buy a home, you can consider some of the government schemes designed to help first-time buyers get on the property ladder. The government recognises that there is a demand in the UK for people to own their own home and has set up several schemes to help those struggling to do so. Note that these options are only available to home-buyers and not to developers.

Right to Buy

The Right to Buy scheme was introduced in 1980 and is still relevant to the stated aim of a recent Housing Green Paper, 'Quality and Choice, A Decent Home for All'. The scheme allows council tenants of two years or more to purchase the home they live in at a price that reflects the rent that has been paid to date and, to date, has helped over 1.3 million council tenants in England buy their own homes. There are two options available under the Right to Buy scheme. Firstly, you can buy your home by paying the full purchase price with discounts ranging from 32% to 70% according to the number of years you have spent living there as a council tenant and subject to a maximum

OTHER SCHEMES

There are a number of other low-cost home ownership schemes available:

- 'Right to Acquire': similar to Right to Buy, giving certain tenants of Registered Social Landlords (RSLs) a statutory right to buy their home at a discount.
- Homebuy: enables RSL and local authority tenants to buy a home on the open market with the help of an interest-free equity loan equal to 25% of the purchase price.
- Conventional Shared Ownership: allows RSLs to build or purchase and then renovate existing dwellings for sale on shared ownership terms. The purchaser buys a share of a property (typically from 25% upwards) and pays rent on the remaining share.
- Cash Incentive Scheme: aims to release local authority accommodation for letting to those in need of housing and encourages owner occupation. The scheme works by paying a grant to a tenant to help the tenant buy a property in the private sector.
- Do-It-Yourself Shared Ownership: offered by a few local authorities and allows people on low incomes access to home ownership. Unlike 'Conventional Shared Ownership' it allows a purchaser to select a property on the open market and then buy it on shared ownership terms, paying rent on the share they do not own.
- Starter Home Initiative: helps key workers on low incomes (such as health workers, teachers and the police) to purchase a house in highly priced areas which are undermining recruitment in their sector.

discount limit for the area in which you live. Secondly, you can use the Rent to Mortgage scheme if you want to buy your home but cannot afford to pay for it all at once. You should be aware that government and council schemes of this kind are not open to property developers.

CREATING AND CONTROLLING A BUDGET

One of the most common and most serious mistakes made by first-time developers is to underestimate the budget. Make up your mind what you are doing and if you really are property developing then that is a business. You must include all your outgoings and costings, allow for contingencies and know where you can make cutbacks if

the budget looks like getting out of hand. Burying your head in the sand and simply not looking at the sums at all because you don't like what you see is not fooling anyone but yourself. An overspend will not go away and managing the money does require organisation and discipline. Don't forget if there is no real profit at the end of the year your new business will not be able to trade.

Cash flow

Remember, cash flow is the key to success or failure. Plan your budget meticulously and itemise in detail the things you will have to pay for. You will find that you end up drawing on the money by degrees. Avoid getting carried

It is absolutely vital to make sure the amount you pay for your property makes it a sound investment

away at the beginning of a project just because your bank balance is looking healthier than it has done in years – you may find that there is nothing left for crucial works later on, leaving you with no alternative but to cut corners to get the work finished. Working out a realistic budget in the first place is the answer to this. It is absolutely vital to make sure the amount you pay for your property makes it a sound investment before you commit yourself; rather than buying something that happens to be unmodernised and then discovering that the cost of the development and the purchase price actually adds up to more than you can sell it for.

How much will it cost?

If you itemise realistically you can work out a sound allocation of costs. The maths may seem a bit overwhelming and the probable costs may seem terrifying but if you are not realistic at this stage you will be in for big trouble later on. The most common expense to overlook is the actual cost of buying, owning and selling the property. You also need to include everything from major repairs and structural alterations to light fittings and bathroom and kitchen fixtures. And don't forget to factor in the cost labour.

Experience will help you know how much something is likely to cost, but before you have built up the experience it is useful to make a detailed schedule of the works that need to be carried out on the property, with drawings if necessary. Then approach builders and collect together your quotes. Go over this budget over and over again and adjust it as necessary. If you have no experience of what these costs are and are not used to working out a budget, it is easy to miss vital items, forgetting to include, say, stamp duty or perhaps even the wiring, and especially forgetting that there will certainly be unexpected expenses on the way.

BASIC RULES FOR A SUCCESSFUL PROJECT

Don't be tempted to spend money on things just because you like them – remember just because it is your taste it doesn't mean it will be anyone elses. Make your money matter – spend where required but not where desired. Other guidelines include:

- Get a survey done. Before you purchase any property, make sure you understand its problems, know what work is needed and whether this is the project for you.
- Get a second opinion. Check what has been sold for what price recently – you can also ask the estate agent you are planning to sell the property through what they think will add value to the property. Consider their advice but don't follow it blindly – above all remember this is not a home for you.
- Be aware of current Building Regulation requirements and adhere to them. Seek advice from the Building Regulations Officer at your local council planning department. It is illegal to carry out work that does not comply with Building Regulations; flouting regulations will almost certainly come up through solicitors and surveyors during a sale and may well affect the ability of a potential buyer to secure a mortgage on the property. Most planning departments are very helpful, so ask their advice.

■ Have integrity in your product. Do a job properly or not at all. Purchasers and certainly their surveyors are not foolish and so don't labour under the illusion that you won't get found out.

■ Design for your market and not for yourself. Whilst keeping the décor as neutral as possible, don't feel as though you have to make the property bland. Create the best possible layout but leave scope for potential buyers not to feel smothered by your flights of design fancy.

Don't forget that however exciting an adventure developing a property may be, it is first and foremost a business and a business needs to be successful – that is, in the not-too-long run you need it to make you a profit. To succeed you must be businesslike from start to finish.

This means having an organised approach to the whole venture, getting advice where it is needed, keeping an efficient office and records and doing things methodically. Then if anything goes wrong, you have your files and records to refer back to, you know how you stand financially, you have advisors' contact details to hand and you should be able to organise yourself out of trouble.

Make lists. Don't rely on your own memory – however well exercised it is it will still let you down now and then! Deal with all potential difficulties before they reach a head. Trust me, they won't go away!

THE TAX SITUATION

Once you have made a profit from any development and sale you will have to consider tax.

Principal Private Residence Relief

If the house is your only home and your place of residence, then you are allowed to sell it on and keep the profit and not pay any tax at all.

Capital Gains Tax (CGT)

If the property is not your place of residence you are liable to pay this tax, although as an individual you are allowed to make capital gain a percentage of the profits (£8,200 in the 2004/2005 tax year) before you are liable to pay CGT. Any gain above this limit is charged at different rates depending on your circumstances (although not more than the top rate of 40%).

Income Tax

A professional property developer has to pay income tax on the profits. Help sheets are available free on the Inland Revenue website covering all these tax issues. Developers with queries regarding the allowability of expenses are advised to seek the advice of their local Tax Office as all cases are different.

> No matter how exciting an adventure developing a property may be, it is first and foremost a business

VAT

VAT is a tax chargeable on taxable supplies made in the UK by 'taxable persons'. All types of supply of goods or services (outputs) are covered by VAT law, whether of a revenue or capital nature. Supplies include the sale, hire or loan of goods. Outputs usually fall into one of four categories:

■ Positive rated: taxable at 17.5% or at a reduced rate of 5% for some supplies including construction work on property conversions, domestic fuel and power and energy-saving materials.

■ Zero-rated: including 'socially or economically important' items e.g. public transport, children's clothing and so on.

■ Exempt supplies including 'necessities' e.g. most forms of insurance, postage, finance and so on.

■ Other: some supplies are outside the scope of VAT e.g. non-EU supplies.

CALCULATING YOUR PROFIT

Make sure you understand the issues touched on above before being able to count your profit. Until you have some experience and a few projects under your belt it is all too easy to miss out details that could prove very expensive in the long run. A good idea is to photocopy the checklist on pages 183–87 and take it with you to each viewing. Tick the boxes and jot in the relevant items as you go round the property. When you get it home it will be an invaluable aid to remind you about each property; you can add details about the alterations that need to be done and work out costings, getting quotes for each job.

The completed charts will help you calculate your renovation budget. Add this sum to the administrative and purchase costs of the property and subtract this figure from the potential sale price.

Calculations about what the development is costing and therefore the potential profit need to be constantly reviewed because things change constantly and you need to be aware of where you will need to make cost cuts as the work goes forward. The initial calculation of your potential profit should be whatever is left after you have taken the purchase price, administrative costs and renovation budget off the potential sale price. The all-important calculation to make here is the total cost of the whole development.

This is a very basic calculation, but it is essential that you remember to include all costs. Don't forget you will be paying more in terms of borrowing if you run over time. The following is an example of how costs are broken down to calculate profit.

PURCHASE PRICE	£80,000
COST OF WORKS INCLUDING CONTINGENCY	£25,000
PURCHASE/SALE, LEGAL AND BORROWING FEES	£15,000
TOTAL COSTS	£120,000
SELLING PRICE	£135,000
PROFIT	£15,000

MORTGAGE PROTECTION

Remember that if you decide to give up your job or are made redundant during your development project or if you become ill or injured, you may have difficulty keeping up your mortgage payments. You cannot rely on the State to help to cover the payments. There is no help for the first nine months of unemployment or disability for mortgages. It may be worth buying extra cover to protect your mortgage payments in case this situation arises. Policies differ, so always check them very carefully.

MONEY CHECKLIST

1 Be realistic about what you can take on financially.
2 Make sure you can definitely access the money for the purchase and other expenses. Research more than one possible lending scheme.
3 Get as much sound financial advice as possible from more than one lender or independent mortgage broker or financial advisor.
4 Make sure you work out a realistic budget. Calculate on the pessimistic side to avoid nasty shocks.
5 Keep detailed records for your accountant to calculate tax owed.
6 Review your calculations as to your spending regularly as the work progresses.

4
BUYING AND
SELLING PROPERTY

4 BUYING

When buying a property there are many considerations, including whether you should buy freehold or leasehold, where you should buy, the problems of finding a solicitor, getting a structural survey and making use of the results. Don't set your heart on one particular property until you have completed the purchase. Many things can go wrong, especially if there is a chain of purchasers, so don't commit yourself to any advance expense that relies on the purchase going ahead. And be patient – the whole process may take longer than you expect.

Buying property can be a complicated and time-consuming process. Each stage of the procedure can be lengthy, particularly if there is a chain of people all trying to buy and sell at the same time. The process may be less complicated if the property you are buying is empty. In England there is always a risk that the sale could fall through at any stage before the contracts have been exchanged. There are a number of reasons why this could happen: if the seller decides not to sell; if the seller accepts a better offer, thereby gazumping you; if you cannot agree to the conditions of the sale; if a survey or homebuyer's report highlight problems with the property; or if you cannot get the mortgage you need.

FREEHOLD OR LEASEHOLD
It is important that you know the difference between a freehold property and a leasehold one.

Buying freehold
Most houses are freehold properties. This means that you legally own and are responsible for the house and its grounds. As such, it is your job to maintain the property and check the professional status of any workmen you employ to carry out repairs. You will need to be aware of any by-laws that may govern what you do, for example whether the property is in a Conservation Area, or whether the building you want to buy is listed. In multiple occupancy properties the residents may join together and purchase the freehold to ensure the property is cared for as they would wish.

Buying leasehold
The majority of flats are sold on a leasehold basis. This means you have bought a lease, which allows you to live in the property for a certain length of time. The actual owner of the building is the person or company who owns

the freehold and you will have to pay them an annual ground rent. They are then responsible for the maintenance and upkeep of the building. For this service they will expect you to pay additional service charges for which they should arrange buildings insurance, cleaning and general maintenance. The cost of extra works, such as the redecoration of communal areas or roof repairs or new lifts will usually be split between the number of leaseholders in the building. On rare occasions, leaseholders may be responsible for all of the maintenance work on the property. Be sure to find out the details of the lease at the viewing stage. Always know what you are buying before you invest.

As with short-lease landlords, there are good and bad freeholders, some more responsible than others. If you have problems with shoddy work, inflated bills and poor management, you can get together with the other leaseholders in your block and present a case to your local leasehold valuation tribunal, a body that deals with disputes over service charges and the purchase of leasehold property by tenants holding long leases.

If the freeholder appears to have been less than diligent, it is worth checking whether it is possible to actually buy out the freeholder or, alternatively, purchase a share of the freehold. This usually happens when all of the leaseholders have got together and formed a company to buy out the freeholder, transferring the responsibilities of the property to the parties who live there and giving them direct control of the property and its maintenance.

FINDING A PROPERTY
First you have to find an area which is suitable for your purpose. Then you have to find the property itself. At first glance there may be plenty of potential properties, but on closer inspection you will probably find that few of these

will be cost effective by the time you've done them up and sold them on. So study the information in this chapter and follow the guidelines if you don't want to make expensive mistakes. The initial stages of sourcing a property are:

■ Researching an area.
■ Finding a property.
■ Viewing a property.
■ Arranging a survey.

You can then proceed with the buying process (see page 87).

The first thing when looking for a property is to choose the area you want to buy in. You may try to find an up-and-coming area but it is difficult to make sure you're hitting it at exactly the right time. Sometimes areas take years to fulfil their up-and-coming promise (see pages 14–15). If possible choose an area near where you live so you can spend time there and really get to know it.

WAYS OF FINDING A PROPERTY
Estate agents

These are the obvious first port of call when looking for a property. Register with all the estate agents in the area who will send details via e-mail and post. You will soon get to recognise the jargon and what to expect from estate agents' descriptions and pick out just those that seem relevant to your project.

Driving round the area

Estate agents are not the only option. A useful way when you are just starting out and if you have time is to drive round a particular area and look at properties with 'for sale' signs outside. You can dismiss immediately those in impossible locations and home in on those that look promising. This may be expensive in time and petrol but can be very educational about an area. For example, if there seem to be many homes for sale in one area, there may be some reason that people are not buying there.

> A useful way is to drive round a particular area and look at properties with 'for sale' signs outside

Local press

Scour the local papers and property magazines for properties, some of which may be for private sale.

Buying at auction

Buying at auction is a way of buying a property at a competitive price. But be warned – buying at auction is a skill that has to be learned. There is much more to this method of buying than turning up and landing a bargain at the drop of the hammer. If you are not careful or have not been to an auction before, you could get carried away and end up bidding over the odds for a property. You must do your research. Find out as much as possible about the property you are interested in bidding for well in advance of the auction day and visit an auction house to sit in on a few property lots before you actually go to buy so that you understand how auctions work. You can find out where and when property auctions are held in your area from the local press or the Internet. The auction process is exciting and it is easy to get carried away.

Always give yourself a top price and do not allow yourself to go over that, no matter how tempted you are. If the bidding gets too high, get up and leave. If nobody else is interested in the property you may be able to pick up a real bargain, although this hardly ever happens. Properties sold at auction can be very risky as they are often run-down properties that require major structural work. If you buy on a whim, you can end up paying well over the odds for a property that turns out to be a liability and not an asset. Remember, once the hammer goes down you are legally obliged to buy the property and you must complete within four weeks.

The Internet

This can be an absolutely fascinating way of looking for property. It can also be very time-consuming. Pick an area and stick to it otherwise you can too easily get seduced by properties not conveniently nearby which would be a drain on your resources and energy and fail to bring in that essential profit.

OTHER WAYS OF FINDING CHEAP PROPERTIES

If you are prepared to do some research yourself there are other ways of purchasing property which can sometimes work out cheaper:

Buying off-plan

This means buying a property that has yet to be built. The best way to find out about these is via the property press. Contact the developers to see computer graphics and artists' impressions of the finished scheme and find out

> # Buying off-plan will give you the opportunity to choose the layout and view you like best

about their previous projects. Visiting these will give you a feel for the developer's design style. Make sure you have a list of agreed internal fixtures and fittings from the developer in writing.

Buying early like this will give you the opportunity to choose the layout and view you like best. You can often get a good deal – the developer usually asks for a reservation fee when you choose your home so they can show their financier they have a certain number of sales. This frees up their cash flow and allows them to offer the property at a cheaper price than when the scheme is completed. If the market is good your investment may have increased before you move in.

You may also benefit from discounted deals your developer can take advantage of for fittings and furnishings with new constructions. These are often fashionable and can also add value to the property. If the area is on the way up, you could be investing where prices are about to rise. However, remember, if the market drops, you are obliged to complete on the home at the same purchase price.

Buying privately

Small ads in local papers and some ads on the Internet offer private sales of property. This could save you a few thousand pounds if the vendor is advertising a property for a quick sale and deducts their saving in agents' fees from the asking price.

Don't assume, however, that a private sale is automatically a bargain. The disadvantages are that it is you who will be working for any financial saving. You may waste time viewing properties that are unrealistically described and will need to deal with the vendor directly. If you decide to pursue a private sale be sure you are clear about what you expect to be included in the sale and confirm any verbal agreements in writing.

Buy ex-council stock

You can still sometimes find brick-built properties with roofs and windows in good condition and lots of private homes nearby.

Buy outside the peak periods

Most people buy properties in spring and autumn so you may find the odd bargain in winter or summer when the few people selling may be desperate to do so quickly.

Consider repossessions

These properties may well be in a poor state of repair but the mortgage lender will be keen to sell as quickly as possible and so a cheaper price may be negotiable (although the law says that lenders must get the 'best price reasonably obtainable').

VIEWING THE PROPERTY

Buying the property will commit you to it. So make sure you buy one that can actually be turned into a saleable product without costing a fortune. Take your time to consider a number of properties in the area and learn to recognise what you are looking at and what you are looking for. Don't jump at the first property you see because it has a pretty front door or an apple tree in the garden. Dress comfortably and wear trainers or walking shoes. Take a notepad and pen or electronic notebook and a camcorder or digital camera to record your viewings as no amount of memory work compares with watching your tour again when you get home; but always ask permission from the vendors first. Don't be rushed – this is an important purchase for you and you need to think it through thoroughly.

View as many likely properties as you can. It's the best way of getting a feeling for when a property is sound and when it isn't, whether it's being offered at a good price

that reflects the standard and size of accommodation on offer locally and you can make sure it is in a location that you like. Be wary of properties on busy roads, flats in basements and properties that need too much expensive renovation. Sometimes such elements can seem to indicate value for money, but often the disadvantages outweigh the advantages.

The exterior

Inspect the exterior of the property carefully. Stand well back from the house and look to see whether it is horizontally and vertically aligned, whether the windows are level and whether there are any major cracks in the brickwork, particularly under windows. These all indicate that there may be subsidence or structural instability. Check that chimneys are standing up straight. Get to recognise potentially expensive works that will be needed from the exterior such as rotten window frames, bad pointing, loose gutters and cracked or missing roof tiles. Look for a damp-proof course. Lack of damp-proofing will have to be rectified and such work is expensive.

The interior

Once inside, check for signs of damp. Get to recognise the smell of damp and rot and watch out for damp patches on the walls or ceilings. Do the floorboards feel spongy when you walk on them? Can you see any fungus or spores lurking in dark corners? Indoors look for unsatisfactory plumbing and check to see if there is an old and inefficient boiler. Look for expensive items that need updating such as new window frames (are the windows double-glazed?), new flooring or a new bathroom suite. Are there enough power points?

Check that the property has been well cared for (and not just had a coat of paint slapped over some chronic problem such as a crack in the wall). In general, if it has been well maintained most problems are likely to have been fixed rather than concealed. Badly done DIY jobs, poorly finished paintwork and attempts to mask problems are all warning signs.

What to ask

Don't be inhibited about asking questions. Ask, for example, about the plumbing, check the age and condition of the boiler and find out when the house was last rewired. Ask what will be included in the sale. For example is the shed in the garden included, the light fittings, any shelves, fitted carpets? If they are included and you don't want them, find out whether you could get a reduction for not including them. Are the walls and roof insulated? How much does it cost to heat the house in winter? Is there a selling chain? If the vendors are waiting to move into another house before they sell, you could wait a very long time before completing.

Second visit

If a property meets most of your criteria on the first viewing, then it's time for a second visit. Use this opportunity to take a very good look at the basic structure and condition of the property. Take a friend or parent with you. A second opinion can be invaluable and may prevent you from getting carried away and making an expensive mistake and it's even better if he/she is a builder or has experience in buying or renovating property.

You should also be aware of any sites surrounding your property, particularly possible development sites and check the planning records for those sites. Planning control seeks to protect residential amenity, e.g. the amount of light into habitable rooms, but there is no right to a view in planning law. So if the unrestricted view of the river, park or clock tower is what you bought a house for, make sure that permission has not been granted for any development in the way (or it has not been identified as a development site in the council's development plan).

THE BUYING PROCESS

Buying a house is a complicated business and the process usually takes a few months. There are six main steps to go through. Making an offer and the whole process usually happens more or less in the following order:

- Getting a valuation.
- Getting a survey or homebuyer's report.
- Doing the legal preparation (conveyancing).
- Exchanging contracts and paying a deposit.
- Completing the sale.

There are many hidden costs along the way. You are likely to have to pay a lot of money on top of the purchase price before you become the actual owner.

Making an offer

This is a process of negotiation and it is rare for the asking price to be the final price. Estate agents deliberately mark the property artificially high since it is taken for granted that negotiation will take place. The first offer is usually 5–10% below the asking price, depending on the perceived level of demand and current market conditions. The two sides then work towards a price somewhere in the middle.

Before making an offer be sure that you know the market value of the property. It's worth finding out what properties have actually sold for in the area, rather than the price that they were valued at. You are not restricted to making an offer on only one property but if all your offers are accepted you will have to make a decision very quickly.

If your offer is accepted it will then be 'subject to contract'. This means you and the seller have agreed in principle to go ahead with the transaction but neither of you is yet legally bound.

When making an offer make sure the vendor and agent are both aware of the terms of your offer. For example, which fixtures and fittings you want to be included and what work you want to be completed on the property before the sale is completed. Make sure the offer is subject to a survey and contract. If the survey shows something that needs doing on the property, renegotiate. If a large amount of work needs to be done on the property this may have been factored into the price, but sometimes it is not. You may be able to negotiate the price more effectively if you make an issue of any repair work and convince the seller that the property is genuinely overpriced.

Ask the vendor to take the house off the market immediately to discourage any further offers and reduce the risk of being gazumped.

VALUATIONS AND SURVEYS

Once you have found a property you want, secured your mortgage and got your solicitor on board it is time to think about the survey. It is tempting to dismiss the need for an independent surveyor's report with so many other costs piling up, but it is your responsibility as the buyer to find out what you are committing yourself to. The seller has no liability whatsoever once the purchase is completed. Surveys are designed to give you the information you need to make an informed and sensible property purchase. The Consumer's Association and the Council of Mortgage Lenders both advise you to arrange a survey before buying a property. I advocate the same. There are three main types of survey: basic valuation, homebuyer's report and full structural survey. When money is tight, the idea of spending more than the bare minimum may not be desirable, but a survey is essential if you are buying an old property or one that needs any degree of renovation. Do not rely on just a valuation.

> # Surveys are designed to give you the information you need to make an informed and sensible property purchase

A VALUATION

A valuation, or 'basic valuation' as it is often called, is an inspection carried out on behalf of your mortgage lender to ensure their investment is sound. In other words, its purpose is to check that your intended property is worth at least the amount they are lending you and to identify any problems that could affect the security of the loan. Your mortgage lender will expect you to pay for the valuation. In addition to the cost of the valuation itself, you may also be charged an administration or arrangement fee by your bank or building society. You are entitled to know the amount of the fee being paid to the surveyor and the amount being retained by the lender.

A valuation is not a survey. It is a limited inspection. A property can have defects that are not of concern to the mortgage lender and therefore won't appear in a valuation report. Furthermore, a valuation does not provide you with any legal recourse as it is for the benefit of the lender only.

One of the biggest mistakes made by first-time buyers is to rely on the information provided by the valuation when deciding whether or not to purchase a property. Before you dismiss the idea of a survey, remember that it does give you a certain amount of legal recourse and is conducted for the benefit of the borrower rather than the lender. Make sure you fully understand what is and is not included in the survey. If you choose to instruct your own independent surveyor, ask about any specific information you would like to know before the survey is conducted, for example whether or not it will be feasible to make structural alterations. You should also mention any specific areas for investigation, such as testing the drains or checking for woodworm. If your surveyor is not qualified to do this, he or she should be able to arrange for another specialist to do it.

Surveyors should comment on all parts of a property that are readily accessible but they are not obliged to inspect areas that are difficult to get at. They won't lift carpets, shift furniture, use a ladder to inspect the roof or move items stored in the loft unless you specifically instruct them to do so. Similarly, since most surveyors are not trained electricians or plumbers, they will not test services such as the wiring and water supply. However, they may comment on their condition. Where necessary, surveyors will recommend that an expert examination be carried out.

Read the terms and conditions of the survey carefully and double-check with your surveyor if you are unclear about anything. Use the results of your survey to make a reasoned and informed judgement as to whether to proceed with the purchase and to assess whether the property is a reasonable purchase at the agreed price. Be clear what decisions and courses of action should be taken before the contracts are exchanged.

FLAT OR HOMEBUYER'S SURVEY AND VALUATION REPORT

The Homebuyer's Survey and Valuation Report (HSV) is a service carried out to a standard format defined by the Royal Institution of Chartered Surveyors (RICS). The HSV is primarily designed for properties built within the last 150 years, which are of conventional construction and in reasonable condition. An HSV does give you legal recourse but is not a detailed survey of every aspect of the property. It focuses only on significant and urgent matters.

An HSV seeks information on the following:
- The property's general condition.
- Urgent and significant matters that need assessing before entering into exchanging contracts (or before making an offer in Scotland) including recommendations for any further specialist inspectors.
- Any significant defects in accessible parts of the property, which may affect its value.
- Results of any testing of walls for dampness.
- General comments on damage to timbers, including woodworm or rot and evidence of damp.
- Comments on the existence and condition of damp-proofing, insulation and drainage (although the latter will not be tested).
- The recommended reinstatement cost for insurance purposes. This means the anticipated costs of reconstructing a building in the event of its damage by an insured risk such as fire. It is not the same as the market value of the property.
- The value of the property on the open market.

Once you have arranged your survey or valuation report, you need to be able to understand the results. The following pages provide examples of a survey and explain the most common structural terms to help you make the most of your survey and ensure you steer clear of expensive mistakes.

Report No.

Voucher No / Case Id.

Instructing Office:

Reporting Office:

Residential Property Mortgage Valuation Report

(Figures in brackets are for Nationwide use)

Inspection date:

BRANCH COPY

1. MORTGAGE DETAILS

Applicant(s) Name(s)

Property Address
inc. postcode

Purchase Price £   Advance Amount £

2. TENURE

Tenure   Freehold (0) / ~~Leasehold (1)~~ or ~~Feudal (2)~~   If Leasehold unexpired term   Years

Rent -   Ground/Chief/Feu   £   p.a.   Fixed/escalating etc.

Maintenance charge   £   p.a.   Other

If shared ownership, what % of the property is being purchased?   %

3. TENANCIES

Is there any tenancy apparent?   ~~Yes~~ / No   If Yes - please give details and rent(s) upon any agreement

4. PROPERTY DESCRIPTION

Type of Property   Detached House (01) ☐   Semi - Det House (02) ☐   Terraced House (03) ☒   Detached Bungalow (11) ☐

Other Bungalow (12) ☐   Purpose Built Flat (31) ☐   Converted Flat (33) ☐

Approx. Year Built   1880   If a flat, which floor is it on?   Is there a lift?   ~~Yes~~ / No

Number of Bedrooms   2   Number of Bathrooms (inc. ensuite bath/shower rooms)   1   Number of habitable rooms   4

5. PROPERTY CONSTRUCTION

Main Building
Construction - Walls   225 mm solid brickwork.   Roof   Pitched and slated.

Garage / Parking Space   ~~Single (1)~~ / ~~Double (2)~~ / ~~Parking Space (3)~~ / None (4)

Is the parking space / garage offsite?   ~~Yes~~ / No

6. SERVICES

Mains Services Available   Electricity / Gas / Water / Drainage / ~~Other~~

Type of Central Heating   ~~None(0)~~ / Full Gas (1) / ~~Full Electric (2)~~ / ~~Full Oil Fired (3)~~ / ~~Full Solid Fuel (4)~~

~~Part Gas (5)~~ / ~~Part Electric (6)~~ / ~~Part Oil Fired (7)~~ / ~~Part Solid Fuel (8)~~

7. NEW PROPERTIES (if applicable)

Name of Builder   NHBC / Zurich / Architect / Other

Are roads / footpaths   made / partly made / unmade   Estimated cost of making up   £

8. BUILDINGS INSURANCE

Estimated current re-instatement cost including site clearance and professional fees excluding VAT, except on fees   £90,000

Floor area - Main Building   75   m²
Garage if not integral   m²
Other Buildings   m²

Does this property need to be referred due to special insurance risks?   Yes / ~~No~~   If Yes - include appropriate key statements in Section 10 - General Remarks

Case Reference: M1066692	Page 1 of 4	M 4 (07-01)

A Homebuyer's Survey and Valuation Report is designed to satisfy you that the property has no obvious structural defects, although the level of examination undertaken by the surveyors is by no means as thorough as that carried out for a full structural survey.

Property Address: 45, Lothrop Street, London   **BRANCH COPY**

9. OTHER MATTERS THAT MAY MATERIALLY AFFECT THE VALUE
(If applicable, give more detail in General Remarks below)

Is the property readily saleable at or about the valuation figure?	Yes / ~~No~~	In the case of flats etc. is proper management / maintenance apparent? — ~~Yes~~ / ~~No~~
Has the property ever been affected by structural movement caused by subsidence, settlement, landslip or heave?	Yes / ~~No~~	Is the risk of further movement one the Society can accept? (If No decline property) — Yes / ~~No~~
Rights of way / Easements / Servitudes / Wayleaves (where apparent on inspection)	~~Yes~~ / No	Building works that may have required Planning Permission / Building Regulation approval — ~~Yes~~ / ~~No~~

Any other important factors?   Yes / ~~No~~   If Yes give details: | Please see GENERAL REMARKS. |

10. GENERAL REMARKS (including the general condition of the property)

The subject property is an ex Local Authority two storey mid-terraced dwelling house situated within an established residential area accessible to all the usual urban amenities of West London.

The property has been maintained and decorated to a generally satisfactory standard and there is one essential repair relating to providing documentation for the underpinning of part of the main front wall.

Limited rising dampness was noted and we would advise that a damp and timber defects specialist inspects the property and carries out any required works.

There is a deciduous tree approximately 5 metres from the building, approximately 10 metres high outside the boundaries on suspected shrinkable subsoil. Trees can cause damage to buildings and services but none was seen. Arrangements should be made for the tree to be kept regularly pruned to prevent it from increasing in size. (continued)

Legal advisers should confirm that all consents have been obtained for the through reception room and the removal of the ground floor chimney breast.

Demand for this property may be reduced because the bathroom is on the ground floor.

11. WORKS TO BE CARRIED OUT as condition of mortgage subject to retention below. (Listing should only include work absolutely necessary to protect the Society's security. The amount of advance must be ignored.)

Provide documentation for the underpinning works.

a)   Name of contractor.

b)   Plans and specifications.
(continued)
c)   Name of owner at time.

d)   Name and address of any insurance company which dealt with a claim.

e)   Engineers report and supervision certificate.

f)   Any guarantees.

Amount of Recommended Retention (minimum retention amount is £1000. This is not an estimate of costs. The Applicant(s) should obtain detailed estimates before proceeding with the purchase.) | £ |

12. VALUATION FOR MORTGAGE PURPOSES - (assuming vacant possession unless otherwise stated)

Is the property a suitable security for the Society?	Yes / ~~No~~
If Yes, valuation in present condition	£
Valuation upon completion of any works required under section 7 or 11	£290,000
If shared ownership, value of share being purchased	£

I certify that I have personally inspected the property and that in making this report I am not contravening Section 13 of the Building Societies Act 1986, or any variation or re-enactment of it.

Valuer's Signature	501163 = 3838	Firm Address	
Name and Qualification Firm's Identity Code			

Property Address: 45, Lothrop Street, London   **BRANCH COPY**

Date		Postcode Telephone Fax Number	

IMPORTANT NOTICE TO APPLICANT(S)

This report has been prepared solely for the Society's purposes. It is not a structural report and is based upon a limited inspection. It may not reveal serious defects and may contain inaccuracies and omissions. It is unlikely to be adequate for a purchaser's purposes and should not be relied upon.

YOU ARE STRONGLY ADVISED TO OBTAIN A FULLER REPORT ON THE PROPERTY.

The Society does not guarantee that the purchase price is reasonable.

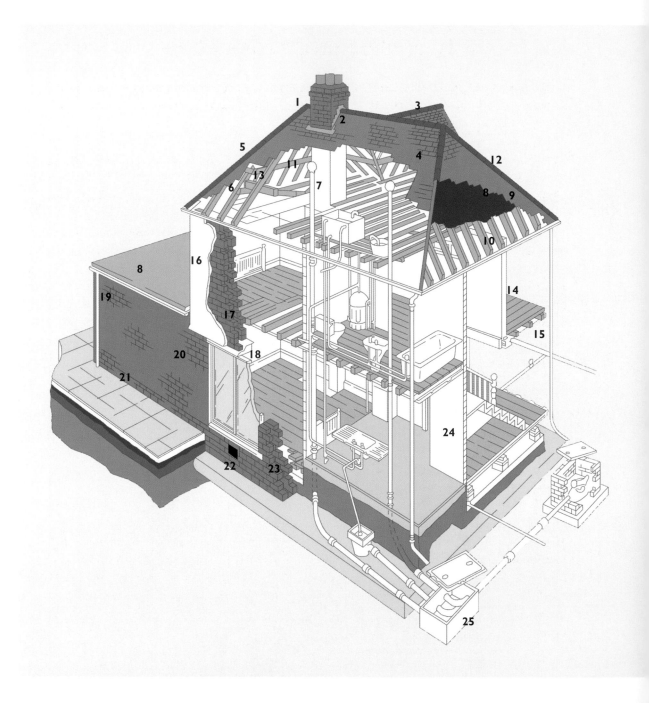

STRUCTURAL ASPECTS OF A HOUSE

The following list of definitions explains some of the official terminology used when referring to a building's structure. Not every building will incorporate all the elements highlighted here but some, such as rafters and slating, will be common to most.

1 **Chimney stack:** the part of the chimney generally built in brick.

2 **Flashing:** generally made from lead, this is placed around chimney stacks. It weatherproofs the angle between the roof finish and any adjoining walls.

3 **Ridge:** the highest part of a roof where the pitches meet, usually covered by ridge tiles or lead.

4 **Slating or tiling:** the outer roof covering.

5 **Pitch:** the angle of the roof slope.

6 **Insulation:** generally a wadding laid over the ceiling joists.

7 **Soil and vent pipe:** the 4in pipe that takes waste from the loo to the main drain or septic tank.

8 **Felt:** material used to cover the battens on a sloping roof. Also used to cover flat roofs, with a layer of stone chippings applied over it.

9 **Battens:** thin strips of wood on the roof to which felt and then tiles or slates are fixed.

10 **Rafters:** the sloping timbers running from the eves to the ridge.

11 **Purlin:** a main horizontal beam in a roof supporting the common rafters.

12 **Hip tiles:** tiles edging the sharp edge of a roof from ridge to eaves.

13 **Strut:** a brace consisting of a bar or rod to resist longitudinal compression.

14 **Timber stud wall:** a wall constructed from a wooden framework and covered in plasterboard.

15 **Floor joists:** the wooden beams supporting the floorboards.

16 **Cement rendering:** the sand and cement covering to brickwork.

17 **Cavity brick (or block) wall:** a wall constructed of two separate leaves with a cavity between them.

18 **Lintel:** a beam spanning an opening of a doorway, a window or a fireplace.

19 **Gutter and rainwater pipe:** used for the collection of rainwater.

20 **Bond:** the pattern of laying bricks in walling. English Bond consists of alternate courses of headers (bricks laid at right angles to the wall line) and stretchers (bricks laid along the wall line); Flemish Bond consists of alternate headers and stretchers in each course.

21 **Damp-proof course (DPC):** a layer of waterproof material in the wall of a building near the ground to prevent rising damp.

22 **Air brick:** a brick with holes in to provide air flow.

23 **Wall ties:** used to hold two sections of masonry together when it is not bonded.

24 **Solid wall:** a wall built of natural stone, brick or concrete block and mortar – often load-bearing.

25 **Manhole:** a hole usually with a flush iron cover through which a person can gain access to a drain or other underground structure.

WHAT'S THE REPORT REALLY SAYING?

The following extracts from a Homebuyer's Report are accompanied by explanations of what the surveyors are actually saying. Some of the terms used may put the frighteners on potential homebuyers, but in many cases the report is just anticipating what might happen in the future rather than stating what is badly wrong today.

UNDERPINNING

We understand that part of the main front wall of the property has been underpinned. Your legal advisors should make enquiries about local authority permission and guarantees for this work.

Many older houses were built with little or no foundations – it is therefore not unusual for some movement to have taken place. The only cause for concern is if the property is unstable or continuing to move, so don't necessarily panic. If it hasn't fallen down yet it is unlikely to do so in the next five minutes, though houses with a history of movement can be more expensive to insure. Do ensure that any underpinning work has been done in accordance with the correct authority.

TIMBER ROT

We found no signs of wood-boring insect infestation. However, older properties such as this one are susceptible to attack and infestation may be discovered when the property is completely emptied.

Without taking pieces of the building apart it is impossible to guarantee the condition of those areas. However, if you do find you have an infestation you will have to employ a specialist to cut away all the decayed timber and ideally burn it.

BRICK COURSES

There is some fracturing and tilting of brick courses and sills which we believe has been caused by old settlement of the building but this is not considered and being long-standing, no remedial work is necessary. Nevertheless, the cracks should be filled to prevent water penetration.

With particularly wet winters and dry summers the ground will expand and contract and as a building is generally rigid it will reflect some of this weather change with cracking – it is wise to repair such cracks, partly to prevent water penetration but as much for cosmetic reasons as any other.

ROOF

The main roof structure appears satisfactory but it sags slightly. This is not unusual bearing in mind the age of the property [c.1880], and strengthening in the form of a pair of struts should be installed in the near future.

As well as pointing out where immediate action is to be taken, a Homebuyer's Report will suggest areas of the property that may need work doing in the future, as here with the suggestion of strengthening the roof.

CHIMNEY

The chimney stacks and flashings (weatherproofing strips) could not all be inspected because of the height and configuration of the roof and we cannot make any detailed comment on these areas. It is possible that defects may exist in these unseen areas. Unless the property is fully inspected before exchange of contracts, there may well be additional costs or repair which must be borne by you.

Any part of the property that has not been inspected MAY have problems – do not automatically assume that because a survey suggests work may need doing it is likely that it will need doing.

DAMP

We recorded high damp meter readings in the main rear wall which may have been caused by the absence of an effective damp-proof course and some repairs/improvements are needed.

There are many causes for a wall to be damp. Amongst them is condensation, rainwater and leaking pipework. But it's worth noting that all forms of damp are solvable.

SOIL TYPE/DRAINAGE

The subsoil in the area is of a shrinkable clay type which can cause foundation movement. The risk is increased if drainage is defective and when prolonged spells of dry weather occur. As movement has occurred in the past, the drainage may well be faulty. You should follow our recommendations in Section D2 in respect of further testing.

Most drains in our towns and cities are now over one hundred years old and as the pipes were built of clay they are prone to fracturing and root penetration through the joints. If you do have a collapsed drain this can be a major, expensive job to rectify.

GARDEN

There is a large tree close to the property which can affect a building's foundations and drainage.

Some trees have a larger root mass than others depending on the type of subsoil, the type of tree and how far away from the building it is. It may not be a problem.

HOW TO READ AND UNDERSTAND A STRUCTURAL SURVEY

A full structural report (or building survey) should include plans, conditions found and report on the past, present and future performance of the physical characteristics of the building. An example of a full structural report could include:

- **Background:** who wants the survey; where the property is located.
- **Circumstances of the inspection:** what the weather was like on the day of inspection. A brief outline of property describing whether services are switched on, furnished or not.
- **Description:** brief history; how the house has been adapted over the years; nearby houses and surrounding area; roads.
- **Construction:** what material the walls and roof are made from; description of timber, concrete used, ceiling construction.
- **Roof coverings:** a detailed description of all the roof coverings including porches, main section and rear sections.
- **Rainwater goods and waste pipes:** detailed description of the efficiency of the guttering.
- **Walling:** detail of walls both internal and external.
- **Joinery:** external and internal joinery including window frames and door frames.
- **Decorations:** summary of how good the paintwork is.
- **Damp proof:** notes on the existence of damp and ventilation.
- **Garage and outbuildings:** description of garage door, function and state of repair.
- **Drainage:** location and state of drains.
- **Site:** description of the level of the site, fences, gardens and nearby road.
- **Roof void:** internal roof description including state of timbers and ceiling.
- **Internal flooring:** description of flooring in all areas of the property including type, finish and state of repair.
- **Ceilings:** what materials they are made from; height and state of repair.
- **Timber infestations:** woodworm, dry rot, wet rot.
- **Electrics:** state of wiring system.
- **Plumbing:** strand of water pressure, location of stop cocks and PVC storage tank.
- **Heating:** type, age, efficiency.
- **Additional enquiries:** any works that will be needed shortly.

FULL STRUCTURAL SURVEY
(ALSO CALLED A BUILDING SURVEY)

This is an in-depth and comprehensive inspection suitable for all properties but especially recommended for the following buildings:

- All listed buildings.
- Properties built before 1900.
- Any building constructed in an unusual way, regardless of age.
- A property you are planning to dramatically renovate or alter.
- Properties that have already had extensive alterations.

A building survey can be as in-depth as you want and can be tailor-made to suit you and your property, but generally includes the following:

- All major and minor faults.
- The implications of any defects and probably cost of repairs.
- Results of testing walls for dampness and testing timbers for damage including woodworm or rot.
- Comments on the existence and condition of damp-proofing, insulation and drainage (although the latter will not be tested).
- Extensive technical information on the construction of the property and details of the materials used.
- Information on the location.
- Recommendations for any further specialist inspections.

HOW TO FIND A SURVEYOR

You may find that your mortgage lender or estate agent can recommend a surveyor. It is worth asking whether they have a working relationship with one. In choosing your surveyor, it is important that you select a surveyor who is a member of the Royal Institution of Chartered Surveyors. They can be identified by the letters MRICS or

> A building survey can be as in-depth as you want and can be tailor-made to suit you and your property

FRICS (or TechRICS for technical surveyors) after their name. Chartered surveyors have undertaken an extensive period of training and all are required to carry professional indemnity insurance. If you do not have a recommendation contact the RICS directly. RICS members are qualified, experienced and are required to give impartial advice. They also carry their own professional indemnity insurance.

Because a full survey is a bespoke service you should discuss your exact requirements with your surveyor before he or she visits the property and you may find it helpful to meet him or her at the property after the survey is complete to discuss the findings.

There are other areas where your surveyor can assist. For example on party wall issues, planning and Building Regulations, preparation of simple structural calculations, preparation of design drawings, and contractual and valuation of works advice.

RICHMOND: THE IMPORTANCE OF A STRUCTURAL SURVEY

Native New Yorker Joanna Stamatis worked in human resources and her husband Brian Walden was a management consultant when they decided to swap their corporate lifestyles to become full-time property developers, taking the opportunity to make the most of Joanna's existing design skills. They wanted to drag a derelict terrace in Richmond into the 20th century. The house hadn't been touched for many years and had a number of serious structural issues. It would be a huge job, requiring total modernisation. Brian and Joanna were convinced they could pull it off and, if they got it right, make a lot of money as Richmond is one of the most desirable areas in London.

The property was near to the park and the river, and only 12 minutes by train from Waterloo. Property prices in Richmond are amongst the highest in the country: houses on the Green fetch up to £7m. Even average price two-up/two-down houses go for just under £400,000. The property Joanna and Brian bought is in an area that attracts high-earning young professionals and young families looking for starter homes.

The property had an outdated layout with three bedrooms but no bathroom upstairs. There was a small bathroom downstairs at the back with a dining room and sitting room in the main house.

PROJECT COSTS	
COST OF PROPERTY	£304,000
RENOVATION BUDGET	£60–65,000
TARGET RESALE	£475,000

This would mean a massive profit of over £100,000, though there was extensive work to be done.

Brian and Joanna's total planned investment was £396,000. If they did stick to this figure and sold for £475,000 they would earn £106,000 gross profit. This was not going to be an easy project, though. As well as general modernisation, there was major building work to do because part of the back wall and the entire front wall had bowed out under the weight of the roof. It was so bad at the front that the first floor joists were no longer bearing into the wall.

THE PLAN

Joanna and Brian had paid for a full structural survey so they bought the house with their eyes open. Although their development did need major building work, they were taking it much further and planned to rip out the whole of the interior. They intended to knock down front and back elevations and rebuild them. They wanted to strip out the downstairs and create a large open-plan living area, filling in the side return with an extension to give access to a new kitchen and downstairs loo. The plan also included an enormous amount of work upstairs. The entire existing layout was to be replaced by two reasonably sized bedrooms and a bathroom.

The building work alone was going to cost £46,000. I wasn't sure the new layout was going to be an improvement. But the stairs came down anyway, along with all the internal walls.

The fireplace was to be replaced by a 'very clean, contemporary fireplace with a Zen basket and pebbles'. The main bedroom was to be Moroccan in style with arched cupboards finished with trellis or fretwork; the other was to be a New England bedroom.

This is how they broke down their budget for the work:

PROPOSED RENOVATION COSTS	
NEW ROOF	£3,500
REBUILD FRONT WALL	£8,000
SIDE EXTENSION	£3,600
REMAINING BUILDING WORK, INCLUDING DEMOLITION, STUD WALLS, PLUMBING AND ELECTRICS	£30,900
KITCHEN	£4,500
BATHROOM AND DOWNSTAIRS LOO	£3,500
MORTGAGE	£5,000
CONTINGENCY	£6,000
TOTAL	£65,000

SARAH'S ADVICE

Like Brian and Joanna, if you are developing an old, derelict property I would strongly recommend you get a full structural survey. Before spending money there are a few simple checks you can do to get an idea of how big the job may be that you are taking on.

Check along the window frames and lintels. This will help you see if the wall is bowing out. If it is you can rebuild it, tie it in and/or underpin. Tying in is cheaper but either way, it is a lot of work.

Cracks in the walls could mean subsidence. Take a good look at the exterior and check the houses next door.

If you are developing an old, derelict property I would strongly recommend you get a full structural survey

The original master bedroom was small but adequate as you'd expect in this type of house. It was then opened up to the rafters, making the room seem bigger. Joanna added her own personal touches including painting the storage lapis blue.

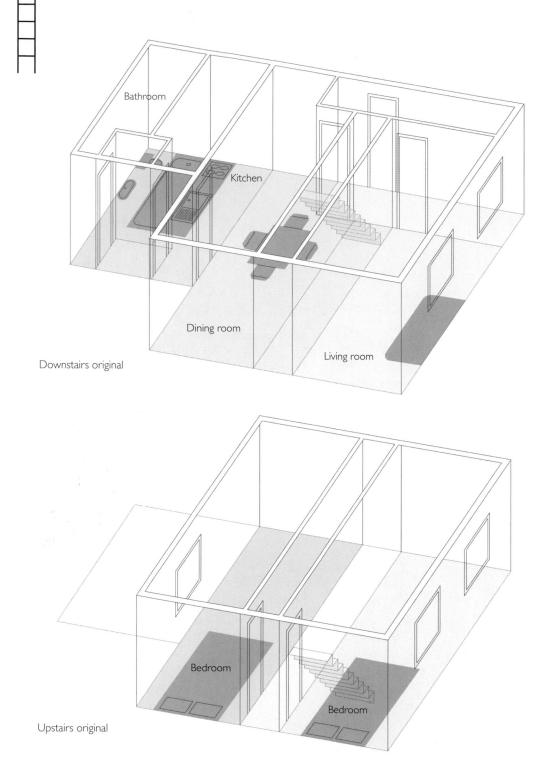

Bathroom

Kitchen

Dining room

Living room

Downstairs original

Bedroom

Bedroom

Upstairs original

The house had a simple layout. There was a small bathroom/kitchen extension downstairs with a dining room and sitting room in the main house. Upstairs there were two identical rectangular bedrooms on either side of the stairs, but no bathroom.

Check the roof. A few damaged slates are easy to replace but they may be symptomatic of a roof that needs replacing. If there are tiles they may be so heavy you often see sagging, which is expensive to rectify.

Watch out for dry or wet rot in the skirting, floorboards and at the bottom of door frames.

Rebuilding the outside walls would be an expensive job but it really needed doing. Certainly they needed a bathroom upstairs, but they were planning a lot more which I didn't think was necessary. The dramatic open-plan space they wanted downstairs would be great, but it would have been much cheaper and just as effective to keep the basic layout as it was. They wanted to put in a new staircase that was less steep in a new position. I felt this was a very pretty traditional cottage in a very popular area – and charming for what it was. Steep stairs in a house like this were normal and the layout could be dramatically improved without this extra expense.

What this house needed was an upstairs bathroom and a good-sized kitchen/dining room to fulfil its

potential. I was worried that Joanna and Brian had not thought the new layout through. You would only be able to get into the bathroom by going through one of the bedrooms and it would be too tiny to take a normal-sized bath. 'We've got around that by using a Japanese tub and making a Japanese-style bathroom,' said Joanna. I personally thought this might be very uncomfortable.

I felt they should have kept the design simple. Once a bathroom had been installed upstairs, the remaining layout could really stay the same. Not only would it be much cheaper, but it would be what a buyer would expect. Joanna's design ideas were all interesting – but not shoehorned into a Victorian terrace in a Conservation Area. They will certainly make a statement, but at a tremendous cost. The £65,000 they had set aside didn't seem much for all the work and planning.

The original tiny downstairs living room certainly benefited from being combined with the dining room, but the layout might have been more attractive with the kitchen/dining room opening onto the garden.

Moving the bathroom upstairs was a sensible move but adding a second loo in such a tiny house was probably unnecessary and ate into the kitchen space.

HOW THE JOB PROGRESSED

Within a week of finalising the plans everything had been stripped out. This turned out to be a massive project. The whole of the ground floor was rotten; the roof needed replacing; and the whole front elevation had to be taken down by hand, brick by brick.

Concrete was laid over the entire ground floor. Joanna was worried about the back wall also being bowed and decided it needed to be rebuilt too. This was not technically necessary but there was no doubt a buyer would be happier with the wall rebuilt.

Brian had no written record of costs. He kept everything in his head, which is no way to run a project. It is impossible to keep track of such a complex project unless you write things down. By now the kitchen had cost £20,000 compared with Joanna's budget of £4,500. The budget started at £60,000 and six weeks into the project had risen to £100,000. At this rate any profit they might make from the project would be negligible. Six weeks into their first development, they were in real trouble, with costs escalating, an enormous loan to cover bills and no income – they decided to sell their own home to release equity so they could finish the project. They now had nowhere to live and were forced to move in with friends.

There was real pressure to get the work finished but their plans got bigger and bigger. They kept adding items such as the flooring that were not in the original budget. The fireplace set them back almost £2,000, new stairs cost £1,200 and the flooring £4,500. Many people interested in this sort of property will want a certain number of traditional features. Period features appeal to a broad market and in these sorts of houses they are often expected. Unlike Joanna and Brian, developers often spend thousands putting such features back in to houses from which they have been ripped.

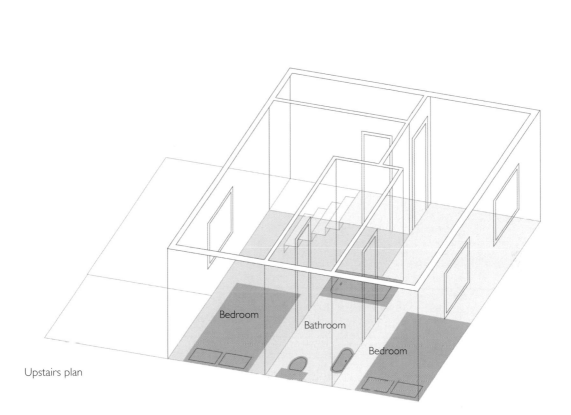

Upstairs plan

Joanna and Brian decided to take up space from both the upstairs bedrooms to create a tiny bathroom between them. This left both the bedrooms much smaller with quite awkward shapes.

Six weeks into their first development, they were in real trouble, with costs escalating, an enormous loan and no income

From reclamation yards you can often get doors for about £50 and there are specialist shops that will reproduce decorative plaster features. As the new centrepiece for the living area Joanna had chosen a very expensive fireplace. This was not in the budget and they had just removed a perfectly good fireplace.

THE OUTCOME

Five weeks over schedule the project was getting to the finishing stages and Joanna and Brian were able finally to move in. The master bedroom was left open to the rafters, making the room feel bigger. The decoration was a fairly personal statement: it's a good idea to build in some storage but perhaps not to paint it lapis blue.

Be careful when adding personal touches – you can limit your market by imposing your own personal taste. The bathroom upstairs was so small that one wall had to be built round the tiny bathtub and the shower was very difficult to get into. No matter how high quality the finish in a bathroom, a tiny bath is likely to put off potential buyers. With the cloakroom installed downstairs there was now not enough room to eat in the kitchen. This tiny two-bedroom cottage didn't need a downstairs loo and would have been better having a kitchen/breakfast room overlooking the garden.

SUMMARY OF ACTUAL RENOVATION COSTS

	ORIGINAL BUDGET	FINAL SUMS
LABOUR AND MATERIALS FOR ROOF, FRONT WALL		
PLUMBING, ELECTRICS, ETC	£46,000	£72,874
KITCHEN	£4,500	£16,500
BATHROOM AND DOWNSTAIRS LOO	£3,500	£4,092
BACK WALL	£0	£4,700
FLOORING AND STAIRS	£0	£5,800
FIREPLACE	£0	£1,900
FURNISHINGS	£0	£9,400
LANDSCAPING GARDEN	£0	£2,500
LOAN FOR TEMPORARY ACCOMMODATION AND STORAGE	£5,000	£11,000
TOTAL	£59,000	£128,766

LESSONS LEARNED

1 *Get a full surveyor's report.* You should be able to calculate how much the development of a property is going to be before you buy it so that you can work out whether it is possible to make a profit.

2 *Learn to how to look at a property with critical eyes.* This applies even if you get a full surveyor's report. Joanna and Brian's whole ground floor was rotten and the whole thing needed to be replaced. This was not taken into account when they were setting a budget.

3 *Use what you have got.* Look at the layout and improve what is there rather than starting from scratch. This tiny house simply needed a normal bathroom upstairs but instead ended up with a tiny sit-up tub accessed through a bedroom. It could have had an open-plan kitchen-diner looking over the garden but instead had a galley kitchen and cloakroom.

4 *Keep an eye on the budget.* Joanna and Brian kept no written records throughout the project and didn't know how much they were spending.

CONVEYANCING

It's easy to become impatient with all the seemingly unnecessary details of buying and selling a property. But don't skimp on this process. You will need a legal advisor, you will need to get the relevant checks done, you will need to include stamp duty into your expenses and you must be prepared for delays as these things work their slow way through the system. Have patience and use the time to work out your development strategy.

YOUR LEGAL ADVISER

Conveyancing is the legal business of buying and selling a property. For this you will need a legal adviser, usually a solicitor, but it is possible to use someone who is registered with the Council for Licensed Conveyancers instead. If you don't already have a legal adviser you will need to find one. Many lenders or estate agents can provide a list of solicitors for you to choose from. You can get details of other solicitors from the Law Society or the Council for Licensed Conveyancers. Solicitors' fees vary so it's worth getting a few estimates. Check that fees include VAT and expenses (disbursements). Don't necessarily go for a solicitor who happens to be nearby or is recommended by your estate agent. Ask friends or relatives whether they have recently used a solicitor for conveyancing with whom they were happy. Your solicitor does not need to be local. With modern technology your solicitor could be several hours' drive away without it making any difference to your working relationship. The most important thing is that they are reliable and efficient as they will be representing your interests. Remember to ask the solicitor for a breakdown of their conveyancing fees before you give them the go-ahead to do any work on your behalf.

SOLICITORS' RESPONSIBILITIES

A solicitor will act on the client's behalf in all matters. The first thing your solicitor will do is get a copy of the Land Registry entry (or the title deeds if the property isn't registered) from the seller's solicitor. These are the legal documents giving evidence of ownership. They are written in legal jargon and need to be carefully examined to make sure there are no unreasonable conditions about how you use the property. If you are buying a leasehold property (which includes most flats) your solicitor will also need to check the lease to find out who has to arrange (and pay for) insuring the building, how much ground rent you will have to pay after the sale, how service charges (for repairs and maintenance) are calculated and whether service charges and ground rent can be increased and if so, how. If there is a problem with the lease it should be sorted out before contracts are exchanged. If you have lost out financially because of your solicitor or conveyancer, you can complain to the Office for the Supervision of Solicitors or the Council for Licensed Conveyancers. You may be able to get compensation (but you will have to pay a new solicitor to help you).

LAND REGISTRY CHECKS

Your solicitor will check with the Land Registry that the seller has the right to sell the property and, when the sale goes ahead, will register your ownership and mortgage agreement with the Land Registry. You have to pay fees for this, which vary depending on the property price and whether the property is already registered or not.

He/she will also carry out local council and other searches. These include: that no alterations have been made without planning permission; establishing whether

To avoid gazumping you may be able to persuade the seller to sign an agreement that the sale can't be called off

the street, pavement and drains are public and council maintained; and finding out whether there are any other expenses linked to the property like a right-to-buy discount that must be repaid. He/she should also check that there are no disputes about things such as noise or parking with neighbours, that the property's boundaries are clear and that there is no disagreement about maintaining them. He/she must also check that a motorway is not about to be built in the adjacent field or that there are any other plans that might affect the value of the property.

The contract is drawn up by the seller's solicitor and involves supplying pre-contract information such as any fixtures and fittings that are to be included in the sale price and answering a standard set of enquires on the property being sold. The solicitor will organise exchange of contracts, the transfer of monies (including a deposit), calling down the buyer's mortgage loan and paying off the seller's mortgage, and will organise the transfer of title deeds, ultimately to the buyer or their lender.

STAMP DUTY
Stamp duty is a government tax that you may have to pay if the property you are buying costs over £60,000. Some areas of the country are exempt from stamp duty. You should pay stamp duty only on the price of the property itself, not on fixtures and fittings such as curtains or

appliances, so it is best to pay for these things separately. The most significant duties are based on the amount of consideration. For land transactions and lease premiums rates charged on the whole consideration are:

UP TO £60,000	NIL
£60,001 TO £250,000	1%
£250,001 TO £500,000	3%
MORE THAN £500,000	4%

PREPARING AND EXCHANGING CONTRACTS
When all the details have been checked, the contract will be negotiated. This stage can often involve long delays as the seller may not agree to everything. For example, you may want to pay less than the price you originally offered, or get the seller to carry out repairs. All the conditions of the sale need to be agreed before contracts are exchanged. Solicitors normally negotiate on your behalf, but they will need to be in regular contact to discuss any changes.

When the contract is drawn up and agreed, you can sign it. The seller signs an identical contract and your respective conveyancers swap the signed documents in what's known as 'exchange of contracts'. At this point both you and the seller become legally bound. You will have to pay a deposit at this stage, usually 10% of the purchase price, but it can be less if the seller agrees. You could lose the deposit if you pull out after exchanging contracts.

GAZUMPING
During negotiations, the seller could accept a better offer from another buyer before you have exchanged contracts. To avoid gazumping you may be able to persuade the seller, through your solicitor, to sign an agreement that the sale can't be called off if contracts are exchanged within a certain time. There may be extra legal fees for this.

HOW LONG WILL IT TAKE TO BUY?

According to research carried out in 2003 in England and Wales, the average time taken from starting house-hunting to completing a purchase is 22 weeks. Remember these are average times, not hard and fast rules – delays over paperwork and other factors may hold up any of these processes.

From beginning your property hunt to your offer being accepted	12 weeks
From acceptance of offer to offer of mortgage	four weeks
From mortgage offer to exchange of contracts	four weeks
From exchange of contracts to completion	two to four weeks

BUYING PROPERTY IN SCOTLAND

The procedures for conveyancing in other countries differ in some respects from those in England and Wales. If you wish to buy in Scotland, for example, there are some marked differences in the way things work.

In Scotland most properties are sold through solicitors rather than estate agents, although the number of estate agencies has increased in recent years. Solicitors are able to call themselves 'Solicitors and Estate Agents' and some set up 'Solicitors' Property centres', where details of all properties being sold by solicitors in the area can be found. The centres are financed by subscriptions from the member solicitors and by charges made to sellers of property – as in the UK, the service is free to prospective buyers. Other solicitors' firms have their own property department and employ sales staff to deal with the non-legal aspects of buying and selling in these offices.

A list of buildings for sale in Scotland with historical or architectural importance is issued quarterly by The Historic Buildings Bureau for Scotland, while all types of property are widely advertised in the Scottish press and on the Internet.

In Scotland, if you are interested in buying a property you have seen at a property centre or a solicitor's you will be directed to the solicitor actually selling it. You will also need a solicitor for conveyancing. English solicitors are not able to practise in Scotland, so if you are relocating from outside Scotland, ask your usual solicitor whether they have a Scottish contact or recommendation.

The Law Society of Scotland also produces a 'Directory of General Services', listing the contact details of practising solicitors throughout Scotland, as well as brochures detailing all of the relevant procedures and legalities. Be warned, there is no scale of solicitors' fees in Scotland – you will have to shop around to get a competitive estimate.

HOW PROPERTIES ARE PRICED

The way that property is priced for sale in Scotland is unique. Generally, properties are presented for sale at 'offers over' a stated figure. Depending on demand for a property, the price eventually paid may be considerably higher than the original figure; it is rare for a purchaser to pay the asking price or below. Sometimes properties are offered at a fixed price, usually because the owner wants a quick sale or the property hasn't sold at an 'offers over' price. In this instance a buyer should be ready to proceed very quickly, as the first acceptable offer at the stated price will secure the property.

THE BUYING PROCEDURE

When you tell your solicitor that you are interested in buying a particular property he or she will 'note interest', that is, tell the seller's solicitor that you are interested in the property. You should then have a chance to make an offer for the property, although the seller is not legally obliged to give you that chance. Don't be inhibited about asking your solicitor as many questions as you need to. Ask your solicitor if the mortgage lender is happy to use the same solicitor as you for their legal work. This keeps costs down. Get an itemised estimate of what he or she will charge before you go ahead.

The process of obtaining a mortgage in Scotland is similar to that in England and most of the major English banks and building societies and all the Scottish banks will lend on the security of Scottish properties. As the buying process can move very quickly it's wise to make sure the necessary loan finance will be available when you need it – subject always to a satisfactory survey on the chosen property.

However, in Scotland it is usual to have a survey carried out before you make an offer for a property. If your offer is accepted you are bound to proceed with the purchase and it will be too late to discover defects or that you cannot get a loan on the property. This does mean that if your offer is unsuccessful you will have wasted the survey fee. Your solicitor will usually instruct that the survey takes place once you have told him or her you are interested in buying the property.

MAKING AN OFFER

When your mortgage company is happy with the valuation of the property, they will issue you an 'offer of advance'. If you are also happy with the surveyor's report, the next thing to do is to make an offer – usually through your solicitor. On a fixed-price property the seller will take the first offer received for the fixed amount. However, most sellers ask for 'offers over' a certain amount and set a 'closing date' by which offers have to be made. Your solicitor will prepare a letter setting out your offer and will send it to the seller's solicitor.

When making an offer you must specify all the conditions under which you want to buy the property and also how much you wish to pay. Prices quoted as 'offers over' usually mean another 10–15% on the price quoted. Your solicitor will guide you on how much you should offer – this is where a solicitor with knowledge of the local market can be particularly useful. In your offer you must also state when you want to move into the property, although this can be further negotiated with the seller at a later date.

ACCEPTANCE OF OFFER

In Scotland, once your offer has been accepted, the property is yours. This is one advantage of the system of house purchase in Scotland, in that it more or less prevents gazumping. When the details of the offer are sorted out between the two parties' solicitors, letters are exchanged between them, which create a legally binding contract. These are known in Scotland as the 'missives' and are the equivalent to the exchange of contracts in England and Wales. So, whether your offer is successful or not, you know where you stand very quickly. This is another advantage to the purchaser in the Scottish property-buying system.

Once your solicitor has concluded the missives, the rest of the purchase goes through. Your solicitor will finish the conveyancing process and you will complete any outstanding loan application papers. Your solicitor will then meet the seller's solicitor and hand over a cheque for the full price in exchange for the title deeds, which he will then hand over to you.

If you buy in Scotland and intend to make the property your principal residence you will acquire Scottish domicile. It is advisable to consult a solicitor at this point, as it may affect, among other things, the way the property is inherited when you die.

A useful address when considering buying a property in Scotland is: HomePoint, Scottish Homes, 91 Haymarket Terrace, Edinburgh EH12 5HE (tel: 0131 313 0044; e-mail: homepoint@scot-homes.gov.uk).

BUYING PROPERTY IN IRELAND (EIRE)

Buying in Ireland is again slightly different to England and Wales and it is important to know where the differences lie and how they will affect you the buyer. Be sure to choose a solicitor who is au fait with the situation in Ireland and has had experience of purchasing properties there so there are no unnecessary hold-ups.

In Ireland it is common to buy a property in a number of different ways: through an estate agent, privately or at an auction. Your solicitor will obtain draft contracts and a copy of the title deeds from the seller's solicitors. You must then sign and return the contract to the seller's solicitor, along with a deposit (which is normally 10% of the purchase price) so that the contracts can be counter-signed by the seller. As soon as these contracts have been signed by both parties and the deposit paid there is a binding agreement requiring the seller to hand over possession and you to hand over the balance on the closing date stated in the contract.

Once a binding agreement is in existence a list of closing documents is set out, all of which must be handed over by the seller's solicitor in exchange for the balance. Prior to closing the transaction your solicitor should make relevant enquiries to establish, for instance, that there are no judgements that are still affecting the property, or orders against the seller or any adverse registrations pending against the property.

Your solicitor will normally visit the offices of the seller's solicitor with a bank draft for the balance. This will be handed over only when the closing documents are found to be in order and the searches are found to be clear. You become the owner when the bank draft is exchanged for all these documents. Keys are then handed over and you can take possession of your new home.

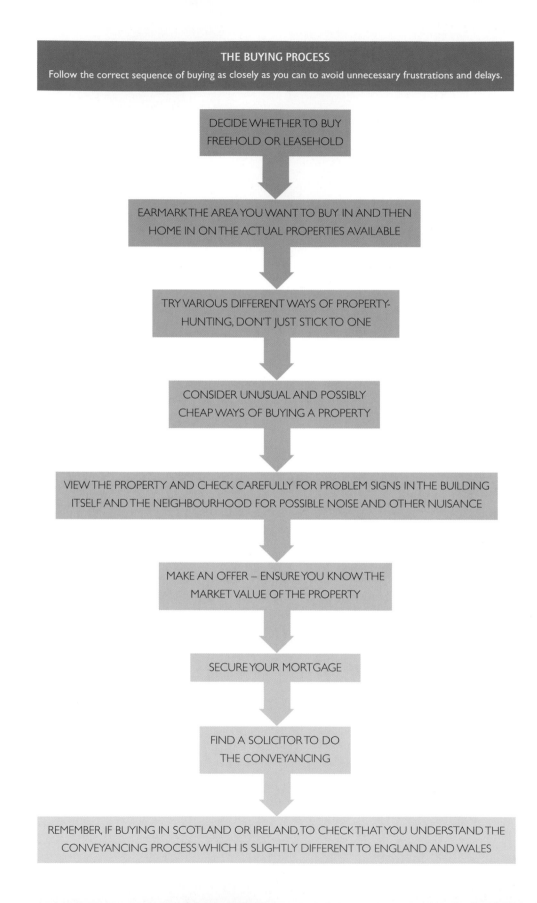

THE BUYING PROCESS
Follow the correct sequence of buying as closely as you can to avoid unnecessary frustrations and delays.

DECIDE WHETHER TO BUY FREEHOLD OR LEASEHOLD

EARMARK THE AREA YOU WANT TO BUY IN AND THEN HOME IN ON THE ACTUAL PROPERTIES AVAILABLE

TRY VARIOUS DIFFERENT WAYS OF PROPERTY-HUNTING, DON'T JUST STICK TO ONE

CONSIDER UNUSUAL AND POSSIBLY CHEAP WAYS OF BUYING A PROPERTY

VIEW THE PROPERTY AND CHECK CAREFULLY FOR PROBLEM SIGNS IN THE BUILDING ITSELF AND THE NEIGHBOURHOOD FOR POSSIBLE NOISE AND OTHER NUISANCE

MAKE AN OFFER – ENSURE YOU KNOW THE MARKET VALUE OF THE PROPERTY

SECURE YOUR MORTGAGE

FIND A SOLICITOR TO DO THE CONVEYANCING

REMEMBER, IF BUYING IN SCOTLAND OR IRELAND, TO CHECK THAT YOU UNDERSTAND THE CONVEYANCING PROCESS WHICH IS SLIGHTLY DIFFERENT TO ENGLAND AND WALES

BUYING CHECKLIST

1 Leasehold or freehold? Understand the difference and the advantages and disadvantages of each.

2 Choose an area. If you will be managing the development, an area close to where you live makes sense.

3 Explore estate agents, local press, buying at auction, the Internet and other purchasing possibilities.

4 View the property. Take your time; if interested view a second time; ask the right questions.

5 Understand the buying process. Organising your finances, making an offer, finding a surveyor, getting valuations and surveys.

6 Conveyancing: understanding your solicitor's responsibilities; preparing and exchanging contracts.

4 SELLING

Selling might be the final step in the property development ladder, but it's one you need to consider from the start. It will be the final test of whether your development has been successful and profitable and the potential resale value of the property will govern how much and what type of development you undertake. As with all aspects of property ownership, selling a house is complicated. Find out what the realistic asking price is for homes in the area and don't go too far above it, particularly if there are a lot of similar properties for sale. Don't plump for the first estate agent you see. Interview three and choose the one that seems most suitable.

Once your property looks irresistible, it is time to get a valuation. Start by choosing your estate agents carefully.

GETTING A VALUATION AND CHOOSING AN ESTATE AGENT

You should ideally look for three reputable agents based in your area to come and give you a valuation of the property. If you bought the property from an estate agent and were happy with their services, then they are a good place to start. To find two others, look at the companies most actively marketing similar homes for sale in your area. Does the estate agent have regular advertisements in the local press, a comprehensive and easy-to-use website with links to property portals and lots of 'sold' or 'for sale' boards dotted around your neighbouring streets? These are all good signs.

To save on time, book in staggered appointments for all your agents to view the property on the same day. Now you have finished the development, you don't want to keep flitting back and forth and you'll want to get the property on the market as soon as possible. When you ring to book a valuation, ask the agent to bring to the appointment details of properties they have recently sold that are similar in size and style to yours. The prices that these homes actually sold for will give you a much better

---

To avoid disappointment try not to be tempted to start mentally spending the valuation figure

---

indication of the current market than the asking prices the owners hoped to achieve. However, before you make those appointments, do your research:

- Look at the local property press, estate agents' websites and property details through the eyes of a buyer.
- Check the sale prices being commanded by properties similar to your own. Get a feel for the market – it may have changed since you bought the property.
- See how many properties similar to yours are currently for sale. This is important: if there is a glut of properties similar to yours on the market, you will need to be even more realistic about your asking price, unless you are offering something extra. Remember the property market works on the laws of supply and demand. The greater the demand for your property, the higher the asking price you can expect to achieve.

Be realistic about your asking price and be wary of an agent who gives an inflated estimate. A common mistake made by home-owners when selling is to be flattered by the highest valuation they receive and choose that agent to sell the property. The reality is that a house is worth only what a purchaser will pay for it, and remember that an estate agent is not a buyer; to avoid disappointment try not to be tempted to start mentally spending the valuation figure. If you have done your research you should be able to spot any over-valuation.

EMPLOYING AN ESTATE AGENT

You've seen three estate agents – now you need to decide which one to market your property with. Do you choose one or several agents to try and sell it? See the table overleaf for a quick run-down of the pros and cons of sole or multiple agents. If you sign a sole agency agreement with more than one estate agent, you may find you are legally obliged to pay fees twice.

METHOD OF SELLING

Sole agent	Joint sole agents	Multiple agents
You instruct only one estate agent to market and sell your property.	Two estate agents market the property for sale and split the fee between them on an agreed basis when one sells it – usually about 75% to the successful estate agent and 25% to the unsuccessful agent.	You employ two or more estate agents to market and sell your property.

PROS

Sole agent	Joint sole agents	Multiple agents
An estate agent will offer you favoured rates of commission if you go solely through them (around 2%+VAT). When the property goes under offer, you will be able to more easily control it being taken off the market and ending the viewings.	Doubles your chances of finding a buyer.	The increased coverage and marketing will get your property seen by a wider market. You pay a commission only to the agent who sells the property.

CONS

Sole agent	Joint sole agents	Multiple agents
You will need to sign a contract to agree that the property is being marketed and handled by only one company for a certain period of time, though how long is negotiable. If you are not happy with the service or decide you want to enlist the services of more estate agents, you will generally need to wait until this period of time elapses before you are able to do so.	An estate agent is less likely to put as much effort into selling your property if there is a chance another agent may find a buyer just as they come up with one. The successful agent has to give a percentage of their commission to the other agent who has done absolutely nothing in terms of their sale – understandably this sits bitterly with many agents.	The rate of commission due to the estate agent is higher – around 3.5%+VAT. If you decide to employ multiple agents, but have received different valuations, you will need to decide on one asking price and put the property up for sale with all of the agents at the same level. It won't look good if home-hunters view your property at one price and see it advertised for another elsewhere. Putting your property up for sale with several agents can send signals to possible home-hunters that it has been on the market for a while, meaning there may either be a problem with the property, or it is overpriced. Neither is appealing to a prospective purchaser.

YOUR ESTATE AGENT

Once you have chosen your agent, you will need to work at building a good rapport with them.

As with any relationship, if estate agents like and respect you, they will do more to help sell your property. And if you are planning on developing property in the local area in the future, then building up a good relationship with an agent you trust is paramount. Whatever your situation you want to get the most out of the agent-vendor relationship, so consider the following points:

■ Commission. In theory an estate agent's commission fee is negotiable. However, don't haggle over 0.5% or 1%. It will make little difference to your gross profit and could scupper your relationship. The last thing you want is for the agent to put less effort into selling the property for less commission.

■ Negotiate a contract. Negotiate to put your property on with an agent for the minimum contract time – usually four weeks. During this initial period the estate agent will have an influx of viewers lined up from their existing database of home-hunters. After this initial glut of viewings, you will be relying on new customers signing up with the agent. If you are pleased with the service the estate agent has offered towards the end of the contract time and with the number or viewings taking place, then extend the contract.

■ Marketing details. When you have discussed the sale price and the commission fee, the estate agent will compile written details and take photographs of the property for marketing. Make sure you are happy with the photographs they plan to use. Check that they were taken in sunlight and are in colour. A bad picture could put off home-hunters from booking a viewing. Estate agents are legally obliged to give correct and accurate details of the property. Mistakes do happen, however,

> # Let the agent conduct the viewings. This will allow the home-hunter to feel comfortable and be objective

so do check the details yourself. Ensure the right descriptions of the property and measurements of the rooms appear. Make sure that the best features are mentioned, as well as sought-after extras like the garden, good storage and parking and the proximity of the property to the nearest travel links and amenities.

■ Viewings. Let the agent conduct the viewings. This will allow the home-hunter to feel comfortable and be objective. It will also mean they can meet the agent who will be negotiating on your behalf if they decide to put in an offer.

■ Communications. Organise a specific occasion each week when you and your agent will speak about the viewings that have taken place. This will allow the agent sufficient time to gather any information ready for your call and save you making umpteen calls while your agent is out of the office. During these conversations, ask for any feedback from viewings and the number of parties that they have shown around the property. Avoid trying to justify any negative criticism to the agent, jot down the feedback quietly and think about it. If you find certain comments crop up time and time again, think about how you could redress the problem to make the property more desirable to viewers, or drop the price accordingly. Respond to any queries the agent has quickly and professionally.

- Building work and guarantees. Keep information about any work you have had carried out on the property in a box file. This should include any certificates for works, Building Regulation and planning permission certificates. Send a full copy of these not only to your estate agent in case of enquiries but also to your solicitor in preparation for a sale.
- Also keep handy the guarantees for any appliances or white goods, any service history you have for a boiler and the manual for how to work the central heating system. These will help the estate agent and the buyer.

YOUR SOLICITOR

A good solicitor or licensed conveyancer (who specialises in property transactions) for your sale is crucial. If you were satisfied with the one you used for the purchase of the property, there will be no problem. If not, you will need to find one you can rely on and fast. (See the section on Buying, page 107, for information on finding a solicitor and the responsibilities of a solicitor).

Remember to ask the solicitor for a breakdown of the conveyancing fees before you give them the go ahead to do any work on your behalf. Find out whether they provide a 'no move, no fee' service – it could save you a lot of money. Do not always be cost-driven with a solicitor; remember, as with most things you will often get what you pay for.

SELLING PRIVATELY

This is another possible option, but in my opinion the pitfalls outweigh the benefits and so I would rarely recommend you plump for a private sale. Although the obvious advantage is that there are no agents' fees to pay, you will have to market the property yourself. This means you need to be incredibly organised and always available to conduct viewings. You will need to negotiate

a sale price yourself, whereas an agent can act as a mediator on your behalf and justify an asking price. You will undoubtedly have fewer resources, and certainly less experience than the agent to carry out all of these important tasks effectively. And remember, there is a lot of money at stake if you get any of these things wrong.

Personally, I would always sell a property I have spent time, effort and money developing through an agent. Don't be fooled into thinking you will save yourself money on commission fees when there are large sums of cash at stake. There is too much at risk if you can't carry out any of the tasks involved in selling as professionally as an agent. In any case, the chances are pretty high that with all of their marketing skills and resources an agent will get more for your property than you would, which will negate any fee you have to pay them.

RECEIVING AN OFFER

When someone decides your property could be their home, they will put in an offer through your estate agent.

You need to think carefully before accepting an offer. If you receive an offer of less than the full asking price it could be because the buyer does not feel that the property is worth that amount. Alternatively, they may be trying to get a good deal, or perhaps be unable to borrow the full amount from their mortgage lender. It is important to gauge your buyer's circumstances. You need to know whether they have a home to sell, whether they have an agreement in principle to a mortgage or how they intend to pay for your property. All of these factors will allow you to weigh up the pros and cons of the offer. If they are part of a chain of buyers and sellers relying on each other, and one sale falls through, everyone else could lose out. Whatever their situation, don't rush into accepting the first offer you receive if it is lower than your realistic expectations. Consult with your estate agent.

They will be working to sell your property as quickly as possible and help you achieve the best price possible, which in turn bolsters their commission fee.

If the offer you receive is a reasonable one, the first decision you will need to make is whether to keep the property on the market or to mark it as 'sold subject to contract'. Generally, the offer will be based on you taking the property off the market, but if you do want to carry out more viewings and continue advertising it to invite more offers, then you should tell the prospective buyer. In England and Wales you can technically accept other offers until the moment you exchange contracts. However, the buying and selling of property in Scotland and Ireland is different from the rest of the UK. If this is something you are not aware of take specialist legal advice.

Ask your solicitor to get confirmation that the purchaser's solicitors have been instructed, and to draw up a draft contract. Your purchaser will generally want to carry out local authority and other searches. Encourage their solicitor through your estate agent and your solicitor to get these requested as soon as possible, as they do take time. The government target is for local authorities to turn around a search within ten days, but in reality it varies between different local authorities from one or two days to several weeks.

Remember, generally abandoning a purchaser in the hope of a quick sale or a bit more money with another buyer is a false economy. The same flaws are likely to show up on their survey too.

VALUATION AND SURVEY

The condition and value of your property is almost certainly going to have to be checked by the buyer. Their mortgage lender will organise a valuation to ensure their investment is safe and the buyer may well arrange for a survey to be carried out.

If the buyer's valuation/survey shows up any problems, your estate agent will advise you on the appropriate course of action to take. This could involve a number of possible options:

- Lowering your price to continue with the sale.
- Taking the property off the market while you fix the problem and putting it back on the market at a later date.
- Arranging for specialist reports to assess the seriousness of any fault found.

THE DEAL IS DONE

Almost there! You've done the hard part and it is now time for contracts to be exchanged between both parties' solicitors. Once you have exchanged contracts, you and your buyer are legally committed to one another and at this point the buyer's deposit (normally about 10%) will be paid into your solicitor's account to be held for you until completion.

Completion – when the transfer of ownership of the property passes from the seller to the buyer – generally takes place about four weeks after exchange of contracts, although it depends on both parties' preferences. The timescale can be longer or it is possible to exchange and complete on the same day.

On completion you will receive from the buyer, via your solicitor, the outstanding balance for the sale of your property, less any fees and your mortgage repayment.

Now is the time for you to take a rest, celebrate or start looking for your next property to develop.

Selling property in Scotland

Scotland has a different system from England and Wales for buying and selling property.

In Scotland, solicitors not estate agents sell the majority of houses. If you ask your solicitor to sell your house, you should expect him or her to provide a full estate agency service. As well as conveyancing, this will include registering your property in the local solicitors' property centre. The solicitor is likely to charge a percentage fee to cover both the selling and the conveyancing and it is sensible to get an estimate for this before going ahead.

You can sell your property through an estate agent but they will normally pass any formal offers that are made to your solicitor.

The next step is to advertise the property for sale – something your solicitor or estate agent can organise for you. In Scotland it is usual to state an asking price and invite offers over this amount. The asking price you put in your advertisement should normally be the minimum figure that you would consider accepting. Your solicitor will advise you on both the price you should ask and the price you should expect to achieve.

When someone is interested in your property, their solicitor will contact your solicitor or estate agent to tell them they have an interested party. Unlike in England, parties have to get a survey carried out at this stage, even before an offer has been made.

If several people are interested in your house it is usual to fix a closing date for offers – a date and time when you will consider all offers that have been lodged. At this point you will have to decide which offer to accept. You are not obliged to accept the highest offer or any of the offers if you do not wish to do so.

Once you decide to accept an offer, your solicitor will liaise with the buyer's solicitor to ensure all points of the sale are agreed. These agreed points are then confirmed in writing and this exchange of letters is referred to as the 'missives'. This process takes only a day or two and it is worth noting that the conclusion of missives constitutes a binding contract from which neither side can withdraw. The short time between offers being made and becoming binding and the absence of gazumping are the advantages of the Scottish system.

When the missives have been concluded your solicitor will finalise the conveyancing. He or she will arrange for the title deeds of the property to be sent to the buyer's solicitor, inform your bank or building society that missives have been concluded and obtain a redemption statement to show the amount of your loan to be repaid on completion of the sale.

For more information on selling a property in Scotland you can investigate the relevant websites listed in the resource list on pages 219–20.

Selling property in Ireland (EIRE)

Selling property in Ireland is slightly different to selling in England and Wales. The great majority of property in Ireland is sold by private treaty, and it is advisable to use an estate agent to conduct the sale for you. It is common in Ireland for agents to also be auctioneers and it is recommended that you choose an agent who is a member of the Irish Auctioneers and Valuers Institute.

Your agent can place a suggested price level on the property on your behalf, though this price is not binding on the seller. Once your property has grabbed the attention of potential buyers, offers will be invited. You would hope to have interest from various parties and to have bid and counter offer at this point. If there is very strong interest in the property, the agent may suggest a closed or private tender. This is essentially a closed competition of final bids from each buyer, with the highest bid winning.

Once you have accepted an offer, it is normal to look for a deposit; usually this is 5% with private treaty sale. Your agent should also ensure that your buyer has funds or an approved loan in place at this point. It is normal to cease to actively market the property at this stage, however the sale is not secured until formal contract documentation has been issued, signed and exchanged by both you and the buyer. Up until this point you may entertain all offers even though you have already accepted an offer. As in England, gazumping does occur.

It is not uncommon for homes in Ireland to be sold by auction, but it is recommended that you employ a combined agent/licensed auctioneers if you choose to sell this way. Check agents in your area and look at the prices they have achieved for homes like yours. There are many good reasons for selling by auction, chiefly that it is quick and you have a defined period in which the sale will, hopefully, take place.

You should expect regular feedback from the agent about how much interest there is in your property and approximately what price you can expect to achieve at the auction. Based on this, you and the agent will be able to set your confidential reserve price just before the auction. During the auction, the auctioneers will try to get your price up as far as they can. Once the reserve price has been met, the auctioneer will let the room know and announce that the property is now 'on the market'. The onus is then on all potential buyers to bid competitively for your property. If the worst occurs and your house does not meet the reserve price and does not sell, your agent can advise you on continuing negotiations with any bidders who are still interested in the property. In this way there is a chance that you can still make a sale.

Once all bids are in, the hammer has gone down and the property has sold, the auctioneer and buyer sign the contract the agent has prepared on your behalf and the sale is unconditional – the purchaser pays a 10% deposit on the auction day and settlement of the balance is normally 30 days later.

SELL THE LIFESTYLE

It is important to remember you are not selling your own home and your own style. You are selling to your target market so don't over-furnish or over-decorate. Do make sure the property is clean, free of clutter and offers prospective buyers a chance for them to see how they can make their own impact on it.

You should know your target market well by now. Your job is to 'tick all the boxes' and provide a few extra aspirational touches at a price they can afford.

It is at this stage of the project that some developers feel it necessary to accessorise each room. Don't be tempted to do this. If you stuff rooms full of your own idea of lovely trinkets, you can needlessly spend a large amount of money, risk putting off viewers with your taste and clutter up the newly decorated space. Keep your look clean and uncomplicated. Furthermore, remember with design, less is more. If you have made a good job of your development and it has a beautiful finish, there is no need to overdo it. You should aim to suggest how the viewer could live in the property, nothing more.

If, however, you have awkward spaces, feel that the rooms need defining or are missing a certain something, look at the following quick, simple tips.

> Make sure that what you do put into a room suggests how that space can best be used

FURNITURE

It is never a good idea to buy a lot of furniture to stage a property you are about to sell. You may not be able to re-use the pieces in your next development and will have to pay to put them in storage. You can present a property for sale with furniture from your own home, pieces borrowed from friends and family or hired specifically for the purpose. If you do need to buy some pieces, then think carefully before each purchase.

Make sure that what you do put into a room suggests how that space can best be used. For example, if you have room for an eating area in a kitchen, add a table and chairs to illustrate the point. If you have a box room, put in a single bed to show that it is big enough to hold one. A small bedroom may be able to squeeze in a double bed, so put one in to illustrate that it's a feasible option. You can pick up second-hand bases and mattresses very cheaply. Swathed in crisp white linen they will look as impressive and inviting as if they were brand new.

However, don't let furniture dominate your rooms. Whatever you do, don't be tempted to fill your rooms with too much, or add pieces that are too large or imposing for the space. You will make the rooms look smaller and moving around the space feel awkward. Arrange furniture to maximise all of the available space and make sure that the colours and styles complement your décor.

CREATE A FOCAL POINT

Use mirrors strategically in the presentation of your property. Placing a mirror in a narrow room will create a sense of depth. In a dark room, it will bounce and reflect light; in a small room, it will increase the sense of space.

If you are short of a great view, cheat by adding a picture or painting from your home or a second-hand shop to create a focal point.

THE FINISHING TOUCHES

Leave bedrooms clean, calm and simple. Dress beds with fresh, crisp linen, preferably white. Keep the kitchen free of clutter – don't be tempted to add china or pots and pans. If you must accessorise, a bowl of fruit, a plant or a bottle of olive oil is enough to add life and colour.

If you are worried the bathroom looks too clinical you can always pop in some towels to soften the look. The living room should feel inviting. Some spaces look best left bare, others need a helping hand. If you have a less-than-desirable view from a window, invest in a simple blind. Think carefully before spending money on having curtains made as you really either need to include them in the sale or risk never using them again. It is better to use fewer pieces of beautiful furniture than lots of tat. Put a table and chairs into a dining room or area – if you do not have a table quite the right size, get a piece of MDF cut to the optimum size and cover with a simple cloth.

Don't put freshly cut flowers around your interior unless you are able to pop in and change both the water and the flowers at regular intervals. Dead or wilting flowers will look and smell terrible. For a low-maintenance alternative, buying plants like lavender or orchids, which need less care, can work out cheaper than replacing flowers several times over and they serve the same visual purpose. Use them to add colour and life to your design where you have dead space or need a focal point.

SELLING CHECKLIST

1 Remember that selling at a profit is your ultimate goal. You will need to be aware of resale prices in your chosen area to calculate your potential profit.

2 Present the property to viewers so that they can visualise living in it themselves: simple, uncluttered and with potential.

3 Go through the correct procedures for selling and make an educated decision about going through a sole agent or two or more agents.

4 Work with your estate agent. Friendly agents are more likely to put their best effort into getting a good deal from you.

5 Remember that in other countries the procedure may differ from that in England and Wales.

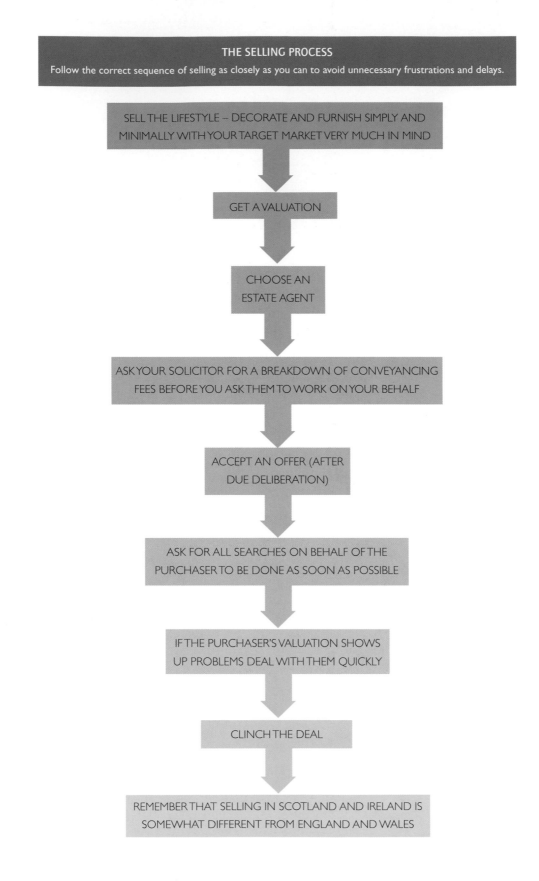

THE SELLING PROCESS

Follow the correct sequence of selling as closely as you can to avoid unnecessary frustrations and delays.

SELL THE LIFESTYLE – DECORATE AND FURNISH SIMPLY AND MINIMALLY WITH YOUR TARGET MARKET VERY MUCH IN MIND

GET A VALUATION

CHOOSE AN ESTATE AGENT

ASK YOUR SOLICITOR FOR A BREAKDOWN OF CONVEYANCING FEES BEFORE YOU ASK THEM TO WORK ON YOUR BEHALF

ACCEPT AN OFFER (AFTER DUE DELIBERATION)

ASK FOR ALL SEARCHES ON BEHALF OF THE PURCHASER TO BE DONE AS SOON AS POSSIBLE

IF THE PURCHASER'S VALUATION SHOWS UP PROBLEMS DEAL WITH THEM QUICKLY

CLINCH THE DEAL

REMEMBER THAT SELLING IN SCOTLAND AND IRELAND IS SOMEWHAT DIFFERENT FROM ENGLAND AND WALES

GLOSSARY OF BUYING AND SELLING TERMS

Asking price: the lowest price the seller of a property has declared he/she will sell at.

Building Survey or Full Structural Survey: in-depth and comprehensive inspection of a property, suitable for all properties.

Consideration: something promised, given or done that has the effect of making an agreement a legally enforceable contract.

Freehold: legal ownership and control of a building or piece of land for an unlimited time.

Full structural survey: see Building Survey

Gazumping: when the seller accepts a better offer from another buyer before you have exchanged contracts.

Homebuyer's Survey and Valuation Report (HSV): a survey carried out to a format defined by the Royal Institution of Chartered Surveyors. It focuses only on significant and urgent matters.

Leasehold: the legal right to live in or use a building or piece of land etc. for an agreed period of time.

Market value: the prevailing price at which properties are selling in a particular area.

Subject to contract: you and the seller have agreed in principle to go ahead with the transaction but neither of you is yet legally bound.

Survey: see Building Survey

Surveyor: a chartered surveyor, who is highly trained in ascertaining the condition and quality of a property.

Vendor: the seller of a property.

Viewing: the opportunity to view a property.

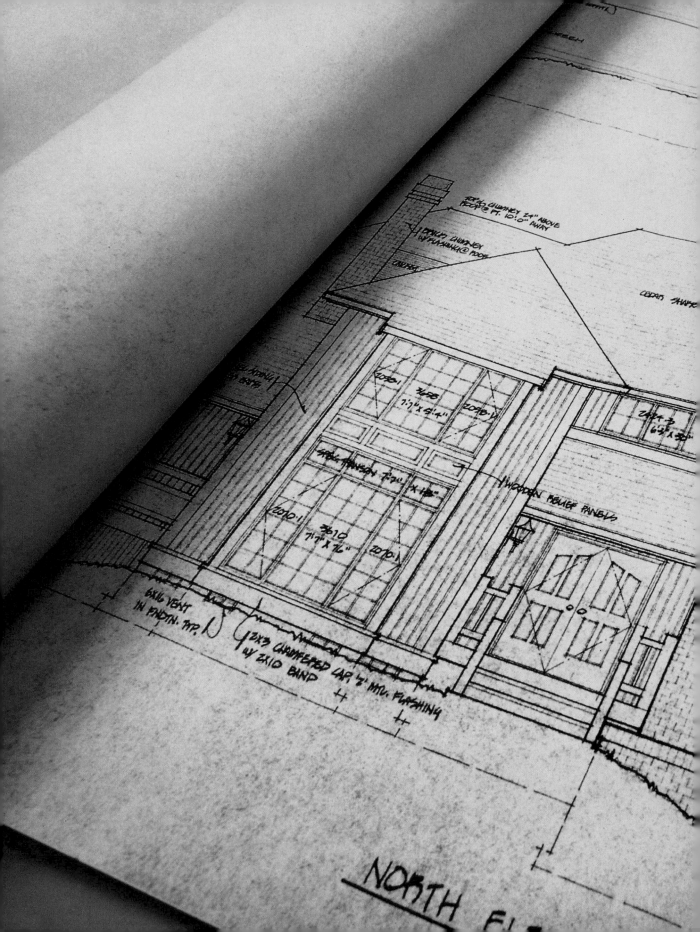

SOUTH ELEVATION
1/4"=1'0"

5
THE
PLANNING

5 THE PLANNING

It is important to make sure that the basic structure of the building is sound before you start planning to alter the interior spaces. Before purchasing the property you should have assessed the extent of the repairs, work and decoration required to make it perfect for your potential market. Don't be daunted by major building works or extensive repairs. Make the property safe and sound first and foremost. If you have done your calculations correctly, you should have the resources to get the job done properly. When viewing a property with an eye to developing it, it is important to understand what potential it already has for your target market and how you can make it most appealing to that market for the least outlay. If you are not experienced in assessing the potential of a property and have little experience in the complexities of building projects, you would be wise to call in a designer or an architect to assess the potential before committing yourself to the building.

DEVELOPING FOR YOUR MARKET

How you design and present your property will strongly influence how well it is likely to sell once it is on the market. To get it right, you must target your design directly to your potential buyer. On average, prospective buyers will take 20 minutes to view a property but have made up their minds whether they want to buy or not within five or ten minutes of viewing. Sometimes the decision has been made even before they ring the doorbell. First impressions stick in the mind, so the importance of the property's outside appearance is obvious – get the front of the property in good order.

Different types of buyers lead different lifestyles and have diverse expectations of what they want from a home. Young professionals, for example, want properties in locations with good transport links, shops and nightlife, while families tend to prefer houses rather than flats and consider gardens a high priority. It is therefore essential to pinpoint your market and renovate your property accordingly in order to achieve your top selling price and maximise your property's potential.

KEEPING WITHIN YOUR BUDGET

It cannot be stressed too much that the first thing to do is work out a realistic budget for your development and then, most importantly, stick to it. Itemise the work you intend to do and cost each individual item realistically. If some things turn out to be more expensive than you planned for, make up for that by saving money on some other item of work. You can often get brilliant ideas from expensive showrooms or magazines and then the skill is to get a very similar effect with less expensive materials using clever design techniques.

HOME IMPROVEMENT GRANTS

The Regulatory Reform (Housing Assistance) (England and Wales) Order 2002 gives local authorities wide powers to provide assistance for repairs, improvements, adaptations and to demolish and re-construct homes. It may be worth finding out if you are eligible for a home improvement grant for some aspect of the work you are considering; grants are generally only available to home-owners, not developers. Each authority will have its own rules about types of help it will offer and about the conditions you must meet in order to qualify for help. To find out if you can get help with home improvements and what help is available in your area, contact the housing or environmental health departments of your local authority or your local Home Improvement Agency.

Help could be in the form of a grant or loan. It could be providing labour, tools or cheap materials to help you carry out the work. It could be providing details of builders who can carry out the work or providing free or low cost surveys or advice in carrying out repairs. For example, you might get a grant through the home energy efficiency scheme, which provides grants to help cover the costs of home insulation and improving energy efficiency.

PRELIMINARY COSTING

Do some serious costing before committing yourself to purchasing any property. Work out the probable cost of renovating the shell of the building, the cost of planning and reorganising the interior and the cost of pulling it all into shape, not forgetting the garden if there is one. Take serious note of items in the survey that indicate work needs to be done. And make sure you understand the terms in the survey and how they relate to the property.

THE STRUCTURE

The basic fabric of the building should be sound before you start on the internal layout. If you find that the roof has to be repaired during the project when you thought you'd get away with replacing a few tiles, this can cost twice as much as if you'd done it first. Drains, damp-proofing and wood rot should all be dealt with as a priority.

ASSESSING THE BUILDING

Before purchasing your property you should have assessed the extent of the repairs, work and decoration required to make it perfect for your market. And before you actually begin on the interior layout and design, you should make sure it is safe and sound and in a good state of repair. There is no point in spending lots of money on cosmetic repairs if you have not carried out the basic repairs required to the main fabric of the building. Ensuring the basic structure of the property is in good condition is one of the most important improvements you will make and potential buyers who are paying a premium for the hassle-free home you are providing will expect just that. If you have done your calculations correctly, you should have the resources to get all necessary jobs done properly.

The first thing is to consider all the things mentioned in the building survey. If anything in this suggests that repairs are needed, these should be done before you even think about any interior planning and design work. The things to consider are, for example, the state of the drains, the state of the roof, damp-proofing, window frames, cracks in walls and pointing of brickwork, and electric wiring. Where indicated by a survey, you should treat against woodworm, dry rot and damp. These things are not cheap but they are absolutely necessary and need to go into your budget reckoning.

Make sure you use suitable materials. For example, roofing slates are comparatively lightweight. If you are replacing slates with concrete tiles, which are heavier, you may have to reinforce the roof timbers to take the extra weight. Once the property is a watertight, functioning shell you can consider how the property can best be arranged and redeveloped for resale.

STRUCTURAL POINTS TO CONSIDER

The difference between new-build and older properties is that new-build will have a consistent construction method throughout, whereas most older properties will have evolved during their lifetime. As a result, older buildings are usually a mixture of original and later construction, often with a combination of different materials, methods and standards.

The periods for the introduction of changed methods and materials are summarised below. These dates are only guidelines as most changes take place over a long period of time, but they may help to eliminate some of the more obvious questions when considering defects in older properties:

Damp-proof courses	1900 to 1920 onwards
Cavity walls	1930 to 1940 onwards
Reinforced concrete floors	1920 onwards
Concrete tiled roofs	Generally from 1940 onwards
Copper plumbing	1945 onwards
13-amp ring mains	1947 onwards

The following are some of the differences you may find between old and new purpose-built properties or within various parts of a refurbished unit:

Foundations

In houses built before 1914 load-bearing brick walls were often built directly off the subsoil without concrete strip footings, or off paving slabs, although sometimes the brickwork of the wall was stepped out at the base to spread the load.

In more recent houses there is always some form of widening at the base of the wall unless it is built on very hard ground or rock.

Settlement and damage to foundations can be caused by movement between old and new foundations or by subsidence (especially in mining areas). The latter can be due to heavy rain or drought on a clay subsoil, or the removal of large trees, which change the water content of the soil in the area of their roots.

Walls

External walls built before 1930 are usually of solid brickwork 9in or 13½in thick. Houses built after 1930 usually have cavity walls or solid walls faced with tiles or boarding. Or they may be built from timber-framed panels or concrete. Many older mansion blocks use solid wall construction although some have a concrete or steel frame with panel walls or brick cladding. A brick facing does not necessarily mean the full thickness of the wall is of brick.

Damage to the mortar between the bricks from weather or penetration by moisture may mean you need to repoint or cut out and replace individual bricks. In the restoration of an old house, badly eroded brickwork may have to be rendered or treated to resist damp penetration.

Installation of a DPC (damp-proof course) became a general requirement in the 1920s.

Internal walls in old and new houses may be constructed from timber-stud, brick, breeze or concrete block. Where new openings have been made through internal walls, the construction above may be supported on timber, steel or concrete beams. In modernised properties walls may have been lined with waterproof lathing to protect internal finishes.

Floors

The ground floor in old houses was often constructed of timber floorboards resting on a honeycomb sleeper of walls. It is important that the space under suspended floors is well ventilated to prevent rot.

Modern houses usually have solid concrete floors. When houses are modernised, ground-level timber floors are often replaced by a solid concrete floor. It is essential to ensure that sufficient air flow has been maintained to adjoining timber floors.

Roofs

As Britain has high rainfall, the most logical roof construction is a pitched tiled roof, which explains the roof style of most of the country's housing stock. If properly constructed, and barring storm damage, this form of roof should last around 80 years without too much trouble.

Older pitched roofs may be tiled or slated and were often built without sarking felt or boards. They may have suffered from years of neglect where rainwater gutters haven't been cleared and lead flashings haven't been maintained; the nails may have corroded and incorrectly repaired roofs may allow water to reach the rafters, causing decay. The problems may well remain if the roof is only repaired rather than totally replaced.

Many extensions to older houses have flat roofs. These generally have a life expectancy of about 20 years. Should a leak occur, the main difficulty is identifying the source as the leak may appear in a ceiling some distance away from the actual defect in the roof.

SPECIFIC FEATURES THAT AFFECT PLANNING

Terraced and other adjoining houses

STRUCTURE

A terraced house is basically part of one long building. You can't enlarge the basement or build a roof extension without affecting the neighbouring houses. Many alterations will require the agreement of your neighbours as well as the local authority. The thickness of the walls and depth and soundness of the foundations will affect what you can do. Both are likely to be sounder in houses built after about 1840. Planning regulations would be unlikely to allow any extension on the front of a terrace. There is more freedom to expand at the back, although many post-1890 houses already have extensions. Most pre-1900 houses have rising damp unless a damp-proof course (DPC) has been injected into the walls.

INTERIOR

There may be ornamental plasterwork, soft-wood panelling and fireplaces with cast iron grates and wood or marble surrounds. The woodwork of the doors and staircases is often high quality and details such as wooden shutters are worth hanging onto. Such features are very popular and are often there for good reasons. For example, shutters are an excellent way of keeping burglars out and the heat in and are often very attractive in their own right.

Detached Victorian houses

Many of the characteristics of terraced houses are shared by detached 18th and 19th century houses, but you don't have to consider these as part of one long building, as in a terrace. When planning your development, however, it's still sensible to consider your house in the context of the style of the houses next to it. Be sympathetic to local styles.

Unusual buildings

The decline of manufacturing industry and the availability of new technology has meant that many buildings not originally built for domestic use are now being converted into homes. From old school houses to railway stations, water towers to windmills, churches, chapels and barns, unusual homes are being created. There are obvious problems with planning and Building Regulations to consider, and many buildings are listed, but they can be the basis for very simple conversions. Light, plumbing and fire exits are the most common problems that need to be overcome. Many of these old buildings are good, solid structures, but they are often derelict and their interior layout may be difficult to organise into a conventional arrangement.

Larger industrial buildings, particularly warehouses, can often be successfully converted into living units. The problem is how to meet the stringent Building Regulations. Window areas are often too small in relation to the floor area; exposed timber beams need to be protected against fire; escape staircases have to be installed; and you need permission to convert the building to residential occupation. Taking on a complete warehouse is not for the first-time developer. But if you can buy early, before the conversion is completed, you may get a preferential price on a unit and then be able to decorate and furnish it to sell at a profit. Living in one large space is very attractive to some people, but many spaces have been subdivided to give a much more traditional feel. What you can do depends partly on the windows. If there are only windows along one outside wall you have little flexibility about how you arrange the space. If there are windows on most of the main walls you have a better chance of creating a worthwhile living space.

BUILDING REGULATIONS AND PLANNING PERMISSION

Building Regulations and planning permission are official ways of controlling the safety and legality of the work and the suitability of any alterations you wish to make. If you do any work that does not comply or without first getting permission you are breaking the law and may have to undo any work already completed.

BUILDING REGULATIONS

Building Regulations have got nothing to do with planning permission. The Building Regulations are a set of minimum requirements designed to ensure that any work you do on the property is safe and legal. They are made by the Secretary of State under powers given by the Building Act. Although it may not be necessary to apply for planning permission to carry out work on your development, any work must always adhere to current Building Regulations.

It is a criminal offence to carry out any work on property that fails to comply. Not only that, but you are legally required to declare any work you have carried out on the property when you come to sell it. If you do not have the correct Building Regulation approval, they may advise their client to insist on a price reduction or, worse still, not to purchase the property at all.

The types of work for which you must have Building Regulations approval include:

- Any extension.
- Loft or cellar conversions.
- Anything that affects the structure of the building such as the removal of a load-bearing wall.
- Bathrooms or kitchens in new locations.
- Installation of new heating appliances (other than electric).
- New chimneys or flues.
- Underpinning or any work that affects the foundations.
- Altered openings for new windows in roofs or walls.
- Replacing roof coverings (unless exact like-for-like repair).
- Installation of cavity insulation.
- Erection of new buildings in the grounds of your property.

Consult the Building Regulations department at your local council planning office before embarking on any building work so that you don't start to do work that does not comply with Building Regulations. Ask for a copy of their guidelines and relevant application forms, depending on the amount of work you are carrying out.

Submit the appropriate paperwork. You will either need to submit a building notice or full plans application with detailed plans, elevations and sections showing all the proposed work and construction details, together with a site plan. You also need to complete a form and pay a fee. A Building Regulations Officer will visit your site to make sure it is running in accordance with the guidelines. You can start work without the go-ahead but at your own risk. Any work that does not comply must be changed and officers do have the power to shut down any site that does not comply or that they consider unsafe. A Building Regulations Approval Certificate will be issued by the department on the satisfactory completion of works. You will need this when you come to sell the property.

PLANNING PERMISSION

This country's planning system is nothing if not complicated, so visit your council's planning department long before you start any improvement work to check what the local position is. For many home improvements planning permission is not required, whilst for others, even apparently quite minor things like replacing windows or decorative wall claddings, you do need to gain planning approval before you can begin. Whatever type of house you live in, the rule is always check with the local planning department before embarking on any work. If you build something which needs planning permission without obtaining permission first, you may be forced to put things right later. This could not only be troublesome but also a very costly mistake.

WHEN YOU'LL NEED TO APPLY FOR PLANNING PERMISSION

The following are common examples of when you will need to apply for planning permission:

- If you want to divide off part of the property as a separate home, for example to create a self-contained flat or bedroom. But you don't need planning permission to let one or two of your rooms to lodgers.
- If you want to build a separate house in the garden.
- If you want to build a parking space for a commercial vehicle or divide the property into separate work and living accommodation.
- If the work you want to do might obstruct the view of the road access.
- If the work would require a new or wider access to a trunk or classified road.
- If you want to extend the property beyond your permitted development rights.

You can make certain minor changes without needing to apply for planning permission. These are called 'permitted development rights'. In some areas of the country these are more restricted. For example in Conservation Areas or Areas of Outstanding Natural Beauty or National Parks (the Norfolk or Suffolk Broads) you would need to apply for planning permission for certain types of work which don't need it in other areas.

HOW TO APPLY FOR PLANNING PERMISSION

If you employ an architect, he or she will generally apply for planning permission on your behalf. If you decide not to employ an architect, here's what you need to do:

1 Phone the council for a planning application form (see pages 134–36 for an example).

2 Draw up relevant scale drawings of your existing and proposed dwelling according to your proposed work. These will be likely to include existing and proposed elevations and basic floor plans. These drawings generally need to be 1:100 in scale and 100% accurate so don't even think of trying to do this yourself unless you are totally confident!

3 Submit the plans and application forms to the council with the appropriate fee.

4 Await the council's acknowledgement of receipt of application.

5 The council will write to the properties in the immediate locality and/or post a notice on your property about the proposed changes. These home-owners have 21 days in which to go online, to the public library or the council to see the plans for themselves and lodge any objection.

6 If the council receives more than two objections then the decision will go to a committee where a decision about the proposal will be made.

7 Planning permission will either be granted or refused, but the planner who is dealing with your application will make a recommendation, which is very often the decision made. If refused, you have the option of taking the council's decision to appeal, but be warned that there is no guarantee that the appeal's decision will be any different and you could end up being liable for the council's costs if you are refused. It may be more sensible instead to listen to the council's comments, revise your plans and resubmit your application.

8 If planning permission is granted and, during work being carried out on the property you want to make any minor changes to the original and approved plans, you must submit the amendment – generally via a drawing – to the planning department. A planning officer, probably the one who dealt with your original application, will decide whether or not these are significant changes requiring submission of a further planning application.

9 If the council feels that the proposed changes are not significant, then they will allow you to start work on the second phase. If it considers they are significant, however, and you go ahead with the new plans regardless, then the council has the power to issue an enforcement notice to stop the work and/or insist on the submission of a retrospective planning application.

10 If you receive an enforcement notice, you are legally obliged to stop work until the appropriate planning permission is gained. If it is not granted, you must undo whatever work has been done so that it complies with your original application, even if this means pulling down thousands of pounds worth of work.

Householder planning application form

1a Your name and address:
Name: ....
Address (with postcode): ....
....
....
....
....
Phone number:...
E-mail address:..

1b Agent's name and address:
Name: ....
Contact name:..
Address (with postcode): ....
....
....
....
Phone number:...
E-mail address:..

2 Full address of the property to be altered or extended
If this is the same as at 1a then write 'as above'

3 Brief description of the proposed building works

4 Type and colour of bricks and tiles (or other materials) to be used on:

Walls:

Roofing:

5 Access to roads for vehicles and pedestrians
Please tick 'Yes' or 'No'   Yes   No

Will you be making a new access to a road or altering an existing access to a road?   ☐   ☐

If 'Yes' please give the name of the road here..
and show details on the plans

A planning application form is far from complicated and relatively straightforward to fill in. Once you have filled out the form you may have to make a number of copies before sending it to the council's planning office. Use this example to prepare yourself for the type of questions you will be obliged to answer when submitting your application.

6   Drainage and flood risk
If new drainage is necessary please tick 'Yes' or 'No' for each question   **Yes**   **No**

Will foul drainage be connected to the main sewer?   ☐   ☐

Will surface water be connected to the main sewer?   ☐   ☐

If you answer 'No' to either or both questions, please send us a supporting statement explaining how you will get rid of foul or surface water

Is the property in the Environment Agency's indicative flood plain?   ☐   ☐
If 'Yes' please send a flood risk assessment with your application

7   Trees and hedges
Please tick 'Yes' or 'No' for each question   **Yes**   **No**

Are there any trees or hedges within, overhanging or next to where you want to build?   ☐   ☐
If 'Yes' please show details on the plans

Does the work involve removing or pruning any trees, hedges, branches or roots?   ☐   ☐
If 'Yes' please describe the work on the plans or in a supporting statement

8   Neighbours
Please tick 'Yes' or 'No' for each question   **Yes**   **No**

Before submitting your application have you

- spoken to the neighbours about your proposal?   ☐   ☐

- shown your neighbours the plans?   ☐   ☐

If 'Yes' to either please say what comments your neighbours made and what, if anything, you have changed as a result

9   Building Regulations
Please tick 'Yes or 'No'   **Yes**   **No**

Have you submitted a separate application for Building Regulations approval?   ☐   ☐

10   Pre-application advice
Please tick 'Yes' or 'No'   **Yes**   **No**

Have you received any advice from us about your proposal?   ☐   ☐

If 'Yes' please give the name of the officer who gave you the advice ....
and enclose any correspondence you have had about the proposal

When you have filled in this form and prepared the plans and supporting information, please complete the checklist below to make sure you send all the information we need with your application. Then sign in the appropriate places below.

Checklist

The checklist is to make sure that you send all the information we need with your application.

	Yes	No
Filled in application form	☐	☐
Correct planning application fee	☐	☐
OS-based site location plan with the site clearly edged in red and other land owned in blue	☐	☐
Site layout plan	☐	☐
Existing floor plans	☐	☐
Proposed floor plans	☐	☐
Existing elevation drawings	☐	☐
Proposed elevation drawings	☐	☐
Supporting statements we ask you for on this form	☐	☐
Two signatures and dates required (see below)	☐	☐

Ownership Certificate
I certify that 21 days before the date I signed this application form nobody except the applicant owned the application site and none of the site forms part of an agricultural holding. (If either of these statements is not the case, please see the guidance notes.)

Signature ....

On behalf of ....

Date ....

Accuracy of information on this form
I have filled in this application and, as far as I know, the information I have given is accurate. With it I apply for planning permission.

Signature ....

On behalf of ....

Date ....

LISTED BUILDING CONSENT

If your property is a listed building, you will need special consent to carry out any building works. Your first step should be to contact your local council before you make an application for listed building consent. The conservation officer will tell you whether your proposals are likely to be accepted. This could save you time and money in the long run. It is also often best to employ an architect who is used to working with listed buildings.

Local authorities deal with all listed building applications and will give you the appropriate form for making your application. The majority of cases are dealt with solely by the local authority but the most important cases are also referred to English Heritage (Notifications) and sometimes to the Secretary of State for the Environment, Transport and Regions (Referrals).

Your application will need to include enough information to show clearly what you intend to do,

illustrated with detailed drawings and photographs. It will usually take at least eight weeks after you send in your application form for a decision to be sent to you. If consent is refused you have six months in which you can appeal to the Department of the Environment, Transport and the Regions. VAT does not apply to the cost of alterations to listed buildings, although it does apply to repairs and ordinary maintenance.

NEIGHBOURS AND PARTY WALLS

Before you start on your development it's best to inform your neighbours about the planned work. Even if what you are going to do is perfectly legal, there's no point in upsetting them. If your plans will affect party walls you may need a party wall surveyor or lawyer.

A party wall is a wall that separates buildings on either side of the boundary. A party structure is a floor partition between flats and maisonettes that are approached by

WHEN YOU NEED LISTED BUILDING CONSENT

If your building is listed, the planning rules are far more rigorous. You will need to apply for listed building consent along with planning permission if you want to:

- Build an extension or addition, including conservatories and sun rooms, alter existing balconies or verandas, build a loft conversion, put in dormer windows or roof additions. In fact, anything that changes the way the building looks.
- Build a garage, garden shed, greenhouse or swimming pool on your land.
- Add a porch to the house.
- Alter terraces, walls or gates.
- Put up satellite dishes, TV and radio aerials.
- Make any significant alterations to the interior of the house. Sometimes this even includes decoration, repair and maintenance.

The Party Wall Act gives guidelines for resolving disputes between neighbours in relation to their party walls

separate staircases or entrances. So, like party walls, they form part of a building. If part of your proposed plans includes work that affects the party walls you will require a Party Wall Agreement.

Works to the party walls are covered under the Party Wall Act 1996, and require certain procedures to be followed. Failure to follow these procedures can extensively delay your project and, in some cases, lead to detailed redesign being required. A chartered building surveyor will be able to give advice in this regard and act as a party wall surveyor.

If you intend to do work that affects a wall between you and your neighbour then you must find out if the Party Wall Act is relevant in your case. If it is, you must inform your neighbours of the work that is to take place. The Act gives guidelines for resolving disputes between neighbours in relation to their party walls. Work under the Party Wall Act includes:

■ Works to an existing wall or structure shared with another property.
■ Building on a boundary.
■ Excavating near a neighbouring building.

INFORMING YOUR NEIGHBOURS

You must serve the notice on your neighbours at least two months before you start the work on party walls or a month for party fence walls or excavations that are close to your neighbours' property. The notice is only valid for one year. Give the neighbours your name and address, the building's address if it is different from your own, a clear statement that your notice of intention to undertake the work is under the Party Wall Act, full details of the proposed works to be carried out and the date you intend to start work.

After the notice is served, your neighbour has up to 14 days to give written consent for the work to take place or to serve a counter notice requiring additional work to be carried out or object to the work being done. If after 14 days your neighbour has not replied you will need to resolve the dispute before starting work.

RESOLVING PARTY WALL ISSUES

If either you or your neighbour have objected to the other's notice, and in the unlikely event that the dispute can't be resolved by friendly discussion, the Act provides for the resolution of disputes through a surveyor who will draw up a document that includes:

■ A description of the work that is to be undertaken.
■ When and how the work is to be carried out.
■ A description of the condition of the neighbour's property prior to the work.
■ Conditions allowing the surveyor access to inspect the work as it is carried out.

The surveyor will decide who pays the fee for drawing up the document, although it is up to the person undertaking the work to pay all costs.

BATTERSEA: TAKING THE NEIGHBOURS INTO ACCOUNT

Thirty-one-year-old Jonathan Moon turned his back on a highly paid career in IT to become a full-time property developer. After nine months of searching he finally found his first project – a second-floor, two-bedroom flat set in a quiet street in Battersea, south London. The house was in a traditional residential area which was also a Conservation Area.

PROJECT COSTS	
COST OF PROPERTY (NOT INCLUDING FEES)	£195,000
RENOVATION BUDGET	£50,000
TARGET RESALE	£300,000
ANTICIPATED PRE-TAX PROFIT	
(NOT INCLUDING FEES)	£55,000

Jonathan had big plans to make his property stand out. His idea was to convert the loft into a brand new bedroom and bathroom and completely revamp the rest of the flat to create a state-of-the-art renovation. 'I think of it as smooth with a feeling of sophistication. Nothing frilly, nothing fancy. I want the worktops to merge with the worktop space rather than having edges and lines'. It was the high-tech gadgets, such as plasma screens and a music system linking all the rooms and even a built-in coffee-maker, that Jonathan planned would bring in more money.

Jonathan was so confident he borrowed £185,000 and used up all his savings to buy and renovate this property.

THE PLAN

When Jonathan bought the flat it was spread over one floor with three smallish rooms at the front. One had been used as a reception room; the others were bedrooms. At the back there was a tiny kitchen with an even tinier shower room off it. The original wooden sash windows had earlier been replaced by PVC windows.

Jonathan was going to entirely change the layout by knocking the walls down between the three main rooms to create an open-plan space comprising a kitchen at one end and a sitting room at the other with no division. At the back of the flat he planned to build out from the old kitchen onto the patio to create a reasonably sized bedroom. By removing the old doorway he would create enough space for a luxury ensuite wet room and still leave enough room for another private terrace. Glass bricks would allow light into the bedroom.

He planned to create a second level, turning the flat into a maisonette by converting the roof space into a master bedroom and bathroom, where there would be plenty of storage and a small roof terrace. Jonathan intended to project manage the conversion himself,

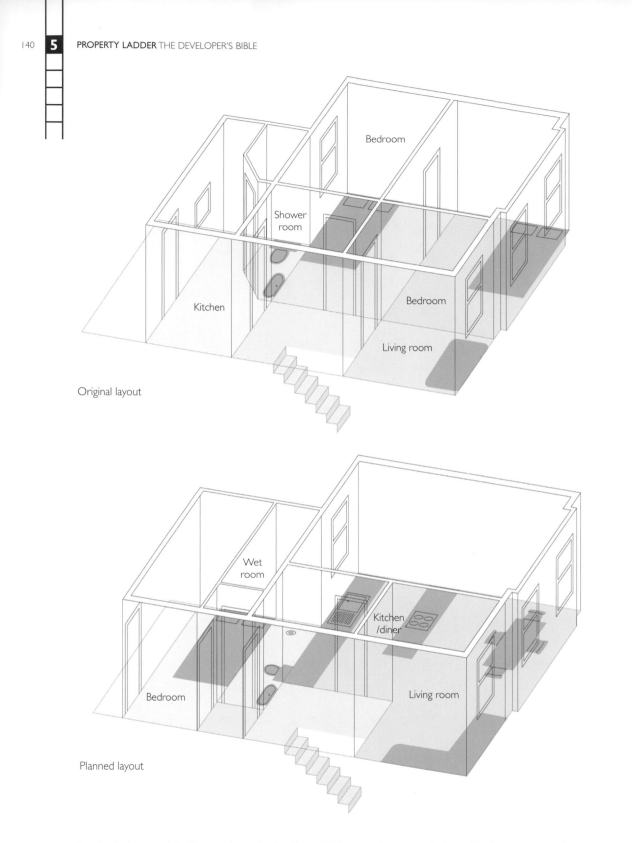

Original layout

Planned layout

Jonathan's flat was originally spread over the first floor with three small rooms at the front. His plan was to turn the main rooms into an open-plan kitchen and sitting room. At the back he planned to create an ensuite wet room and a small terrace.

Jonathan knocked down the walls between the three main rooms to create an open plan kitchen/living room with a contemporary finish. It looked spacious and modern – but cost twice the budget allowed for it.

although he had never done anything like this before. To convert the loft he needed to put in three huge steel girders which would be sunk into the party walls shared with his neighbours.

This is how he broke down his budget for the work:

PROPOSED RENOVATION COSTS	
CONVERTING THE LOFT	£25,000
BUILDING WORK	£10,000
NEW KITCHEN	£4,300
NEW BATHROOMS	£2,100
DECORATION	£3,500
FLOORING AND CARPETS	£1,500
TECHNOLOGY	£3,000
CONTINGENCIES	£600
TOTAL	£50,000

SARAH'S ADVICE

I was worried about Jonathan taking on the role of project manager. This was going to be a big job and he was completely inexperienced in this kind of work.

Jonathan's plan for the new living area would create a real feeling of space. Ideally I thought he could have made it even better by adding sliding doors so that the space could be divided, which would make the area more flexible. I was pretty sure that Jonathan was making the flat how he would like to live himself with 'all mod cons' including his surround-sound system and lights that would come on automatically as you walked in through the door.

I didn't think that his £50,000 budget would cover the costs. In this sort of development the gadgets were unlikely to add to the value to the property. I thought it would be a good idea to reinstate the original sash windows, since this was a Conservation Area, and save money on the technology, especially considering the size

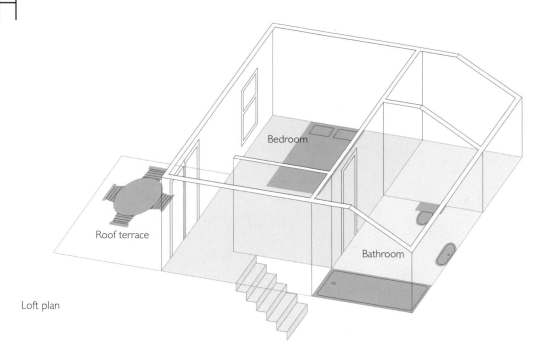

Bedroom

Roof terrace

Bathroom

Loft plan

Jonathan planned to convert the roof space into a master bedroom and bathroom with plenty of storage and a roof terrace.

of the job he was taking on. The market who would pay for extra gadgets were more likely to be in a development with parking and a gym.

Jonathan's idea of having a glazed wall to the bedroom would be very effective, but I felt it might be better to have a completely glazed end wall. The converted loft space with its own ensuite bathroom would be a selling feature and having two small terraces would add value and appeal to his market.

A loft conversion is a good way of adding value, but you must do your homework first. Check with local agents to make sure there is a potential market for it. Check how much it will add to the value so you can be sure it will make a profit over the cost. Extensions are most effective when the original property is not balanced. If it has more bedrooms than reception rooms or large reception rooms and few bedrooms, creating extra rooms can work well. Older houses with bigger roof spaces are easier and cheaper to convert.

HOW THE PROJECT PROGRESSED

Jonathan's team of Polish builders got off to a flying start, tearing down walls and stripping the whole interior of the flat. However, Jonathan neglected one important thing: to get permission and Party Wall Agreement from his neighbours to sink the new supporting steel girders into the party walls. The girders were already in by the time his, by now irate, neighbours complained. The party wall surveyor was concerned that the scaffolding was now resting on someone else's only recently repaired roof so the work ground to a halt. The longer the situation continued, the less work there was for the builders to do and what work there was now had to be done in the wrong order, costing time and money.

Jonathan had to acknowledge that his project would probably cost a little more than the £50,000 originally budgeted. In a more buoyant market, he could probably have recouped the money from the extra gadgets he was intending to install but in a soft market getting an unusually high price would be difficult. He remained convinced that everything about his property was so special that he would make his ambitious asking price, but just down the road a similar two-bedroom flat with original features, a new kitchen and its own private garden had just sold for £255,000, that is £45,000 less than Jonathan wanted for his. Prices for similar properties in the area suggested that he would have to drop his price in order to sell.

Five weeks into the project, there was still no agreement from the neighbours and eventually work came to a complete standstill and the builders left the site. Jonathan was spending more money every day on mortgages and loans. The Party Wall Agreements were now the bane of his life. 'I thought I'd ticked all the boxes but I now realise the one issue I neglected was the most important – getting consent to do the works.'

Jonathan realised he needed to dig an inspection hole in the downstairs neighbours' garden so that a district surveyor could check whether the foundations were deep enough to carry the weight of the building work. But relations with the neighbours were further soured when during drilling, some dust and debris fell into their flat. Even worse, six months after he began the development the already-pretty-alienated neighbours reported a leak into their bedroom from Jonathan's flat, making their newly decorated flat uninhabitable.

Nine weeks after starting work the neighbours finally gave their verbal permission to dig the hole, but no signed permission was forthcoming for a further four months. Finally the insurance company sorted out the neighbour's redecoration and temporary hotel accommodation and work could progress. Structural work on the loft and new extension could now continue, and Jonathan could start on the rest of the building work and plastering. This was a very big step

Jonathan built out onto the patio to create a bright, airy bedroom with huge windows and an ensuite wet room which still left space for a small private terrace.

Jonathan converted the roof space into a master bedroom with its own bathroom. It had plenty of storage space and the luxury of a small roof terrace from which there were good views. This would be a great selling feature.

forward. But Jonathan had planned on finishing the work within 12 weeks and it had already taken 24. With the loft conversion well underway the builders were finally able to start on the small rear addition. Here Jonathan created a second bedroom with its own wet room. After over a year with no money coming in, all his savings were used up and his sports car had to be sold. He rented out his home in Clapham and moved a mattress into the Battersea flat. He needed to sell as soon as possible.

THE OUTCOME

By the time they'd finished the builders had been working nights as well as during the day and were exhausted. But Jonathan had transformed three small rooms into a great open-plan kitchen/living area. The kitchen had a contemporary finish with stainless steel and granite. Hardwood floors and light, white surfaces accentuated the feeling of space making the room feel bigger. It did look great but cost an amazing £10,000 – twice the allotted budget.

The tiny bathroom and kitchen at the back had been replaced by a bright, airy bedroom with huge windows overlooking its own private terrace, just as Jonathan had envisaged. But he had spent thousands on the sort of high-tech gadgets he would like in his own home and it was difficult to see how he would make the money back. The biggest change and the biggest expense was the roof. Storage had been fitted into the roof space and there were great views from the roof terrace. The original budget for the roof had been £50,000 and amazingly, despite all the delays, the builder had stuck to the fixed fee.

SUMMARY OF ACTUAL RENOVATION COSTS		
	ORIGINAL BUDGET	FINAL SUMS
BUILDING AND DECORATION	£38,500	£38,500
KITCHEN AND BATHROOMS	£6,400	£14,955
TECHNOLOGY	£3,000	£8,500
FLOORS AND CARPETS	£1,500	£4,748
CONTINGENCY (PARTY WALL & INSURANCE)	£600	£14,354
TOTAL RENOVATION COSTS	£50,000	£81,057 (£89,500 INCLUDING FEES)

LESSONS LEARNED

1 *Notify the neighbours.* It is essential to create good relations with your neighbours from the start. Make sure you notify them of your plans and get any necessary permissions. Jonathan started off on the wrong foot with his. Party wall legislation is there to protect people from damage by neighbours working on walls they share. Try to meet all your neighbours at the start of the building work. Let them know exactly what you intend and what your timescale is. Try to minimise the disruption to their lives. Their co-operation is very helpful when developing.

2 *Make sure you have the skills for managing the project.* Plan meticulously for every contingency.

3 *Adhere to Building Regulations.* Seek advice from the Building Regulations Office at your local council planning department. It is illegal not to secure the correct Building Regulations approval for works done – not doing so can also impact on the survey or the ability of a potential buyer to secure a mortgage on the property.

THE RIGHT TO LIGHT

In the case of any extension, neighbourhood Rights to Light can limit the height and position of the proposed building work and in certain cases actually reduce the site value. Rights to Light are difficult to track; they can be registered, granted by deed or simply acquired after having a minimum of 20 years enjoyment of light through a window or opening. The general rules for neighbours' Right to Light are:

■ The reduction in light must not make the property less fit than it was for its purpose.

■ The amount of 'appropriate' light may vary depending upon building, use and even region.

■ The amount of light considered to be sufficient will tend to vary depending on the use of the room.

In reality, Right to Light actions are rare. But anyone planning to extend a building should be aware of the quite remarkable impact not only on the property, but also on their finances, if a dispute occurs.

THE DESIGN

Designing a conversion is a complex business. Both wiring and plumbing may have to be completely rethought to fit in with a new layout, for example, and this will be costly. Certain things such as installing insulation will be worth doing, but beware of fitting expensive luxuries, like a sauna, which may have only minority appeal.

THINKING AHEAD

Obviously the quicker you manage to turn a property around, the quicker your new business will become viable. But be careful not to get so carried away by the idea of doing up tatty properties and selling them for a huge profit that the cost of your improvements actually eats into or destroys your profits. While some areas change their ownership profile fairly quickly, others can take many years to gain a new image. Indeed, there's a chance they may never do so. You certainly don't want to over-develop and end up with a property that has cost so much to revamp that you need to charge way over the local market value to try and recoup your costs.

Keep all improvements to a level that sits comfortably in the area and save your fantasies about whirlpool baths and games rooms for another day. In fact, the most common mistake made by property vendors is a simple matter of failing to clean and clear any clutter from the property before showing it to potential buyers. Simple design and a good finish do not necessarily need to cost a fortune and this, together with a spotlessly clean property, is much more important than throwing money away on fancy plans.

INCORPORATING THE SERVICES

The wiring, but more noticeably the plumbing, can present real problems if you are going to alter the interior spaces of your property. The location of these services is crucial to the overall plan – for example, it will affect where the kitchen and bathroom should be located in the property for greatest economy. At an early stage you should plot the existing power points, boilers, soil stacks and drainage runs on your plan. This should help you decide where the highly serviced rooms should be. There may be a choice of suitable positions. If not, adding extra foul drainage, for example, could prove costly.

JOBS WORTH DOING

It is always worth carrying out essential repairs to roofs and windows, and fitting sound wiring. Central heating and good insulation are also always worth installing. A well-designed central heating system that is beautifully fitted will not only run economically but is also a good selling point, along with a well-painted front door with good quality door furniture, an undamaged doorstep and front steps and a neat front garden. Apart from that, the key to getting it right is knowing your market and exactly what prospective purchasers want.

Modernising a kitchen or bathroom is a good selling point but can be an expensive process. Installing a second bathroom is often a good idea, particularly if you are designing for a young family, but this also has the potential to be expensive.

If you buy a property with a good quality but tired kitchen, updating it without replacing it may take pressure off your budget, and a well-presented kitchen will always help when you come to sell. Wooden doors can be painted, for example, to freshen them up and give a more contemporary look. First make a key on the surface with a fine sandpaper, apply a base coat of multi-purpose primer and finish with a good-quality eggshell paint. Complete the look by adding new handles. Many hardware stores have ranges that look luxurious with an affordable price tag. Replacing a worktop can also make a dramatic difference if it is past its best. Paint walls and ceiling a clean neutral colour to brighten and freshen the room. If your tiles look tired, then consider re-tiling, regrouting or freshening the grouting with a good scrub of bleach.

Don't forget the kitchen floor. Re-tile, lay a fashionable linoleum or use varnish or floor paint on boards. Putting down good flooring in fairly neutral colours can be expensive but is often worth it as it will finish the whole room off beautifully.

JOBS NOT WORTH DOING

Like many decisions to do with your development, your market will help you decide what is or is not worth doing. Always think carefully before you start installing expensive luxuries. Saunas, jacuzzis, water features, tennis courts and swimming pools all fall into this category. Equally think before fitting UPVC double-glazed windows – in the right market they will add value, in the wrong area they will detract from the value. Even a conservatory, if built in the wrong manner for the wrong property, will detract from the value at worst and cover its cost at best.

MAKING THE MOST OF PERIOD FEATURES

When you purchase a property for development that is in a bad state of repair, it is tempting to rip everything out and start again. Salvaging what you have, however, can not only save you money but also appeal to your market. Period features, if they were fitted when the property was built, will not only fit its style but generally add to its value. If your development is a period property there is a good chance that the buyer will be wanting just that, both inside and out. So think before you rip out any original features. If they are damaged, can they be restored? Check what is waiting to be rediscovered beneath 'modern improvements' and see what you can do to salvage them. The following are all items that, if in good condition, would probably be worth keeping:

Cornices
- Cornices, the carved or moulded plaster strip where the wall abuts the ceiling and central ceiling roses, vary from the simple to the florid.
- If the original cornicing is damaged or crumbling you can hire a specialist to make a mould of a good part of it and repeat the pattern in plaster to replace the damaged area. You can remove all the cornicing and

CORNICE

DADO/PICTURE RAIL

FIREPLACE

PERIOD DOOR

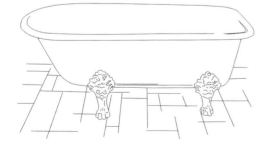

PERIOD BATH

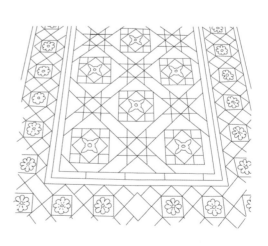

FLOORING

replace it with one that is a traditional standard moulding. Do not be tempted to replace the original cornicing with cheap, mass-produced coving as it will look out-of-keeping with the style of the room.

Dado and picture rails

- Dado or chair rails were devised to prevent the backs of chairs from damaging the wall and are about 90cm (3ft) up the wall. They make an attractive visual break, particularly in a high wall and offer opportunities for using a combination of colours in the decoration.
- Picture rails are fixed to the wall about three-quarters of the way up and were originally designed to hang pictures from. Like dado rails they are a decoration in their own right, especially on a high wall.

Fireplaces

- Even if the property is centrally heated and needs no fireplace, a traditional fireplace can emphasise the good points of a period house and act as a rather more attractive focal point than a television.
- Good stonemasons or marble restorers can restore chipped or broken surrounds – always get a quote before you commission one. In general, wooden fire surrounds were originally painted. If you think yours would look better with a wood finish, the surround can be carefully stripped and treated.
- If you knock two rooms into one and therefore have two fireplaces in a sitting room but are short of a fireplace elsewhere in the property, you can always move the secondary one into a new position and leave a hole for a grate in its place.

Floors

- Exposing and restoring original flooring utilises what you already have and can add real value to a property.

To revive hardwood floors give them a vigorous scrub with a mix of one part turpentine, one part methylated spirits and one part vinegar. Finish with two or more coats of floor polish.
- If pine or deal floorboards are worn you can sand them and finish with a sealant clear varnish. Beware, though, that sanding will remove the distinctive colour achieved by decades of wear.

Doors

- If you have period doors but need them to be fire doors to comply with fire regulations you can buy intumescent paint, which is fire-resistant. Together with door closers, larger door stops and intumescent smoke seals these should satisfy the regulations.
- Victorian houses and some 1930s houses may still have original stained-glass surrounds to the front door. These can be very attractive, particularly if they match others along the street, so don't be in a hurry to remove them.
- If your property is a 19th-century terraced house it may have one large room at the back and another at the front connected by double wooden doors. This is a feature well worth keeping. The rooms can be divided or opened up at will; no expensive conversion is needed and the doors themselves, if original, will only need stripping and repainting.

The bath

- If your property contains a cast iron or roll-top bath sitting on decorative feet that looks like it has seen better days, think before you skip it! The original is much more desirable than modern plastic. Never attempt to move a roll-top bath yourself. They are very heavy and you could damage your property as well as your back!

Put yourself in the shoes of your target market and ask yourself how the spaces would work best

- A tatty bath can look like new again with either a professional polish or re-enamelling. Then add a set of shiny new taps.

Shutters

- If you find that your property still possesses shutters you should certainly keep them. They are now seen as a valuable asset for both security and aesthetic reasons. It may be necessary to have them stripped, repainted and re-hung, but they are attractive and practical.

Staircases

- The staircase is the first thing you see in many houses. The shape and details, the newel posts, the balusters and the shape of the treads will be very characteristic of the period of your house. Think carefully before you alter an original staircase. Not only will you alter the proportions of the interior but your new staircase will have to comply with Building Regulations.

Lighting

- The lighting you choose should complement the basic characteristics of the house. Fittings don't need to match the period – as especially in older properties light fittings were limited – but they do need to enhance the rooms. In older houses, it is often better to use a traditional option (such as a chandelier or simple gas-style fitting) or a much more modern alternative that does not try to fight with the original design. Simple spotlights on a ceiling with delicate moulding sensitively done can avoid detracting from the property's original architecture.

SPACIAL SOLUTIONS

A large number of British houses are spatially challenged by the terms of today's lifestyle. Over half of Britain's housing stock was built before World War II and the average living room is a mere 4.5 x 4m (15 x 13ft), but with efficient modern heating today's home-buyers are now looking for as much space as they can get for their money. So, what's the answer? To make a limited area feel spacious you will need good design to make the very most of the way it looks. You can't make a room physically larger without knocking down walls or building an extension, but you certainly can make it feel bigger.

Even if you decide to employ an architect or interior designer to plan your design, it will help you to understand the spaces and possibilities if you sketch a floor plan of the property. Go round the property with your sketch and review what you like about each room. Are the rooms a pleasing size and shape? Do they connect up well? Then go around and list the least attractive elements of each room. Is it too dark? Is there an ugly view? Does a fitted wardrobe take up too much room? Is there an obvious and practical solution? Put yourself in the shoes of your target market and ask yourself how the spaces would work best.

MAXIMISING SPACE
Using colour for a feeling of space

- Pale, light colours generally help to increase a sense of space. Shiny surfaces reflect light so consider using an eggshell or gloss paint – be cautious, though, as the shinier the surface the better the finish you need.

Space-making floor treatments

- Whilst laying the same flooring throughout a property unifies it, you can often make a room with different areas (i.e., kitchen and dining area) actually feel larger if you change the floor covering for each area.
- The heavy textures and dark colours of dark-coloured carpets and rugs absorb light like a sponge. For a small space choose hard, shiny floor coverings such as wood, resin, tile or slate. These materials will bounce light and sound, making the space feel larger than it actually is.
- The direction in which you lay a floor or patterned covering can have an impact. Vertical lines accentuate length and depth, horizontal lines accentuate width.
- Removing the skirting from a room will increase the sense of space, but you'll need an exceptional and very contemporary finish to carry off this look.

Ceilings

- Tall ceilings and smooth surfaces increase the sense of space. The shiny, swirl patterns of an Artexed ceiling, for example, visually drip and will make it feel lower than it really is. You can plaster and skim over Artex to visually push the ceiling back up again.

Make the most of light

- The more daylight that fills a room, the more space there seems to be. Where you can, add a window to a dark or small room, or increase the scale of an existing one.
- Keep window treatments simple and uncluttered. Big bolts of fabric and heavily draped curtains fill up visual space and cut down the amount of light that filters through the windows.

- Sight lines and views, especially of outside space, have the effect of visually expanding our immediate surroundings and taking them beyond actual walls. If you are deprived of a view, use an old Japanese trick. Place an eye-catching object just outside the window, such as an ornamental tree, a brightly coloured sculpture or planter. Your eye will naturally be led to the object, thereby extending the sense of space by proportion and line.
- Light shining upwards and bouncing off a white ceiling increases its intensity and will give a gentle but effective light as well as increasing the feeling of space.

Mirrors and pictures

- Use mirrors and pictures to reflect light. Place them strategically to reflect doors or paintings in a long, narrow room or passage. You can also use them like windows, reflecting corners and vistas from a room to make the whole space feel bigger.
- If you have a low ceiling, place a large picture in the middle of the most dominant wall. The picture will draw your eye, detracting from the height of the ceiling.

Sight lines and views, especially of outside space, have the effect of visually expanding our surroundings

Stripes and lines

- Wallpaper with vertical stripes draws the eye upwards, and can increase the sense of height; though take care you don't make the room feel like a candy box.
- Dado rails and wallpaper with horizontal lines visually increases the width of a room and will help to make tall, narrow rooms seem better proportioned. Be very cautious about using horizontal lines, however, as most ceilings are not high enough to create a spacious effect.

Furniture

- Generally, you should only use pieces of furniture that are in proportion to the scale of the room. A large sofa in a small living room, for example, will often swamp the room and make it feel cramped. Very carefully chosen, though, a beautiful piece of furniture or a painting that is out of proportion can actually enhance the room in an 'Alice in Wonderland' manner.
- Moving the furniture slightly away from the walls will reveal more wall space and make the room seem bigger.
- Less is more. The fewer things there are in a room, the greater the sense of space. Beautiful design requires restraint and with a development you are merely suggesting how the prospective buyer might use the space and don't need to stuff rooms full of furniture.

Doors and doorways

- Doors and doorways can have a huge impact on the way we perceive space. Take a tip from grand stately homes. If you are completely renovating a period property, align doorways to create longer sight lines. While this can be expensive, it is worth considering if you are already replacing walls and doorways or changing the structure of a building.
- The best space is the most flexible space. With every square foot costing more each year, we need to make

> Generally, you should only ever place pieces of furniture that are in proportion to the scale of the room

maximum use of our space. While many people want open-plan living, at times we also need to be able to shut away a home office or children's area. Sliding doors that disappear completely into a cavity wall are ideal. They maximise the sense of space by opening up rooms, yet can close off the space when privacy is required. Avoid using cheap door systems. A sliding door must feel solid and slide easily.

Storage

- Storage helps to keep a space clutter-free. Consider installing concealed storage with generous built-in cupboards and built-in units that will keep surfaces clear and utilities hidden.

HUMANISING LARGE SPACES

Sometimes 'homeliness' is more important than a feeling of space. This is usually true for very tiny spaces such as a loo or attic workroom. You can achieve this by choosing a rich, strong colour instead of a white or pale one. But you have to be sure about it. If in doubt, try the colour in your own home rather than testing ideas in a development where you want to appeal to the broadest section of the market possible.

Sometimes, however, vast open spaces can feel much too large. They make us feel vulnerable and unable to relax. The answer is to visually cordon off sections of the room, using colour and furniture.

A rich, dark colour will add warmth to a large space but also tends to have the effect of bringing walls in. This can be particularly useful if you have a room with an irregular shape. A long, narrow room can appear squarer, for example, if you paint the furthest, smallest wall a dark colour to bring it closer to the eye. Strong colour on the long walls, on the other hand, will give a long, thin corridor effect. Use larger, more monumental pieces of furniture to zone specific areas within an over-large room.

MAJOR IMPROVEMENTS

Altering the basic layout of a property can be a good idea if you can be sure that the end result will be a much more satisfactory home. In most properties, whilst you may be able to make dramatic changes, this may not be best for your market. If there are large bedrooms but only one bathroom, consider stealing a corner of a bedroom and creating an ensuite shower room. A cloakroom can often be tucked into spaces like the cupboard under the stairs, depending on drainage runs. Roof space, with the correct Building Regulations approval, can be used for anything from a study to a child's bedroom.

KNOCKING THROUGH

Where rooms are small and you want more space it is usually possible to knock down a wall between two rooms and create a larger one. You will need to comply with Building Regulations to do this and also take advice from a structural engineer, who will calculate the size of any supporting beams required.

SPLITTING UP ROOMS

If the property has large rooms and you want to divide them, you will need some form of partition. If you are merely building a stud wall to create two bedrooms out of one, or to separate a kitchen from a dining area or a study from a living area, this is fairly straightforward and you can probably do it yourself. If you are creating two separate rooms out of one, you may need to get Building Regulation approval.

EXPANDING INTO THE LOFT

Lofts, even if the ceilings are low, can provide quite large rooms if well converted. It can be difficult to gain planning permission to raise the ridge height of the roof unless a precedent has been set elsewhere on the street. You will need to get into the roof space and work out whether you feel there is enough space and head height to justify the expense. Loft conversions are not cheap but it is a way of adding extra square footage to a property whilst only losing the area taken up by the new staircase.

Although they charge a premium, it can end up cheaper to get a specialist loft conversion company to carry out the work as they are geared up to tackle the specific work involved. When getting quotes, ask the companies if you can see an example of their work. Get two or three estimates, as these may vary considerably and check exactly what each covers, looking especially carefully at the clauses about insurance. Agree everything with them in writing, including the size and frequency of the stage payments you will have to make.

If you are going to organise the loft conversion yourself or even do it yourself, you must take advice from an architect, surveyor and/or structural engineer. The work will have to comply with Building Regulations and in certain circumstances you will need planning permission. A professional will be able to advise about this.

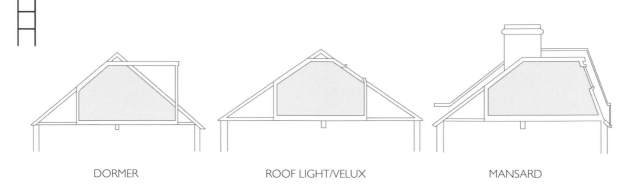

DORMER   ROOF LIGHT/VELUX   MANSARD

The three most common types of loft conversion are: dormer (a projecting upright window in a sloping roof); roof light or Velux (a window in the roof at the same angle as the roof); and mansard (a roof with two pitches, the lower part of the roof being steeper than the upper slope).

REGULATIONS THAT LOFT CONVERSIONS MUST ADHERE TO

There are strict regulations about the conversion of an attic space into a habitable room. Because you are effectively adding another storey to your living space there are fire regulations to which you must adhere. This generally involves creating a route of escape down through the house that is protected against fire. This route cannot pass through another habitable room. You will need to either fireproof existing doors or install fire doors with self-closers along this route to meet the necessary regulations. A Fire Protection Officer or Building Regulations Officer will need to be satisfied that your changes comply with regulations.

EXTENDING AT GROUND LEVEL

Extending the property at ground level can make all the difference to the feeling of space. You may want just a few metres extra to fit in a porch for coats and boots or a downstairs cloakroom or to build a full-scale conservatory with doors opening out onto the garden. Whatever you want, there are a number of factors to take into account, and it really is best to get some expert advice.

If you plan a substantial extension you will certainly require planning permission, though smaller extensions may lie within your permitted development rights. As a general rule, you will find it difficult to get approval to dramatically extend the roadside elevation or raise the

ridge line of your house. Any proposed roof terrace is unlikely to be approved if it overlooks neighbouring gardens. Bear in mind that planning guidelines often change and you will need to check with your local council to keep up to date or employ an architect who will be familiar with the guidelines and can help you come up with a proposal that is more likely to be approved.

The next thing is to complete an application form and prepare detailed drawings. An architect or surveyor is the best person to do this. They will also know about planning permissions and Building Regulations and will apply for them on your behalf. Copies of these will be put on display in the public register for anyone to look at who thinks they might wish to lodge an objection. Some local authorities also publish details of proposed extensions in the local newspaper to notify people of proposals that the authorities think might affect them.

As a general rule, you will find it difficult to get approval to dramatically extend the roadside elevation

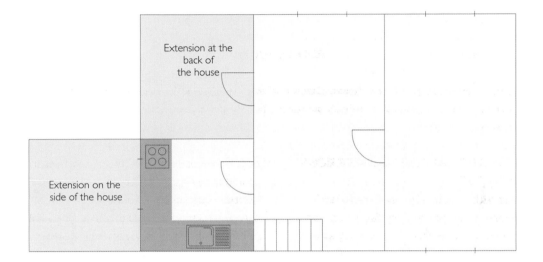

Extension at the
back of
the house

Extension on the
side of the house

Extension on the side
and back of the house

Adding an extension to a two-up/two-down property can be carried out in a number of ways: building out at the back or the side (top), or building a complete wraparound construction (bottom).

SPECIAL REQUIREMENTS OF BUYING TO LET

Before you embark on any renovation project, you need to know who your market is and how to target their needs accordingly. Refurnishing a buy-to-let property is no different, but it does have some particular requirements of its own. If you are wanting a more contemporary finish and are feeling uninspired, hip hotels or trendy restaurants can really help with ideas (as well as providing the perfect excuse for some rather glam nights out!). The actual finishes and furnishings might not be within your budget but you can borrow some ideas, look at the different materials and see how the professionals put a look together.

For the more expensive end of the contemporary market it is important to offer tenants luxurious extras, but these don't have to cost a fortune. Start with the basics – good, effective lighting is crucial, as is making the space as user-friendly and flexible as possible. Try and keep your colour palette limited and apply different finishes rather than different colours.

Preparation is paramount. Before you invested in a buy-to-let property you should already have thought long and hard about the current use of the property, its future prospects, as well as looked at the amenities provided by the local area. You will have determined which type of person these particular attributes appeal to and researched how much you are likely to achieve each month, to make sure your investment is financially viable.

Finally, and most importantly, you will have checked that there is a demand for rental property in the area. Now as you carry out refurbishment you need to tailor the layout, style and facilities to fit that market.

MATCHING THE PROPERTY TO YOUR MARKET

Make sure you have your potential purchaser clearly in mind and tailor the décor and furnishing to their tastes. Any prospective buyer will want to feel they can impose their own tastes, so keep the décor simple, the finishes first class and the furniture to a minimum. If designing for rent, keep everything sturdy and easy to replace.

First of all you need to know your market. Think about what basic things your target tenant will want and expect from a rental property. A corporate client is likely to want all the gadgets and mod cons with a particularly high-spec finish. The student market, on the other hand, will opt for more basic budget accommodation and a simple decoration scheme.

Check that there is currently a demand for your type of property on the rental market. Look at similar homes available to rent in your area and seek advice from a letting agent. You should have already done this before you purchased the property, but if time has lapsed since you exchanged contracts, the market may have changed. You need to be up to speed on current rental values so that you can budget for your design scheme accordingly. Planning carefully from the outset will keep you focused on your market and help you stick to your budget.

DESIGNING FOR RENT

Whatever your market, design and spec, there are some general rules that will stand you in good stead when furnishing a buy to let.

Décor

Keep your décor light and bright. As most tenants will only stay a year or so, you need to be able to appeal to a much broader market than for sale. (Any tenant will want a little leeway to add his or her own personality and taste, even if only for a short time.) For walls, stick to one colour throughout, preferably a neutral one. You will find this is easy to maintain and touch up between tenants, it is inoffensive to all and maximises the sense of light and space the property offers. Avoid loud colours and patterned papers, both of which rely on the tenant having the same taste as you.

Flooring

Partly for ease of maintenance and partly to pull your scheme together, think about continuity. Laying the same flooring throughout, for example, helps the rooms to flow. Using different flooring will visually break up the space; in an open-plan space this can work to your benefit, giving the effect of two rooms whilst borrowing the extra space for a sight line.

Think carefully about the type of flooring you use.

- Carpet is an affordable option that appeals to most people. If you do choose carpet, avoid light colours as marks show more easily and it is best to go for a relatively cheap carpet that can be replaced every few years rather than spending a fortune on an expensive one that is likely to be damaged anyway.
- Solid wood and laminate floorings are easy to maintain and keep clean but whilst they are still popular at the moment, they may date fashion-wise in a relatively short period of time.
- Think twice about fitting wood flooring or carpet in bathrooms as they require the user to take a certain amount of care. You will find ceramic tiles or linoleum more durable and water resistant.

Kitchen

Think practical and clean. If installing a new kitchen choose a simple, light-coloured modern design that is easy to maintain and keep clean. Buy affordable kitchen units that you can replace every few years. For worktops, avoid materials that damage, stain or burn easily such as wood, as tenants are less likely to take care of them. Make sure you install a splashback for the sink and cooking area to prevent walls getting greasy and grubby.

Make sure all appliances are in full working order or replace them between tenants – leave a photocopy of the instructions and keep the originals in your filing system. Ideally, have a freestanding rather than integrated washing machine and fridge so that if anything goes wrong with either, you can slide it out easily for repairs or install a replacement.

Bathroom

For bathrooms stick to a simple white suite and provide plenty of splashbacks. Most tenants like a good shower, so if you are able to fit one easily, do. If the room has a tired but perfectly good bathroom suite for your market, don't go to the expense of changing it. Think about scrubbing it up and just replacing the tiles, taps, a shower curtain and lavatory seat to give it all a fresh feel.

Ventilation and extraction

Make sure all your rooms have adequate and efficient ventilation and extraction. This will help to prevent the build up of cooking smells and condensation and prevent damp and mould, especially in the bathroom.

Furniture

Consider wear and tear when buying the furniture for a furnished property. Choose upholstery in dark colours to minimise staining and go for heavy fabric. Leather may sound like an expensive option but it has become much cheaper in recent years and it will get better and better with wear. You might also find a good piece second-hand, though again be aware that its style may be out of fashion before the piece wears out. Heavy canvas is another option. Washable loose covers are a good idea for chairs and sofas. You can also protect pieces with a proprietary stain repellent.

Note that as landlord, you are responsible for ensuring the upholstered furniture and soft furnishings you supply, whether new or second-hand (unless antiques), comply with the latest fire-resistance standards. The regulations apply to beds, mattresses and headboards, sofas and armchairs, and loose and stretch covers for furniture. They require that soft furniture has fire-resistant fillings and that the fabric has passed appropriate match-or-cigarette-resistance tests. You can obtain further information by contacting your local Trading Standards Office or the Department of Trade and Industry (DTI).

PART- OR FULLY FURNISHED?

Don't assume that you have to provide totally furnished accommodation. If the lease is as long as six or 12 months, part-furnished is as much as the tenant is likely to want. This means a fitted kitchen, bathroom, beds, sofas and table and chairs. (Do be aware of a landlord's obligations regarding furnishings and fire regulations – see above.) Furnished and unfurnished properties generally command a similar rental price, but some areas and some properties will tend to let more easily unfurnished and vice versa. Do your research, get it right for your market and, if in doubt, consult a letting agent.

Think sturdy if you need to buy furniture.
- If buying new tables and chairs go for simple and durable, although old school or church chairs from a junk shop can look great in a country-style kitchen.

Students and professionals will want a simple style – for a contemporary look buy copies of designer pieces that you can replace once they go out of fashion. Robust and grand antique pieces will look and wear perfectly in most period properties, especially in larger family units.
- You may want to invest in one piece that sets off a room, like a large mirror. It may be worth spending the extra money on this, depending on your market.
- If you decide to let a property part-furnished, make sure you either have fitted wardrobes or provide freestanding ones.
- If buying new beds, buy at the cheaper end of the market and replace them often. Mattresses will become marked before they wear out – replace them regularly regardless of whether they are worn out.

Window dressings

You can buy very reasonable ready-made curtains or blinds – it is best to get a plain colour rather than a pattern as this appeals to all markets.

Accessories

Do not be tempted to fill a rental flat with trinkets – accessories are for your own home, not a rental flat. The tenants will want to surround themselves with their own possessions, not yours.

If the lease is as long as six or 12 months, part-furnished is as much as the tenant is likely to want

---

MAKING THE MOST OF THE PROFESSIONALS

As a first-time developer you cannot possibly expect to have all the skills needed to see the whole project through to a successful conclusion, so it's important to know when to call in the professionals. Architects have an understanding of the potential of spaces and can transform a property from the ordinary to the extra special.

EMPLOYING AN ARCHITECT

Architects have trained for seven years. Don't under-estimate their skills. Much as you wouldn't try to mend a broken leg yourself but would go to a doctor, if you have a reasonably sized building job, unless you and your builder are extremely confident, you will need to get an architect on board.

You should certainly employ an architect if you intend to carry out any major architectural or structural changes to your property. They will tell you whether what you are proposing is possible and how to achieve it, and will advise on the best approach for your particular property and your purse strings. They will also advise on how to achieve more light, space or rooms in your property, all of which can add value. A good architect's recommendations and results can be wonderful, but their skills of course come at a cost.

Even if you don't employ an architect, if you are making structural changes you will need to enlist the services of a structural surveyor. For insurance reasons, a structural surveyor will generally need to be employed directly by you, although they will also work closely with your architect, project manager and builder.

Before starting out, sit down and have a think – be objective and make sure that the proposed architectural/structural changes will increase the market value of your property by an amount that covers both the cost of the work and provides you with an additional profit for your efforts. If it does, go ahead and apply for any necessary planning permission.

FINDING AN ARCHITECT

- As with builders and other contractors, it is always good to have a personal recommendation. Ask friends and professional contacts whether they know of anyone who has recently used an architect whose residential work they were particularly happy with.
- Seek advice from the RIBA (Royal Institute of British Architects). The organisation offers a telephone and Internet service that helps match an RIBA-registered architect to the job you propose. To help clients who are embarking on a building project for the first time, the RIBA publishes a standard form of agreement entitled 'Small works (SW99)', designed for use on projects where the cost of the building work is not expected to exceed £100,000.
- Alternatively, ask at your local planning department if they know of any architects they could recommend.
- Next, make a call to several architects and arrange some meetings. You want to get an idea of costs and see whether you can communicate clearly, and exchange ideas on a level you are happy with. You will also want to check their availability upfront, so that you don't commit to them only to discover you incur delays while they finish another project.

ARCHITECTS' FEES

Architects' rates vary as much as for any other professionals. If you want to hire one just to draw up plans for planning permission, their charges will start at around £55 per hour for this service. An architect who works with you on the project from concept to completion is likely to charge anything from 10% upwards of the total cost of your renovation works and will carry out a similar role to that of a project manager.

A new edition of The RIBA's Client's Guide to Engaging an Architect was published in May 2004. The introduction to this makes clear that there are no 'standard' or 'recommended' fee scales and that the fee is dependent on the specific requirements of the project and the client.

The guide starts with an explanation of the need for a written form of appointment between you and your architect, preferably a Standard Form of Agreement (SFA). It explains the main purpose and content of the appointment document including defining the extent and type of services to be provided, copyright, fees, dispute resolution, determination of the agreement and what is required of both client and architect.

The section on fees sets out a range of options for fee calculation including percentage of construction cost, lump sums, time charges and the new 'value-added' concept of fees. It also highlights the fact that fees are a matter of calculation and negotiation based on the services to be provided by the architect, the procurement method, the programme, and the cost, type and complexity of the project.

Fees for work to existing buildings (refurbishment and extensions) are likely to be between 40% and 60% greater than the fees for new-build work. There is no guidance on hourly rates since the wide variation in hourly rates between different sizes, types and locations of architectural practices and between different sizes, types and locations of project make this unrealistic.

PLANNING CHECKLIST

1 Assess the extent of repairs, work and decoration required to make the house right for your market, taking note of all the things mentioned in the building survey.

2 Make sure you comply with Building Regulations and that you get any necessary planning permissions. Do this as early as possible because the relevant consent may take some weeks to come through.

3 See that you are on good terms with your neighbours. Alienated neighbours can be very obstructive.

4 Make sure your design will not be so expensive that it gobbles up all your potential profit.

5 Make the most of period features. Don't rip everything out without a thought as many items will be an added attraction for potential buyers.

6 Tailor the property to your market and if you are buying to let, remember that this market has particular requirements of its own.

7 Find a reputable architect and/or builder. Discuss the project with them before you appoint them and choose the one you think will understand what you want; don't necessarily go for the cheapest.

GLOSSARY OF TERMS USED FOR GAS, ELECTRICITY AND WATER SERVICES

Ampere (amp): the rate of flow of electricity through electric wires.

Circuit breaker: a safety device which opens (breaks) an electric circuit automatically when it becomes overloaded.

Direct cylinder: hot water cylinder where the water is heated by an immersion heater.

Electrical cables: cables for carrying electricity which come in various sizes depending on the load required.

Expansion pipe: this rises vertically from the water cylinder and allows pressure in hot water systems to discharge safely if the system overheats.

Fuse: the weakest link in the electric circuit. Its purpose is to cut off the supply should a fault occur.

Fuse box (or consumer unit): a box housing fuses or circuit breakers for the electric installation in a building.

Indirect cylinder: water is heated by the boiler and passed through a coil within this cylinder. This hot coil then heats the water in the cylinder. The hot water then comes out of the taps.

Junction box: a box containing a junction of electric cables.

Meter: instrument for recording the amount of gas, electricity or water supplied to a home.

Ofgem (Office of Gas and Electricity Markets): the regulator for British gas and electricity industries, operating with the gas and electricity markets authority.

Ring main: an electrical supply serving a series of power points and returning to the original source so that each power point has an alternative path in the event of a failure.

Stopcock: main valve where the mains water supply can be cut off in the event of major plumbing problems.

Storage tank: the main cold water storage tank, generally supplying bath, basin and loo.

Volt: unit of electrical potential.

Watt: unit of electrical power, the rate at which electricity is produced or used.

GLOSSARY OF ARCHITECTURAL AND BUILDING TERMS

Architrave: a decorated wooden strip that runs around a door, window or panel.

Baluster: the upright in a staircase or balustrade that supports the horizontal top rail.

Bargeboard: a timber piece fitted to the outer edge of a gable, sometimes carved for decorative effect.

Bay window: a projection within a wall to form a window.

Bow window: a window projecting in a curve without increasing the floor area.

Casement window: a window opening on side or top hinges.

Column: a structural or decorative vertical element, usually circular, supporting or framing the upper parts of a building.

Corian: very tough, man-made material used for worktops.

Cornice: decorative moulding strip usually made of wood or plaster that runs round the wall of a room, just below the ceiling.

Curtilage: the area within the boundaries of a property surrounding the main building.

Dado rail: a wooden rail fixed horizontally onto the wall, usually about 1m (3ft) above the floor. The area below is usually panelled or given a different paint treatment to the area above.

Damp-proof course (DPC): a layer of impervious material laid in a wall to stop damp.

Dormer windows: vertical windows that project from a sloping roof. They can provide the necessary height to turn an attic into a habitable room.

Eaves: the lower, overhanging section of a pitched roof.

Engineering brick: an extremely hard brick used mainly in engineering structures such as bridges or piers to support beams.

Fanlight: a window over a door, often semi-circular with radiating glazing bars.

Footing: a foundation.

Foundation: concrete base upon which the walls and structure is built.

French window: fully glazed, hinged door.

Gable: the triangular part of a wall under the inverted 'V' of the roof line.

Glazing: fitting glass into windows or doors.

Gutter: a channel running along the eaves for conveying away rain water.

Habitable room: any room intended to be used for sleeping or living purposes.

Hipped roof: a roof sloping at the ends as well as the sides.

Inspection chamber: manhole for the inspection and maintenance of foul drains.

Joists: beams supporting a floor or roof.

Laminate: the layering of material pressed and glued together to create a tough surface material or beams. Used for kitchen work surfaces, for example.

Leaded light: a windowpane subdivided into small squares or diamonds by lead strips (known as cames).

Linoleum (lino): form of flooring made of cork and linseed oil, similar to vinyl but warmer to the touch.

Lintel: a structural beam above an opening such as a window or door.

Listed building: a building officially recognised as being of particular historic or architectural interest. Permission is required for alterations or repairs.

Load-bearing walls: walls that are necessary for holding up the building.

Mansard roof: a roof set back from the building frontage, usually behind a parapet and rising in two pitches to form an increased attic space.

Mezzanine floor: an extra floor between two floors. Sometimes used in just a portion of a room to create a balcony.

Mouldings: decorative plaster or woodwork detailing (on cornices, arches, ceilings and so on).

Partition wall: a wall erected to separate two areas of a home, but which is not part of the structure of the building.

Mullion: a vertical piece of stone or timber dividing a window into sections.

Pantile: a clay roofing tile with an 'S'-shaped profile.

Party wall: the dividing wall between properties.

Patio door: sliding glass door, usually in a metal or UPVC frame and double-glazed, leading onto a patio or garden.

Plan: a drawing as seen from above.

Plinth: the widened base of a column or wall.

Pointing: treatment of joints in masonry by filling with mortar to protect against the weather.

Polystyrene: man-made insulating material in the form of boards.

Polyurethane: plastic resin used in paints and varnishes; in extruded and foamed form it is used as an insulating board.

Rafter: one of a series of structural roof members spanning from an exterior wall to a centre ridge beam.

Reveal: the area of masonry or frame visible between the outer face of a wall and a door or window which is set back from it.

Roughcast: a type of render for plaster or concrete with a rough surface finish.

RSJ: Rolled steel joist or beam supporting a floor or roof.

Sash window: a window that slides vertically on a system of cords and balanced weights.

Seal: a barrier.

Semi-detached (Semi-D): a house joined to another house on only one side.

Skirting: a wooden strip running along the bottom of a wall, where it meets the floor.

Soffit: the underside of eaves or other projection.

Softwood: wood from a cone-bearing tree, such as pine.

Splashback: a surface fitted behind sanitaryware to protect the wall against splashing.

Stack: the part of the chimney visible above the roof.

Stock brick: a traditional clay brick used in house construction. May be yellow or red.

Stucco: plaster used for coating exterior walls.

Suspended ceilings: false ceilings that can lower the height of a room and conceal light fittings/wiring.

Tanking: a method of lining a room below ground level with a non-porous skin to prevent damp.

Terraced house: one of several houses joined together in a row.

Tongue-and-groove (T&G): wooden boarding, which fits together to make an economical form of panelling. Often used below dado level in a room.

Transom: a horizontal framing bar in a window.

Weatherboarding: overlapping timber boards used to clad the outside of a building.

Trim: see architrave.

UPVC: plastic material sometimes used instead of wood for window and patio door frames.

Vinyl: tough but flexible plastic material used to provide practical and waterproof floor coverings and tiles, particularly for kitchens and bathrooms.

6
ON
THE JOB

6 ON THE JOB

The attractive part of a development project may be the planning, but its management is just as crucial to success, if not more so. Managing the restoration or conversion of any building is an extraordinarily complex business and it is vital to set up a workmanlike environment from which the whole project can be directed with efficiency and precision. To be a good manager you need to be disciplined and orderly, good with figures, good with people, good at juggling priorities, dates and order of work, and at keeping an eye on the budget. If you do not feel up to all of this, employing an efficient manager will save money in the long run. It is still important, however, that you keep in touch with what's going on from day to day.

MANAGING YOUR DEVELOPMENT

Making sure your development runs smoothly, on time and to budget requires many different skills and also a sound knowledge of what's involved in the whole process of working on site. It is unwise to take on this task yourself if you also have a full-time job.

The success of a development is partly dependent on a smooth running site. Whether you choose to develop one property at a time, or several concurrently, you will need to do some careful planning to ensure that your site(s) stay on schedule. The first decision you should make is whether to oversee the development yourself or to employ an experienced project manager. On a larger site you really need a site manager who is on hand every day. On a job where you are subcontracting work to a number of different tradesmen such as joiners, plumbers, electricians and decorators, it can be difficult to co-ordinate their activities and ensure that the work progresses smoothly. Depending on the time you are able to devote to the project and your experience, paying someone to do either or both jobs for you is a sensible idea and will help avoid the whole project grinding to a halt.

THE BUILDING CONTRACT

If you are paying someone else to run a job for you it is wise to have a contract (for example in line with the JCT Agreement for Minor Building Works 1998 Edition) drawn up for the whole project. One possibility is to download a free, ready-made contract at the Federation of Master Builders website (www.fmb.org.uk). The following are the kinds of things that should be covered by the contract:
- Detailed schedule of the works to be carried out.
- Contract clauses: these should provide an outline of the responsibilities of the firm tendering. It is often easiest to have an 'all materials included with the

exception of' list to avoid the chance of any potential misunderstandings about the work.
- Insurances: to be the responsibility of the main contractor from hand-over to completion. The contractor must indemnify the employer against damage to neighbouring property, damage or injury caused to workmen, other persons or things or any claim under common law arising from the works; the contractor must submit evidence of insurances before starting work.
- General quality of work: the works must be carried out by appropriately skilled labour and executed in accordance with accepted good practice of the building industry and to the satisfaction of the contract administrator. Sub-standard work to be re-done at the contractor's expense. Handling, fixing or application of all proprietary materials to be in accordance with manufacturers' instructions.
- Protection: the contractor to provide for storage of on-site materials and their adequate protection and security. New and existing structures and finishes to be adequately protected during the course of the contract.
- Waste and nuisance.
- The contractor will remove rubbish and waste material regularly from the site and keep the works clean and tidy, and will manage the parking of works vehicles and offloading of materials so that this does not cause obstruction to road-users.
- Tools, scaffolding, and strutting: the contractor will provide all necessary tools and provide and erect any

necessary scaffolding and other supports necessary to preserve the stability of existing structures.
- Facilities/temporary work/services.
- Agreements as to the provision of water, electricity and other temporary facilities while the work is in progress.
- Building control: contractor to be responsible for gaining a completion certificate for Building Regulations stating that works carried out complied with current Building Regulations and have been signed off by the Building Regulations Officer.

- Party Wall Agreements: to be responsible for complying with Party Wall Agreements and planning permissions.
- Sub-contractors: the contractor to enter into agreements with his sub-contractors which embody the same conditions for which he himself is responsible and provide any facilities necessary for them and to agree all working details and dimensions with them.
- Variations: not to be carried out without the written consent of the contract administrator and prices of any variations are to be agreed before proceeding.

WHAT'S INVOLVED IN SITE OR PROJECT MANAGING?

Project managing is one of the most important roles on-site. The responsibilities of a project manager include:

1 Running the site from the beginning to the end of the project.
2 Ensuring that the site complies with legal requirements.
3 Ensuring the site is safe.
4 Hiring all the sub-contractors and tradesmen needed for the job.
5 Scheduling their works in sequential order and making sure the work is carried out within the budget and time-scale agreed with the owner of the property.
6 Paying the sub-contractors' wages and complying with current sub-contractor tax regulations.
7 Ordering all the materials required.
8 Arranging for the right supplies to arrive at the right time.
9 Making big decisions, but also clearing up the site and ensuring tea, coffee and loos are available.
10 Usually being on-site approximately six days a week for at least several hours, arriving around 7.00am. The project manager is inevitably the person putting in the extra labour if things run behind schedule.

A project manager needs to understand their role as well as have a lot of time, energy and the right contacts. They also need the personality to run the site like a military operation, as well as developing a good working relationship with everyone involved with the project. A happy team means you are more likely to get good results and swift work, all of which will get you nearer your profit faster.

If you are contemplating being your own project manager, look at yourself realistically and ask whether you have all the necessary skills, as well as the time and money.

CAN YOU AFFORD TO SPEND ADEQUATE TIME ON-SITE?

If you are committed to another full-time job, then the answer is most probably 'no'. If your working hours are flexible then you must think of project managing one site as a full-time job, no less. In my experience, you will not be able to work elsewhere for a large chunk of the day and simultaneously fit in working on-site, overseeing labour and ordering materials into 24 hours. Rule number one is to be realistic about what you can take on.

CAN YOU AFFORD TO GIVE UP THE DAY JOB?

It is essential you are realistic about how much profit you need to make a year to provide yourself with an income before you think about developing full-time and giving up the day job. You may like the idea of being your own boss, but it is not an easy option. The workload associated with this role means that project managers usually command a payment of at least 10 if not 20% of the value of the project. To save this money, many first-time developers try to oversee the project themselves. But this is the case only if things run smoothly on-site. Inexperience can result in hiccups, a lack of planning early on or even partway

through a development can cause overruns in budget and schedule, all of which can have costly consequences. Rule number two is to take a long look at your salary. If you are earning enough to pay a project manager, then question why you shouldn't.

If the building work you plan to have done is relatively minor (lasting just a few days) you should at least draw up a very basic contract between you and the builder. The following page illustrates the type of contract you can put together.

EXAMPLE OF A BASIC BUILDING CONTRACT FOR MINOR BUILDING WORK

Name of builder ....

Address ....
....
....

Name of client ....

Address ....
....
....

Description of the work ....
....
....
....
....
....

The work will take approximately .... to complete

Quotation ....

VAT ....

The price ....

Signature (builder) ....

Signature (client) ....

Date ....

DEFINITIONS OF TERMS AND EXPLANATION OF SOME OF THE CONDITIONS FOUND IN BUILDING CONTRACTS

Consents: Unless otherwise agreed, it is the responsibility of the client to sort out any planning permissions and Building Regulations clearance. If the builder suffers any loss as a result of these consents not being obtained, a claim for damages may be made against the client.

CDM: The Construction (Design and Management) Regulations 1994.

Changing the work: If a client wants to alter the work as specified in the original contract this will need to be put down in writing and signed by the client and the builder.

Clearing the site: Before the job begins the builders have to provide a list of goods, materials and fixtures that they will remove from the site before the job can be carried out. And agree to return them when the job has finished.

Conciliation: The client and builder agree to go into conciliation in the event of any dispute arising from work covered under an insurance policy such as MasterBond.

Defects liability period: Some contracts will include a guarantee period (of, say, six months) covering against faulty workmanship or materials.

Delays and disruption: The builders have the right to adjust the pre-agreed price if delays and disruption occur due to actions carried out by the client.

Interim payments: These may be required if the contract period for the work is longer than 28 days.

Leaving the site: At the end of the job the builders agree to clear away any surplus materials, rubbish and tools.

Materials and goods: The builders agree to use new, good-quality materials on the job but do not accept responsibility for the quality of any goods and materials provided by the client.

Services: Unless they are not available, the client must agree to provide basic amenities for the builders including washing facilities, water, electricity and storage space.

Sub-contracting: Will state whether or not this is allowed on the job. It usually is, but the builder will state liability for all work carried out by the sub-contractors.

The Work: The work carried out by the builder. Sometimes this will contain a design element and, if so, this will be stated in the contract.

Termination of contract (by builder): This clause will cover the conditions under which the builder has the right to terminate the contract before the agreed end date of the work. It includes the client hindering the builders' work or obstructing the site, the client failing to make the interim payment and the client becoming bankrupt.

Termination of contract (by client): This clause will cover the conditions under which the client can terminate the contract. It includes the builders failing to work steadily, failing to work at all for a consecutive number of days and the builders becoming bankrupt.

Transferring insurance money: The client must transfer any insurance money or local authority grant to the builder and this will go towards working out the price of the job.

Withholding payment: The terms under which the client can refuse to pay after the due date has passed. Will usually state that the reasons for withholding payment have to be put down in writing.

WINCHMORE HILL: MANAGING THE BUILDER

Sharon Lennon and Mark Standing are designers of shop and bar interiors. They both gave up their jobs to become first-time developers, hoping for a better quality of life. They wanted to be in charge of their own time, spend less time travelling and have a less stressful pace of life. They both gave up work before they found their first property and it was some time before they managed to buy.

They took out a large business loan to pay for creating a fantastic modern family home from a tired Edwardian house, hoping that their eye for detailed design would help them make money from developing the property. They wanted to have it modernised and back on the market within three months. The house needed complete redecoration, a new central heating system, a new bathroom and shower room and they wanted to build a large extension on the back to make the kitchen bigger, and to sort out the back garden.

PROJECT COSTS	
COST OF PROPERTY	£375,000
BUDGET	£40,600
TARGET RESALE	£500,000

If they managed to stick to these figures it would earn them £85,000; they would then need to take off all their professional and legal fees and tax. Other houses in the area were fetching £485,000 but they were confident it would be 'the best house in the street by quite a large margin … people are used to seeing good design in bars and hotels so we are going to deliver as much as we can of their design dream.'

THE PLAN

The property was a large, five-bedroom house over two floors. Downstairs there were two big reception rooms and at the back a mishmash of small outdated rooms, a tiny basic kitchen, pantry, dining area, an outside loo and an outside shower. Upstairs at the back of the house there were two small bedrooms together with a bathroom and separate loo. At the front there were three more bedrooms, two good sized and one small double. There was no doubt that the layout needed improvement.

Mark and Sharon wanted to move the bathroom from the back to the front of the house. They tried to squeeze another bathroom into their plan but in the end decided it was best to have 'just one glamourous sexy bathroom'. At the back of the house they wanted to knock the corridor, the old bathroom, the loo and the back bedroom together to make one good-sized but slightly awkwardly shaped bedroom. The smallest bedroom was to be fitted out as a study.

This is how they broke down the budget for the work:

PROPOSED RENOVATION COSTS	
BUILDING	£10,600
PLUMBING	£7,500
DECORATION	£4,500
FLOORING	£4,500
ELECTRICITY AND LIGHTING	£5,000
TILING AND SPLASHBACKS	£1,500
DOORS AND SUNDRIES	£1,000
ROOF	£500
GARDEN	£500
KITCHEN	£5,000
TOTAL	£40,600

SARAH'S ADVICE

Mark and Sharon really had their work cut out as this was going to be a massive job. The house had not been touched in 35 years and needed total modernisation.

Mark and Sharon wanted to arrange the smallest bedroom as a study, but it is best to show that a small bedroom can actually fit a bed in, then people can use it as a study if they wish. Because it was so small, people might have difficulty imagining it as a bedroom if it was furnished as a study. And the property really needed to be marketed as a four-bedroom rather than a three-bedroom house.

They wanted to move the only bathroom from the back of the house into one of the front bedrooms, which meant there would still only be one bathroom in this top-spec house. I felt this was a mistake – the loo and the bathroom could have been knocked together and an ensuite shower room added to the master bedroom. A five-bedroom, two-bathroom house is very likely to be worth quite a bit more money than a four-bedroom, one-bathroom house.

Mark and Sharon decided to have one big glamorous bathroom rather than two smaller ones.

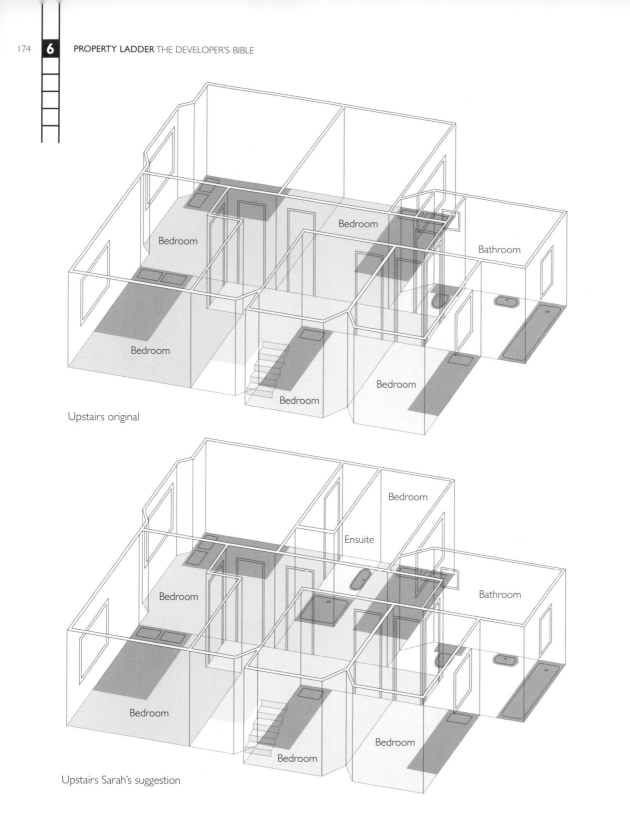

Upstairs original

Upstairs Sarah's suggestion

Mark and Sharon wanted to have four bedrooms. That only left room for one bathroom, which they wanted to move from the back to the front of the house. I thought one bathroom was not enough for five people and that the existing loo and bathroom could have been knocked together and an ensuite shower room added to the master bedroom.

The ground-floor extension would certainly add value to the house. But make sure before extending that you do your research. Talk to your local agents and find out whether your plans will make your property worth more than the works cost. Also check to see whether this will make your property the most expensive in the street. Check what the extension will be used for – turning a tiny kitchen into a kitchen diner in a big family house to improve basic amenities will add most value. Sharon and Mark's extension would not leave much money for anything else but would be a vast improvement, though £500 seemed an amazingly small amount for the garden. My advice with a family house would be not to leave the garden as an afterthought. Treat it the same as any other room in the house Young professionals want a low maintenance garden, children want somewhere to play, and everyone wants to entertain. A quick tidy-up and a bit of decking was not going to be enough.

All this work was going to come at a price. I didn't think they had budgeted enough. Considering the finish they wanted and that they were not going to do any of the work themselves, their budget of £40,600 did not seem at all realistic.

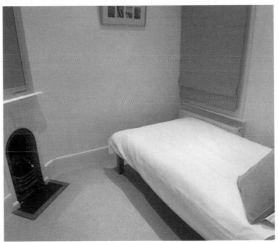

Mark and Sharon planned to turn the smallest room into a tiny study, but in the end they took my advice and presented it as a small extra bedroom.

HOW THE JOB PROGRESSED

Mark and Sharon gave themselves 12 weeks to do the renovation and get the house back on the market. They wanted to use this project as a showpiece for future developments. The pressure was on to get as much done as possible.

Although Mark took on the project managing himself he was due to go away for two weeks for his 40th birthday. One of the most important elements of this build was the kitchen extension, which would now have to take place while he was away. This meant that the crucial fitting of the huge steel beam which was to take the weight of the entire back wall was left in the hands of Ken, the builder. Mark and Sharon had also arranged that a local client for whom they were designing a bar/restaurant would oversee the work while they were away on holiday.

When the RSJ arrived for the extension Ken found that it was too deep to be hidden in the thickness of the floor void between the ceiling of the kitchen and the

> # When the RSJ arrived for the extension Ken found that it was too deep to be hidden in the thickness of the floor void

floor of the room above, so it either needed to stick up through the bedroom floor or down into the kitchen ceiling below. He was sure Mark wouldn't want it protruding down from the new kitchen ceiling so as he had to make a decision one way or the other decided to opt for a projection up through the bedroom floor. His guess was wrong, though, and when Mark got back from holiday and found the beam projecting above the bedroom floor he was not at all happy and there was a furious row. Ken agreed to drop the steelwork down

The original poky little kitchen space was moved out into the extension and then totally transformed into an efficient, spacious and well-fitted kitchen.

ON THE JOB177

into the kitchen for no extra cost and put the communication breakdown down to experience.

Nine weeks into the project the work was on schedule but not on budget. The tiler failed to turn up so a new one had to be found who charged an extra £400, but at least the floor was ready for the new kitchen to be fitted. Mark and Sharon were doing the right thing in trying to save as much as possible on items such as some of the floors and the lighting. With no option they began to cut down on the things that would have made the project ultra-luxurious.

But they had to be careful not to lower the value by compromising the quality of the final finish. They were relying on the kitchen to sell the property. It was unfortunate that Mark was away for two weeks during a crucial part of the work. It wasn't easy to get hold of him by phone, so important decisions that should have been his had to be taken by the builder. In the long run this held up the work, caused bad feeling and was detrimental to the smooth running of the job.

THE OUTCOME

By the 15th week the project was pretty close to completion. Mark and Sharon now had a stylish four-bedroom contemporary home. Their eye for design did make the house look great and the luxury bathroom was superb, although I still felt that the house would have been even better with an ensuite as well. They took my advice on the study and made it into a small bedroom.

The downstairs area of small, outdated rooms was extended to create a state-of-the-art kitchen/dining room.

SUMMARY OF ACTUAL RENOVATION		
	ORIGINAL BUDGET	FINAL SUMS
BUILDING WORKS	£10,600	£14,550
DECORATION	£4,500	£5,500
TILING	£1,500	£1,900
ROOF AND SUNDRIES	£1,500	£1,800
KITCHEN	£5,000	£6,800
GARDEN	£500	£4,000
ELECTRICS	£5,000	£4,800
PLUMBING	£7,500	£6,300
FLOORING	£4,500	£3,700
INTEREST ON LOAN	£0	£6,000
LEGAL FEES AND STAMP DUTY	£0	£21,000
TOTAL	£40,600	£76,350

LESSONS LEARNED

1 *If you're going away, leave someone in charge who will regularly visit the site.* As project manager of a development, being away while crucial work is being done means that adequate contingencies have to be put in place to ensure that all work is done to your satisfaction. When crucial decisions have to be made it is best for them not to be left in the hands of the builders alone.

2 *Keep on good terms with the builders.* In spite of Mark's row with Ken over the steel beam, Ken did lower the beam without charging any money for the sake of goodwill. Although it took an extra three days it was not nearly as expensive a mistake as it might have been. When the first tiler failed to finish, it cost an extra £400 for the second tiler to do the work.

3 *Make sure you sell the house at its full potential.* Mark and Sharon wanted to set up the smallest bedroom as a study, but fortunately changed their minds and let viewers see it as a bedroom which they could turn into a study if they wished. They needed four bedrooms for this big family house and it would help them to appeal to their market.

DOING YOUR OWN SITE/PROJECT MANAGEMENT

Are you disciplined, efficient, good at figures, unflappable and used to dealing with personnel? Then you may make a good site/project manager. You will also need to have plenty of time, be able to show up during the day to receive deliveries and talk to the workmen. The following are all things you need to think about.

There is a lot to be said for handing over the stresses of the day-to-day running of a project to an experienced manager. However, if you feel you are up to the challenge and are committed to doing it yourself, here are some tips to help you get off to a good start.

- Get your site organised as soon as contracts are exchanged. Source your materials now and find the right contractors and tradesmen for the job as soon as possible.
- Have back-up tradesmen and builders on standby. Ask friends or fellow-developers for recommendations. Keep a database of contact details just for your development projects and start to build up good contacts. You never know when you will need them.
- Using your schedule of works, draw up a chart of what works need to happen on-site and when. This will allow you to order materials at the right time. Too much

arriving too early will result in a cluttered site. Not only will you have a security risk, but you will also find that you have to constantly shift heavy items from room to room so tradesmen can do their work. Doing this also increases the risk of the goods being damaged. Too much too late means that jobs come to a standstill and your schedule slides. If you are sourcing materials from overseas check that the shipping time fits with your schedule. Consider using self-storage.

- Be crystal clear with all tradesmen. Always work out exactly what you want done before you request a quote for a job, however small. Prepare two copies of the details, including detailed drawings – give one to the sub-contractor, keep one for yourself and file the originals. Many problems with craftsmen are due to vague or incomplete initial instructions – nobody can read minds, so if it matters to you exactly how things are done, draw a plan and write down instructions.
- Control your sub-contractor's costs. Always negotiate fees upfront and stick to a written agreement, unless unforeseen circumstances arise and you change the work that needs to be done or how it should be carried out – in which case be fair and agree on an extra payment.
- Keep on top of all the work that happens on-site so that you can be sure you are happy with the quality of the work. Always pay contractors on time but make sure you are happy with the results of their labour before doing so.

> Be crystal clear with all tradesmen. Always work out exactly what you want done before you request a quote for a job, however small

- Be organised with your paperwork, especially if there is a lot of it, and keep a constant eye on your budget.
- Be realistic about your capabilities. If you are new to developing, don't try to dabble in complicated building processes or difficult features. Avoid a renovation project that you think might be too big for you to handle.

MANAGING MORE THAN ONE PROJECT

If you have built up some experience developing property and several suitable ventures become available, you may decide that you're able to develop more than one property at once. While doing so may spread your financial risk it will also increase the chances of things going wrong. Here are some tips for keeping things running smoothly when you can't be in several places at once.

- Think carefully before you take on multiple projects. Get some financial advice and make sure that you don't overstretch yourself. Think about what will happen if both sites do not sell/rent. Cash-flow is key.
- Make sure you employ a very capable site manager on each site to keep things running smoothly and to ensure that the site is kept tidy.
- Keep on top of your paperwork and your budgets. If you don't know what you have spent on which site, you don't know whether it will make a profit.
- Avoid robbing Peter to pay Paul. If one site is running over budget, don't be tempted to steal funds from another to make up the difference.
- There are a number of positive implications with several sites simultaneously. Consider bulk buying, for example. You can negotiate better discounts if you buy a large quantity of materials at the same time, so get organised.
- Keep a cool head. If you come across a problem, stop and think logically before you act upon it, even when time is key. It is always costly to go back on a decision. Sometimes a brief pause to think can save you thousands of pounds.

GETTING ON WITH THE JOB

This is where all your skills in organising and scheduling will have to come into play. The order of works is complex and seldom runs smoothly. Having a detailed schedule of work will help to keep the work on target and if a particular job gets held up, there should be something else that the builders can be getting on with.

SCHEDULE OF WORKS

Before any work begins, draw up a schedule of works and a budget. It is essential that you get organised at the very beginning of the project so that you don't lose momentum along the way. Decide what needs to be done and find out exactly how much materials and labour will cost. Be strict with yourself and make changes only in areas that will make your property more marketable. Don't be tempted to take on work that will burden your budget unnecessarily.

Plan out everything on a big wall chart. In addition, make lists of the work to be done and details for each job, including when you have employed contractors and when you expect deliveries to arrive. Make sure that things happen at the right time; doing so means that you won't book in the plasterer before the electrician is finished or the kitchen fitter before the units arrive, for example. Remember every extra day you add to the schedule puts a strain on your budget.

HEALTH AND SAFETY ON SITE

There are strict Health and Safety regulations that must be complied with under the Health and Safety at Work Act of 1974 which applies to any place where a work activity is undertaken. The regulations are numerous but there are many that will apply to your particular site, for instance the Construction, Design and Management Regulation 1994 and the Construction, Health, Safety and Welfare Regulation of 1996 amongst others. I would suggest that you either ring the Information Line on 08701 545500 to ask for advice or visit their website on www.hse.gov.uk where you can find free leaflets that can be printed out on the health and safety requirements for all sorts of areas of construction and employment, from required facilities on site (such as clean toilets and drinking water) to when and where hard hats are required.

ORDER OF WORK

This list of work to be done will help you plan how to tackle your own particular project. You can tailor it to suit your own needs.

Preparation

- Clear furniture, carpets, etc.
- Protect other areas from dust and debris.

Demolition

- Make sure floors, partitions and walls are correctly supported where load-bearing sections are to be altered or removed.
- Demolish unwanted structure; strip redundant and disconnected plumbing, electrics, fittings and finishes and remove rubbish.

Special treatments

Each of the following jobs can be undertaken by specialist contractors who will be able to provide guarantees against work carried out that can then be passed onto your buyer.

- Hack off plasterwork to a metre high in the areas requiring remedial work for rising damp.
- Install damp proof course.
- Lift floorboards and carry out timber treatment if necessary (to stop OR prevent woodworm and beetle attack).
- Expose any dry rot and cut back all timber past the affected area by recommended amounts before the area is sprayed.
- Sweep chimneys and flues and reline if required.

Basic construction

- Lay the groundwork for drains, foundations and incoming services.

Adding services

- Water, gas, electricity and telephone supplies to be arranged.

Building

- Build new brickwork of any extension (incorporating new damp-proof course) with lintels, door and window frames and make provision for external meters, extractors, waste pipes, etc.

- Raking out and repointing brickwork (including chimneys), or hacking off and re-rendering external walls.
- Pour ground floor slab ensuring correct damp-proof membrane and insulation is used.
- Fill in after groundwork around building.
- Erect any new internal walls, incorporating suitable insulation.
- Replace timberwork as required.
- Carry out any required replastering.
- Joinery as required.

Water/plumbing

- Mains supply to be fitted to the property.
- Run pipework for hot and cold supply to kitchen, bathrooms, outside tap as required.
- Run pipework to all radiator points.
- Install hot and cold water storage tanks if required.
- Install and connect boiler (if gas, must be done by a CORGI-registered plumber).
- Carcass out bathroom and kitchen in preparation for installation of fixtures.
- Run waste from bathrooms and kitchen.
- Install bathroom fittings and connect.
- Second fix kitchen once it is fitted.

Gas/electricity/telephone

- Run all pipework required for gas fires, boiler, oven and hob as required.

- First fix all wiring (run all cables without connecting up to supply).
- Second fix wiring (fit all light fittings, switches and sockets, test circuits and finally connect to the supply).
- Fit new consumer unit if required.
- Fit alarm (if suitable).

Floors and roofing

- Re-roof or build new roof structure where required, install insulation.
- Fit soil pipes, vent pipes, rainwater pipes and gutters.

Finishing: first finishes

- Decoration, tiling, door and window furniture to be fitted, skirting, architrave to be fitted, cornicing where required, floor tiling or finishes to be laid.

Fitting out

- Installation of kitchen and bathroom units, wardrobes, cupboards, baths, showers, loos, radiators, cookers and other appliances.

Decoration

- Preparation: sand and fill, hang lining paper where required, prime and undercoat.
- Final finishes: finish paint colours and wall coverings.

External works

- Clear site of debris.
- Hard and soft landscaping.

SCHEDULE OF WORKS CHECKLIST

EXTERNAL RENOVATIONS

	PROBLEM	SOLUTION	COST
Roof repairs			
Chimney removal, repair, alteration			
Painting			
Windows			
Guttering			
Repointing or rendering			
Extensions or building works			
Demolition			
Skip hire			
Other			

GARDEN

Hard landscaping (new fencing, patio, decking or paving)			
Soft landscaping (new lawn, shrubs, plants, trees)			
Structures (shed, garage, outbuildings)			
Other			

ENTRANCE

Front door			
Door surrounds			
Porch			
Flooring			
Paintwork			
Staircase			
Other			

TOOLS AND EQUIPMENT

Hire			
Purchase			

LABOUR COSTS INCLUDING VAT

SCHEDULE OF WORKS CHECKLIST

INTERNAL RENOVATIONS

	FLOORING (e.g. concrete, wood, carpeting)	WALLS AND CEILINGS (e.g. plastering, hacking off, replastering)	DECORATION (e.g. walls, ceiling, woodwork)	
Bedroom 1				
Bedroom 2				
Bedroom 3				
Bedroom 4				
Bathroom 1				
Bathroom 2				
Study				
Loo				
Utility room				
Kitchen				
Dining room				
Reception room 1				
Reception room 2				
Hallways and landing				
Contingency fund – 10%				
TOTAL COST				

	TILING (e.g. splashbacks, flooring, fireplace surrounds)	WINDOWS (e.g. replace, repair, install new roof lights, check locks)	ELECTRICS (e.g. run cabling, light fittings and switches, sockets, phone points)	PLUMBING (e.g. radiators, boiler, bathroom, kitchen)

INTERNAL RENOVATIONS

	JOINERY (e.g. general and detailed work: hanging doors, boxing, skirting, cupboards, shelving, etc)	BATHROOM SUITE (e.g. bath, basin, loo, shower, taps and wastes)	NEW KITCHEN (e.g. work surfaces, sinks, taps)	
Bedroom 1				
Bedroom 2				
Bedroom 3				
Bedroom 4				
Bathroom 1				
Bathroom 2				
Study				
Loo				
Utility room				
Kitchen				
Dining room				
Reception room 1				
Reception room 2				
Hallways and landing				
Contingency fund – 10%				
TOTAL COST				

	WHITE GOODS (e.g. cooker, washing machine, dishwasher, fridge freezer, microwave)	GENERAL MAJOR WORKS (e.g. demolition of internal walls, installation of new internal walls, new building work such as extensions and loft conversions, new floors laid)

WHO DOES WHAT?

Unless you are trained or very experienced it makes sense to employ an architect and a main contractor to organise and oversee any major or structural work associated with alterations and improvements. And it probably makes sense to get professionals to do the majority of the rest of the work. If you are reasonably well organised and practically minded, you should be able to do some of the minor work yourself such as stripping out and basic joinery. But it is most unwise to attempt to replace a roof or move a staircase without any experience. You may consider it too expensive to employ others but in the long run it would be better to modify your plans than to embark on major works yourself and end up unable to complete the job, or worse, hurting yourself.

I would always say if in doubt get the professionals in, but if you really want to and if you're confident enough to tackle any electrical or plumbing work, it is essential both that you are very careful and that you have it checked by a professional − all gas work needs to be carried out by a CORGI-registered plumber and new kitchens and bathrooms need to comply with local Building Regulations. A mistake in the wiring can cause a fatal accident with electrocution or a fire. The important thing is not to take on more than you know you can manage.

WHO DOES THE WORK?

If you do decide to get the work done by others, make sure you choose people who are skilled, experienced and competent in the particular job you want them to do.

1 Major building work: you will need a main contractor, bricklayer, roofing contractor or specialist loft/basement company.
2 Air conditioning, plumbing and central heating: you will need a plumber, central-heating engineer or central heating supply company.
3 Electrics/electronics: electrician, telephone engineer, security company.
4 Gas installation: CORGI-registered gas installer or plumber.
5 Woodwork: carpenter (structure), joiner (fittings and fixtures), specialist timber treater.
6 Glazing: a glazier.
7 Fittings and finishes: painter and decorator, plasterer, carpet fitter, tiler.

If the job needs skilled work, it may be wise to check that the person you employ is a member of the relevant trade association, though this is by no means a guarantee either way. This means he/she should have completed certificated training, should be working to certain codes of conduct set by the association and hopefully will give the possibility of arbitration should anything go wrong.

Before embarking on a job ask yourself some questions. Is this work necessary? Can I carry it out myself? Do I really want to do it? Would it be cheaper, in the long run, to employ a professional to do the work? Be realistic about what you are competent to do.

FINDING A BUILDER

Choosing a good builder is essential to the smooth and swift running of any development. The bottom line is that you need to build a reputable team you can rely on and trust to get the job done. The best way to source a good builder I think is to get a referral from family and friends who have recently had similar work done. Otherwise check with a trade association such as the National Federation of Builders (NFB), which can advise you on how to source a reputable, quality tradesman and work with them to get the best results. The NFB has membership criteria covering workmanship, financial status, and health and safety, and also operates a Code of Practice to try to help safeguard customers. Its members are encouraged to provide references from customers, suppliers and financial institutions. No guarantee of workmanship is given, but it is better than opening the Yellow Pages! There have been cases of bogus builders fraudulently claiming membership of official trade associations, so call the association and make sure they are bona fide members.

When you've got some builders' names, ask three to quote for the job:
■ Prepare a detailed schedule of works you want done throughout the property. Include drawings where necessary, be specific and give as much detail as possible. Give a copy to each builder and ask them to give you a quotation.
■ Encourage each builder to submit an itemised quote for the project. When you receive an itemised quote, you will be able to see where and how to reduce costs –

if necessary by deciding to do more of the project yourself. You can try haggling, but be aware that if you force the price down too far it may not be possible for the builder to make his profit. You may come unstuck at some point in the project as there is no reason why he should work on your project for nothing. The harsh reality is that most building work will cost what it will cost – the only way to reduce costs is to do less work.
If one of the three quotes is dramatically less than the others be cautious about automatically going with it – ask your architect or surveyor why they might vary so much. Check them over to see if there are major differences in what they are planning to do. Spending more money at the outset can sometimes save a lot of trouble and frustration, not to mention money in the long run. A builder who gives a very low quotation may well realise halfway through that it was an unrealistic figure, leaving him with no profit – this is where problems will start to set in and it may even end up with them leaving the job unfinished.

Whilst accepting a higher quotation does not definitely guarantee that work will be completed within a specified time, with a healthier profit margin for the contractor they are more likely to be on your job than another. In the long run a smoothly run site will save you money. Ensure that you are given a quotation not just an estimate before a builder begins work. An estimate is an approximate guide to what you can expect to pay, whereas once he has given you a quotation for the work this is the amount that a contractor is expecting to be paid for the job.

Insist that the builder provides a written quotation and signs your contract. If the works are quite major, ensure that the contract states when stage payments should be made, after specified parts of the work are completed. See pages 167–71 for information about building contracts.

PAYING THE BUILDER

On small contracts, lasting less than four or five weeks, most builders will not expect payment until after work is complete. On bigger jobs it is usual to make interim payments as work progresses: you pay agreed percentages of the total estimated cost at specified stages of the work. Some estimates will include 'provisional sums'. These are normally used for work the builder has to sub-contract and has not obtained firm estimates for. Always make sure you are consulted before a provisional sum is converted into a firm price.

FINDING A PLUMBER

In order to estimate for a plumbing installation, plumbers need to be supplied with a detailed specification indicating which fixtures are to go where. Get at least two or three estimates and try to use firms that have been recommended to you by people who have used them. Alternatively, the professional body of the UK plumbing industry is the Institute of Plumbing who can give you the names of registered plumbers in your area. All members are encouraged to adhere to the Institute's Code of Professional Standards.

FINDING A GAS FITTER

CORGI (The Confederation for the Registration of Gas Installers) is the national watchdog for gas safety in the UK and the leading authority on gas safety issues and registration schemes. It provides members of the public with details of local registered installers and investigates gas safety-related complaints from the public.

FINDING A GLAZIER

The Glass and Glazing Federation is a trade association and the leading authority on flat glass, glazing, window and home improvement plastics. Members work to a Code of Good Practice and to the Federation's technical standards. It will give advice on types of glass and names of local members in your area.

FINDING AN ELECTRICIAN

Always use a professional. All work must comply with local codes. The Institute of Electrical Engineers is the main body regulating training and codes of practice for electricians and if you use a member you will have recourse to the institute should anything go seriously wrong. The Electrical Contractors association encourages its members to provide high quality, good value and safe installation and provides education and training. Members follow a Code of Fair Trading.

INSURANCE AND BUILDING WORK

When having work carried out on your property you should first check to see if the contractor has public liability insurance. This will pay for any negligence on their part that results in damage to your property or injury to you or your colleagues. Legally they do not have to have this insurance, but it is sensible for them to have it. If a long leasehold tenant is carrying out work on a property, a landlord is likely to ask for insurance. But for a freeholder it is a personal choice. It is advisable not only for cases of poor workmanship but also for accidents, not to mention third party liability (for an extreme example, if scaffolding collapsed, causing injury).

SOURCING MATERIALS

Finding suitable materials at a reasonable price is important, but they must also come from reputable suppliers who can deliver on time. Finding materials abroad is possible though the Internet, but beware that transport costs don't add too much to the price. Check as many sources as possible since prices can vary quite a lot.

There are various ways of sourcing materials. Local suppliers are often the most convenient and can order items they don't have in stock. However, if you are looking for bargains, it may be worth searching on the Internet and comparing prices. The following are useful general sources:

BUILDERS' MERCHANTS

The traditional builders' merchant sells sanitaryware, kitchen units, brassware, decorating materials, plumbing supplies, timber, doors, roof tiles and most of the basic things that builders require, although the choice may be limited. A builders' merchant may be anything from a small local firm to part of a huge national chain and can supply almost everything the trade might require. Prices are negotiable depending on the quantity. For general building supplies, cement, timber, plasterboard and sheet products, concrete blocks, bricks, concrete and steel lintels, concrete sills, damp-proof course, roof claddings and so

on, they are convenient and often hard to beat on price because of their bulk buying power. However, there are some things they may not stock, such as a full range of decorative mouldings and good-quality wood, which is often better bought in one large load from a specialist timber merchant.

LARGE DIY RETAIL OUTLETS

Nearly every town has its out-of-town retail park with at least one huge supplier of DIY goods. Their main advantage is the hours they are open – if you run out of undercoat at 6pm on a Saturday night and were hoping to finish the decorating by Monday morning, they are a lifeline. They are not always as competitive as traditional builders' merchants in price or choice terms for basic building materials such as cement and plasterboard but they are often excellent in their choice of wall and floor tiling, budget-made hand tools, small timber mouldings, light fittings, electrical goods, bathroom suites and other items that builders' merchants may not carry in stock.

LOCAL HARDWARE SHOPS

There are many successful small high-street shops selling everything from tap washers to wood stains, small bags of cement, light bulbs and garden equipment. Prices may not always be as cheap as the big DIY chains but they are often surprisingly able to come up with items you want and may be convenient if you want, say, a set of wall plugs in a hurry.

Local hardware shops may not be as cheap as the big DIY chains but they often have the items you want

READY-MIXED CONCRETE SUPPLIERS

If you require a large quantity of concrete in one area (i.e., a new slab) you will probably want your concrete pre-mixed and delivered to site and poured into position. It is faster, the quality is consistent and it generally works out cheaper than mixing your own on-site. Ready-mixed concrete is sold by the cubic metre and the rate will vary depending on the distance from the depot and the type of mix ordered.

SAND AND AGGREGATE SUPPLIERS

Like so much in the building trade, sand and aggregates are usually cheaper in bulk. Most areas will have a quarry firm or haulage contractor who will supply in bulk.

CRUSHED STONE SUPPLIERS

A good source of hardcore for filling in foundation walls underneath a concrete floor slab. Crushed quarry stone is the main medium but you can use any suitable sized inert material, which may be quarry stone, crushed concrete, brick rubble or other materials which can be compacted to form a firm base for the concrete slab. Different areas of the country have different facilities for the supply of hardcore and you will need to investigate what is used, or is available most economically, in your own area. Crushed stone is comparatively cheap and the price depends more on the haulage distance than the actual cost of the stone.

GLASS MERCHANTS

Most double glazing in windows and outside doors requires specialised machinery and manufacture and installation. Local glass firms usually stick to small repairs and replacements or single glazing or have to 'buy in'. As from 1 April 2002 Building Regulations require that replacement windows or doors must obtain Building Regulations consent and have their installation inspected to ensure compliance with relevant regulations on conservation of fuel and power, and protection against impact.

PLUMBERS MERCHANTS

Suppliers not only of all plumbing fittings but also of a wide range of bathroom accessories from taps and shower heads to baths, basins and shower cubicles, radiators, water tanks and boilers, often at good prices.

PLANNING FOR CONTINGENCIES

With anything as complicated as a development project, there are bound to be occasions when things don't run smoothly. It is important that you think ahead and work out what these might be and also to earmark part of your budget to make sure you can cope with the extra cost any delay or reworking of a project may incur.

The sort of things that may cause problems are:
- Altering the specification or anything in the contract you have agreed with the builder.
- Delay in getting permissions such as Building Regulations approval or Party Wall Agreements. This may hold up a project for weeks.
- Delays in deliveries of materials or equipment which means work cannot go ahead as quickly as planned.
- Extra expenses incurred through having to hire equipment (such as scaffolding) or doing work (such as repairing the roof) that you had not foreseen.

CATERHAM: SELF-MANAGING AND LIVING ON SITE

Gina Reedy turned her back on a career as an employment lawyer and bought a three-bedroom house as her first development. She intended to live in the property with her husband Steve and two children Jessica and Dominic while she developed it. They sold the family home and used their capital to buy the house. She planned to project manage and do as much of the work as she could herself and gave herself four months to get the house finished and back on the market. 'It's a new business venture for the whole family, so I'm remembering all the time that it's a business and not my home,' she insisted.

Caterham is a desirable area for Gina's target market. It's easy to commute to London and only minutes from the M25. It has a villagey feel with plenty of countryside on the doorstep. Properties similar to Gina's range from £300,000 to £500,000 so she would have to make her development really stand out. It was on a good road, though, and close to a popular school. But that was no guarantee she would get the top price for her property.

PROJECT COSTS	
COST OF PROPERTY	£372,000
RENOVATION BUDGET	£18,000
TARGET RESALE	£450,000

This would be a fantastic profit if it all went according to plan. However, the house had an awkward layout and needed a complete overhaul including new windows, a new bathroom, a new kitchen, entire redecoration, new plumbing, and some new wiring, and to sort it out would be really difficult for £18,000, not to mention all the fees and costs!

THE PLAN

The house was built in 1958 and not much had changed since then. It had two big reception rooms at the front. At the rear was a large, awkwardly laid-out kitchen, a separate utility room and a small shower room. Upstairs felt much smaller. There were three average-sized bedrooms, a small family bathroom and a separate loo just outside on the landing.

Everything in the house had a 1950s feel, especially the kitchen with its floral tiles. It was a real museum piece. Gina didn't want the retro look and intended to rip out everything and put in a new kitchen. Her plan was to knock the kitchen through to the utility room to create a large kitchen/diner.

She also wanted to open out the entrance by turning the stairs, and open them to the second floor to let in more light and give a feeling of space. She planned on creating an ensuite for the master bedroom by dividing the smallest bedroom, which would leave that room barely bigger than the bed. Gina knew that four-bedroom houses sold for more money and desperately

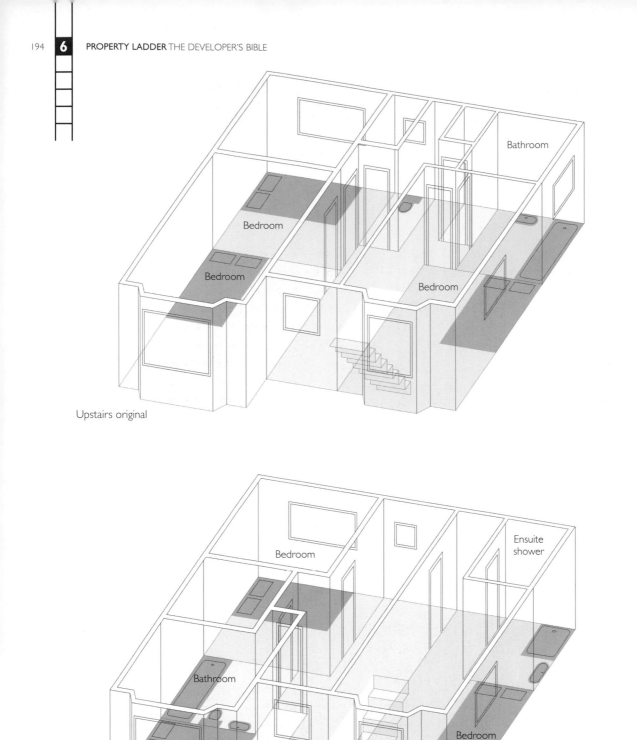

Upstairs original

Upstairs plan

Gina wanted to have four bedrooms although she knew there was not enough space. She decided to divide one bedroom to make room for a new bathroom and add an ensuite shower room to the smallest bedroom, making it even smaller.

wanted to make it four bedrooms despite not really having enough space.

This is how she broke down the budget for the work:

PROPOSED RENOVATION COSTS	
BUILDING WORK	£8,500
BATHROOMS	£2,500
DECORATION	£1,500
KITCHEN	£3,000
CONTINGENCIES	£2,500
TOTAL	£18,000

But the jobs kept changing and there was a phenomenal amount of work to be done.

SARAH'S ADVICE

People often think that living in your development will be easy but it is actually really tough living on site; the work takes longer and keeping the house habitable can cost more in the long run.

I thought creating a kitchen/diner was a great idea which could have been even further improved. Her plan kept the work space where it was and put the table and chairs in the old utility room. This would be cramped and would look onto the garage. If she'd swapped them round she'd have had more space for the table which, if French doors were added, would then overlook the garden. Gina would need to find a way of creating a luxury look within her budget. You can take design ideas from luxury kitchens and with enough thought create something spectacular – think about using more affordable materials which are cheaper such as slate, glass and ply. If you don't have much to spend go for simple and neutral and then splash out on accessories such as tiling or worktops. If you spend money on the detailing, even the cheapest units can look amazing.

Changing a staircase is always an expensive procedure to carry out and in this instance would take up valuable bedroom space from the upstairs floor. Gina had big ideas on a little budget and her ideas didn't stop at the

Gina altered the staircase to make the entrance lighter and more spacious. This was successful aesthetically but it was expensive and took up valuable bedroom space upstairs.

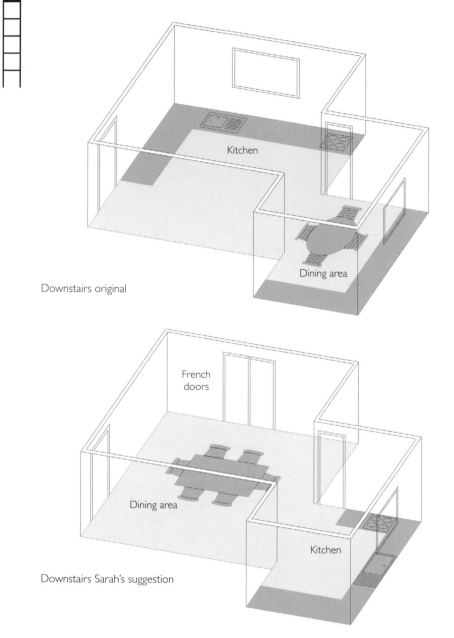

Downstairs original

French doors

Dining area

Kitchen

Downstairs Sarah's suggestion

Gina's plan kept the work space where it was and the table and chairs were squeezed into the old utility room. I thought she could have swapped them round and installed French doors so the table would look out onto the garden.

stairs. She needed four bedrooms, a bathroom and one ensuite, but her plans were awkward. Gina could have created the extra square footage by building an extension above the kitchen but she wasn't able to afford the extra cost of this.

Gina had invested a lot of money in a big development and although she was supposed to be project managing the job she seemed unclear as to what she wanted to do. Gina's basic planning was vague, jobs kept changing and her budget was totally inadequate – she hadn't allowed anything for the new staircase, re-running concealed pipework, changing radiators or doing the garden. Her budget was not based on firm research – it could equally have been £5,000 or £50,000.

HOW THE JOB PROGRESSED

Gina originally intended to do a lot of the work herself but she had no idea how much she had let herself in for. She would have to get someone else to do the stripping out, the labouring and plasterwork. Even without a schedule the builder was hard at work and the house was in chaos, covering the family's possessions with dust. The old kitchen was removed – but there was a seven-week delay before the new kitchen arrived.

Six weeks into the project Gina still didn't know what the exact layout of the house would be so the builders could not give her an exact price. Gina therefore still had no idea how much the project was going to cost. She was also unsure whether to add an ensuite or not, though if one could be fitted it would be likely to really add value.

Living in the property was really difficult for Gina and the family and she found it hard to not get personally involved in the house. Project managing had been more difficult than expected and there was a real danger that it would cost her dear. Extras such as buying radiators had not been factored in and at this rate she could have ended up spending more than the property was worth. Despite her tiny budget Gina was determined to change the stairs. A simple off-the-peg staircase is cheaper than one with twists and turns that has to be specially made. If Gina could turn the stairs without spending a fortune the house would be much improved but losing the fourth bedroom would be a consequence. Cleverly, Gina hunted around and found an affordable staircase, and it looked brilliant. She took great care in measuring correctly so that when it arrived it fitted perfectly. Spending all her £2,500 contingency money was worth it but there was nothing to spare if anything went wrong elsewhere.

As with most sites, unexpected things do crop up and unfortunately a problem was discovered with the upstairs brick walls, which were not properly supported

The original family-sized bathroom was spacious and practical. The ensuite was a good idea but made the bedroom so tiny there was barely room for the bed.

The old utility room was very small and the open-plan kitchen/dining room was definitely an improvement, but would have been even better had the table looked onto the garden.

from below and had begun to drop. Gina had to call in a structural engineer who inspected the upstairs internal brick walls. The surveyor advised either putting in a small steel beam or rebuilding the wall. The new wall cost £3,000 and the surveyor's report £253, neither of which were in the budget. Every pound Gina spent ate into her dwindling profit margin. The house was in total chaos, the plastering was taking place and there were no stairs so they were all living in two rooms downstairs. Finally Gina had enough and despite the cost moved the family into a hotel for a break.

Upstairs Gina had now decided on a completely different layout, this time for the best. Gina had accepted a fourth bedroom was not going to fit in so there were two small bedrooms and the family bathroom on one side and the master bedroom with an ensuite on the other. Despite adding £5,000 to the budget the layout was vastly improved.

THE OUTCOME

Gina had got rid of all the original floors, architraves and doors from upstairs. But downstairs the parquet, fireplaces and door furniture were still there. Keeping a period look may be cheaper than putting in new items. You can pick up more 1950s retro items from specialist shops, junk shops and car boot sales. Gina did decide to keep many of the original features and keep the rest of the house relatively neutral.

The house had really been transformed inside though not that much had been done to the large front garden. The garden is a real selling point for a family house. Don't forget that a large percentage of viewers will have made up their mind before they even get to the front door whether they want the house.

SUMMARY OF COSTS		
PURCHASE PRICE (INCLUDING STAMP DUTY AND FEES)	£387,000	£387,000
BUDGET ROSE FROM	£18,000 TO	£26,000
SELLING FEES, AROUND		£15,000

This means that Gina would have had to sell the property for £428,000 to break even – £3,000 more than the top valuation for a three-bedroom house at that time. Fortunately, she didn't actually have to sell and decided to stay put and enjoy the lovely home she had created.

LESSONS LEARNED

1 *Make up your mind and stick to it.* You need to be very clear at an early stage what you want to do. If you are indecisive you may end up spending any profit. The golden rule is to decide what you want to do and how much it will cost in time and money before you even buy a property. Unfortunately, Gina had no clear idea how long the work would take or how much she wanted done. Though she bought this property intending to make money out of it, the reality was that she paid too much for it and never really took control of the job.

2 *Think about whether you really want to live on site.* It's very hard living on site, and you have to realise it is a site. Gina had family belongings everywhere which made it difficult for work to take place, let alone for the family to live there. Pack the stuff away and label it clearly. If you have a garage or roof space to store things get it all in there before work begins. The trick is to keep out only the barest essentials.

3 *Remember your market.* I would never criticise anyone for making a home for their family but do not confuse that with developing.

FINISHING THE PROJECT

Having survived the stresses and strains of buying and developing your property the final finishing off may seem easy. However, it is important to get this cosmetic part right or you may put potential buyers off. Don't discard all the period features – many people will expect them in a traditional property.

For many, especially first-time developers, the final decorating is the most interesting and exciting part of the whole project. But remember, just as you planned the interior spaces for your target market and not for yourself, you should also be decorating for your target market. Who have you decided you are going to sell to? Be quite clear about this, but at the same time don't be too specific. Every buyer wants to put his or her own personality into their home. What you should be providing is a beautifully designed blank canvas on which they can do this.

RETAINING THE CHARACTER OF THE ORIGINAL BUILDING

Glass

Glass can enhance natural and artificial light in many ways. Glass bricks built into a wall can lighten up a dark basement surprisingly well. Glass can also be used to add decoration to your home. The Victorians loved stained glass and put it in porches, front windows, front doors and lamp shades. Designs were often influenced by Art Nouveau style. Many glass manufacturers produce decorative glass in different forms.

Stained glass panels in or surrounding front doors

During the 19th century stained glass was able to be mass produced and therefore became much cheaper; as a result it became more and more popular. Early on in the century narrow blue or red glass framing panels were popular, as were panels with etched white stars at the

corners. Later, houses in the Arts and Crafts style used subtler colours in leaded lights. Then, as the century turned and the feminine and rather romantic detailing of Art Nouveau arrived, these were often replaced with sinuous floral patterns. As laminated or toughened glass was not around at this stage, and it was generally thinner than much of the glass used today (3–4mm), there is often concern over security – to make it more secure you can back the glass with toughened burglar-proof translucent plastic.

Wood

A traditional house will often have a lot of wooden surfaces, from floorboards to fireplace surrounds and panelled walls. It is usually wise to keep as much as you can of the original wood, which will be sympathetic to the design and date of the building. Different woods have different characteristics.

Even if you have to remove some of the wood, you can replace it with wood that, even if not exactly the same will still be in keeping with the house and may even add to its attraction. For example, teak has strong chemical properties which make it resistant to decay which is why it is used for roof claddings and window frames; African woods often have perfume-like aromas; maple is a rich, golden colour; and oak has been used for centuries for anything from structural work to furniture, panelling and fine floorboards.

Wooden window shutters

Internal wooden shutters can still be found in some of the larger Victorian houses. Sometimes they fold right back against the wall, some fold back into the window reveal. There are sliding shutters that work in the same way as sash windows and run back into a cavity in the wall above or below the window. Apart from being attractive in their own right, such shutters act as another form of insulation.

Wood panelling

Wood panelling is one of the most attractive finishes for a wall and was used in traditional homes, partly to act as insulation and partly to show off the beauty of particular woods. Manufacturing developments have made this a fairly inexpensive finish – large areas can be covered in veneered plywood sheets which come with a variety of surfaces. The best quality have a real wood veneer.

Alternatively tongue-and-groove boards (also known as matchboarding) are usually made of white wood or knotty pine. They are very suitable for small Victorian homes in bedrooms and bathrooms. There is no need to panel a whole room or even a whole wall. You can panel up to dado rail height or inside an alcove or a section of a wall where a feature such as a fireplace has been removed. Tongue-and-groove panels can be painted in a variety of colours, often adding interest to very small rooms without being too fussy.

Wooden floors

Wood has been used for centuries to create attractive floors. Parquet flooring would hardly be cost-effective in most houses. Solid wooden boards are available in oak and other woods, again they may not be cost-effective for the developer. But you can sand and seal old floorboards or replace old boards with a wood block or wood strip floor, available in various woods and very easy to lay.

Plaster

Plaster and decorative mouldings have existed for almost as long as the bare walls they embellish and decorative plasterwork can be a good indication of the age and importance of a house. The Victorians turned the craft into a mass-production industry, making thousands of mouldings, which could be ordered from books.

During the 1960s many mouldings were ripped out or hidden behind partition walls and suspended ceilings, but the current popularity of classically proportioned walls means there are now plenty of choices for replacing mouldings, from traditional designs to modern ones.

Friezes, cornices and ceiling roses

The early Victorians often imitated earlier classical designs, creating elaborate cornices and friezes, some very ornate. Later in the century the designs became much simpler. Cornices and friezes were cast in moulds and a sort of papier maché was often used for ornamental cornices and ceiling roses. Plaster cornices can be cast to match specific designs and are expensive, but there are good standard designs available at a reasonable cost. Avoid resorting to coving in a Victorian house – it would not have originally been used and it looks entirely inappropriate. Keep decorative plasterwork in proportion with the house – if in doubt go to your local library to check on what the detailing in a house such as yours would have been.

Wallpapers: Anaglypta and Lincrusta

Victorian wallpaper producers developed imitation panelling and moulding in embossed papers which were sold under the trade names Lincrusta and Anaglypta. These were much cheaper than, and eventually almost completely replaced, wall plasterwork. By the end of the 1800s nearly every home had their Lincrusta paper below

STAINED GLASS PANEL IN DOOR

CEILING ROSE

CERAMIC TILES

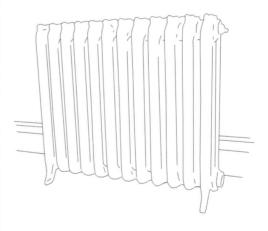

RADIATOR

the dado rail or above the picture rail. The main part of the wall was covered in machine-printed patterned paper. Similar but lighter and more pliable embossed Lincrusta and Anaglypta papers are available today to give an original look to Victorian houses.

Often new layers of wallpaper were simply pasted over old layers, so in many unrestored Victorian houses layers of original wallpaper can still be found. Reproductions of these old styles are available in many colours and ranges today so it is relatively easy to reproduce the look, especially if you have some original paper as a model.

Ceramic tiles

Ceramic tiles are durable and many have survived since Victorian times. Nineteenth-century tiles were often in strong colours. They can be found on fireplace surrounds and in bathrooms. Fireplace tiles were often in bold floral patterns, sometimes with a raised image. Bathroom tiles were often dark green with a frieze. You can get modern reproductions of Victorian tiles, inspired by the designs of the time so it is not difficult to replace any damaged areas. However, some damage can be acceptable to old tiles and adds to the period feel, whereas new tiles if not of the same quality can often detract from the overall effect.

Radiators and screens

Cast-iron radiators were a spin-off from Victorian railway station architecture. Original Victorian cast iron radiators are now difficult to find except in architectural salvage yards and they are not always the most efficient way of providing a warm atmosphere. But there are companies producing efficient and modern look-alikes of the originals.

Grilled radiator screens were introduced by the Victorians as a way of hiding the massive heating contraptions of many larger houses. You can get copies of these today in various designs, often in MDF.

The bathroom

The Victorian roll-top bath has made a dramatic comeback. If you find one in the property you buy, consider making the most of it by cleaning it up and creating a Victorian bathroom round it. Built-in bathroom suites in mahogany will create the right environment.

There are faithful reproductions of traditional baths, basins, lavatory bowls and cisterns as well as fittings such as taps and showerheads. Highly glossy ceramic tiles should complete the effect.

During the early part of the 20th century bathrooms were often panelled in tongue-and-groove boarding and painted white. Square pedestal basins work well in bathrooms built between the wars, and bold black and white colours give a good '30s feel.

Tiles

The choice of tiles is important. Dark green and cream were typical late 19th-century and early 20th-century choices of colour. Narrow border tiles were often used at dado or cornice level.

DON'T FORGET THE GARDEN

Many people embarking on property development dismiss the garden as an unimportant detail. This is a big mistake. Gardens can make or break a potential sale. A front garden is the first thing a viewer will see and if it looks drab or neglected it will immediately colour the viewer's impression of the whole property.

The garden is one of the main attractions for many people, not only retired people and young families but also young couples who see it as an extra space in which to entertain and socialise. So it is important not to fit it in as an afterthought.

GARDENS AND THE LAW
Access to Neighbouring Land Act 1992

This gives limited right of access to a neighbour's garden/land to carry out 'basic preservation works'. The Title Deeds may contain a right to do so to maintain drains, pipes and wires, particularly if yours is a house on a new estate. The right given by the act has strict rules attached to it. Written notification must be given to the next door garden owner and it is enforceable by Court Order if access is denied.

WALLS AND FENCES

- You will need planning permission if you want to build a fence or wall 1m (3ft) high where it is next to the public highway or public footpath. On the other boundaries you will need planning permission if the fence is higher than 2m (6ft) high. You should always enquire of your local planning authority before erecting a fence or wall.
- Don't be tempted to put spikes or broken glass or barbed wire on top of a wall or fence to deter trespassers. If the deterrent causes a nuisance or by your negligence, injures a passer-by, then they may be able to sue you and if it is considered to be excessive you could be open to a criminal prosecution for an injury caused.
- If you build a wall or fence without permission on your neighbour's land you have committed legal trespass. Your neighbour can then obtain a court injunction against you telling you to remove the wall and sue you for damages.

TREES AND SHRUBS

- A tree or shrub belongs to the owner of the land it grows on, even if its branches or roots go over or under adjoining land, although you are not allowed to go onto your neighbour's land or to lean over it to cut your hedge without his/her permission. Even so, if falling leaves from your tree block your neighbour's gutter which results in water damage, you could be liable for the cost of the damage.
- Branches that overhang your neighbour's land are trespassing on their air space. The neighbour can chop

If your tree roots cause damage to a neighbour's house you could be liable for the cost of repairs

the branches back to the boundary but must return the lopped branches to you. If your neighbour lops beyond the boundary, then it is a trespass. It is always best to discuss the matter with your neighbour first.

■ The local authority can make a tree preservation order to prohibit felling, topping, lopping or uprooting certain trees. You can be fined up to £20,000 for ignoring this. Always check with the local authority before getting rid of a tree. Trees in a Conservation Area have their own regulations protecting them.

■ Roots can often lead to substantial damage by growing under the foundations of a building and sucking up all the moisture in the ground. If your tree roots cause damage to a neighbour's house you could be liable for the cost of repairs, the reduction in the value of the house and any other expenses directly arising from the trespass. Willows, cypresses, oaks, elms and poplars are among the worst culprits and have the ability to affect foundations on clay subsoil up to 30m (100ft) away.

By creating a garden plan you can get your ideas on paper, which will help you focus on who you will be selling or renting to.

CREATING A GARDEN PLAN

Do not underestimate the importance of the garden or put off dealing with it until the last minute. A garden can make or break a sale and one that has obviously been neglected or used as a tip for workmen's rubble can only be a disappointment to possible purchasers. What a garden is able to provide is greenery, privacy, somewhere pleasant to sit or to entertain, a space for children to play, shade on a hot day and extra useful space – it has the potential to be one of the most seductive areas in your development.

To draw up a plan, measure the space and draw a rough sketch that includes the doors to the house and windows looking out onto the garden. Then sketch in the sort of garden that would most suit your target market. Remember that a diagonal division can make the garden seem bigger and groups of tallish shrubs or small trees (very closely planted silver birches can provide a pleasant grove and will not grow too tall) will conceal the edges of the garden and again make it seem bigger. A patio area at one end will be necessary and you can add other seating areas elsewhere in the garden to catch the sun at different times of day. Why not add a fountain or other water feature, or perhaps a barbecue and a small bed for herbs near the kitchen door?

Remember to take your potential market into account when drawing up a plan. A pond is not a good idea if you are thinking of selling or renting to families with young children. Similarly, affluent business types may not appreciate masses of lawn that will need to be cut regularly and they will often prefer the convenience of a low-maintenance surface instead.

PRESENTING YOUR PROPERTY TO POTENTIAL BUYERS

When the work is truly completed and the property ready to sell, your role still hasn't finished. Put yourself in a prospective buyer's shoes and give the whole place a thorough inspection. Outside, mow the grass; indoors, clean the place from top to bottom. The immediate impression should be of somewhere cared for and welcoming.

PRESENTING TO SELL

After months of research, planning, careful budgeting and serious amounts of hard work, you will be itching to know whether all your efforts have paid off financially. In short, you want a sale.

No matter what the property market is doing, the good news is that you have a head start over a great deal of the competition. Having just totally refurbished a property you will have taken care of the practical improvements and the design of the space. You won't have any clutter, pieces of unwanted furniture or too many nick-nacks in the space, all of which can be a real turn-off to potential buyers. Furthermore, if you have done your research, your property will be targeted directly at your particular market, their wants and their needs. In other words, your property should already be highly marketable.

You will, however, still need to make an effort! This is the final phase in the development, but it is an important one. Use my three-stage strategy to get things looking great before you book in any valuations:

- First impressions and outside appearances are crucial.
- If it doesn't move, clean it!
- Suggest the lifestyle that could be lived in the space.

OUTSIDE APPEARANCES

If you have spent months concentrating on the interior of the property, you must make sure you have not forgotten the outside. If you have a front garden, you should have planted any new shrubs and bulbs and done any landscaping a while ago so as to give the garden time to mature. The finishing touches should be to mow the lawn, sweep any pathways and keep them clear of weeds and litter. It may sound obvious, but make sure the skip will be collected in good time and that any dustbins are emptied and tidied away. Next, check any impact the adjoining properties have on your presentation. If your neighbours have left a settee outside for the council to collect or have left a pile of rubbish on view, offer to remove the offending items on your next visit to the local tip. Your aim should be to get viewers from the road to your doorway and create a great first impression of a well-maintained and tidy home.

Does the front door need painting or need new door furniture? This is now your last chance to remedy things if the entrance looks dull or if the development work has taken its toll.

Next, get all of the windows cleaned, inside and out. It makes a massive difference to be able to see out from the inside, not to mention the difference more light makes to the interior.

IF IT DOESN'T MOVE, CLEAN IT!

Your next task is to get rid of all of those months' worth of builder's dust and bring out the best in your fixtures and fittings. Try to set aside at least a whole day for cleaning unless you choose to call in a professional cleaning company.

Invest in two pairs of industrial-strength gloves, oodles of cleaning products, brand new dusters sponges, tea towels and any specialist products you may need like fluid for polishing stainless steel splashbacks. Remember to bring the vacuum, a mop, bucket and dustpan and brush from home. Now photocopy the cleaning checklist and take it with you so that you remember everything that needs doing. Forget trying to beat estate agents to viewings in order to grind fresh coffee, bake vanilla pods and fresh bread! The old clichés may be appealing, but they are also highly impractical! Your property should smell clean, when you've finished with it – all you need do now is open all the windows to let in some fresh air.

CLEANING SCHEDULE

- Start at the top of the house and clean each room from top to bottom, literally! This way you can ensure that you catch all of the dust as it works its way down the property when you disturb it.
- Remove any rubbish or leftover tools from the property, then start by cleaning the highest surfaces, such as the tops of wardrobes and light fittings.
- Wipe over any pieces of furniture, shelving, door frames and window ledges with a damp cloth to remove layers of building dust, dirt and grime before dusting.
- Clean and polish any pieces of furniture and vacuum upholstered furniture.
- Polish door handles and other fixtures such as light fittings. Wipe clean any lamp bases and light bulbs. Polish any mirrors and pictures.
- Check that there are no signs of any paint on the light switches and sockets, door or window furniture. Gently scrape off any excess paint and wipe them over with a damp cloth.
- Use a damp cloth to clean inside any cupboards, cabinets or wardrobes. Viewers always have a desire to open these and you want them to be greeted with a fresh smell and dust-free appearance.
- Check that all lights are fitted with working bulbs.

Many professionals choose to view properties after work, in fading light.

■ Make sure your bathroom suite is immaculate. Scrub and shine up your bath, basin, shower and loo, inside and out. Polish taps and mirrors.

■ Get the most out of your kitchen. Make sure the oven, hob, fridge and washing machine are all clean and sparkling. Work surfaces should be spotless, taps and door handles should shine. Wipe down cupboards inside and out – your viewers are bound to check out the storage.

■ Dust all the skirting boards and both the fronts and backs of radiators.

■ Finally, turn your attention to the floor. Vacuum all of the carpets and any rugs. If you have just had carpet fitted, make sure you suck up any bits left by the fitter. If you have recently polished or painted wooden floors, vacuum them before mopping them with a suitable cleaner. In bathrooms, vacuum tiled or vinyl floors to get rid of building dust before mopping them with floor cleaner. Don't forget the stairs. If you are not satisfied with the results in any room, do it again, as a clean floor makes a huge difference to the look, smell and feel of a room. If the floor colour is light, it needs to be ultra clean to maximise that reflective surface and bounce light around the room.

MANAGING A BUY TO LET

If you are selling your development, your hands-on role ends once you have sold the property. If you have bought to let, your on-the-job role is a long-term prospect. One option is to use a managing agent, who will take on many of the stressful aspects of letting, but check on their services and fees before deciding on one.

BECOMING A LANDLORD

To develop property, you need to adopt a myriad of roles and successfully juggle them. If you decide to buy to let, you will need to add 'landlord' to your repertoire of skills. Knowing what to charge for rent is important. Look on the Internet and in letting agents' brochures to see the rental prices commanded by similar properties.

Being a landlord no longer means that you have to find a tenant, organise the legal paperwork, deal with problems and maintain your property all on your own, unless you choose to. There are a number of routes, services and agents available to help you let out your property and manage it. Of course, they all come at a cost.

Depending on your situation, you may choose to go it alone – finding your own tenant and manage all

aspects of the property yourself – or to employ a letting agent, who will be able to provide one of the following four options:

■ Introduction service. The agent simply finds you a tenant – approximate commission is 10% of the monthly rental income.

■ Introduction and rent collection. The agent finds a tenant and administers rent collection each month – approximate commission is 12.5% of the monthly rental income.

■ Full management service. The agent finds a tenant, administers rent collection and manages the property, including any necessary repairs – approximate commission is 15% of the monthly rental income.

■ Full management service, plus rental guarantee. The

A LANDLORD'S RESPONSIBILITIES

Whether you employ a letting agent or not, there are still some responsibilities which you, as a landlord, will need to undertake by law. It is important that you know what these are and act on them.

- You will need a certificate to prove that any gas appliances and gas boilers are safe.
- You will need to ensure that there are adequate fire escapes and fire extinguishers and that you meet all fire regulations. Check with your council as different rules govern different types of property.
- All soft furnishings and upholstered furniture must comply with fire regulations and be made from non-flammable materials.
- You will need buildings insurance to cover the property. Take the opportunity to have additional clauses added, which protect the tenant against injury while staying on the premises as well as protecting the property from any malicious damage that occurs under the tenant's care.
- I would also recommend you have an electrician service any electrical appliances or plugs. Although this is not currently mandatory, changes are anticipated in the near future. Make sure you know your obligations.

agent finds a tenant, administers rent collection and manages the property, including any necessary repairs, plus guarantees a percentage of the rent – approximate commission is 17% of the monthly rental income.

FINDING A GOOD MANAGING AGENT

Essentially you should look for an agent who is active and proactive in your local area. If you are going to hand over a percentage of your hard-earned rental income to an agent you want to have full confidence in their ability to fulfil the services you require.

Visit three local agencies, with a clear idea of the role you wish them to take on and how many of the responsibilities you are happy to look after yourself. Then ask them the following questions:
- How do they market the lets in their area? Their answer will give you an indication of the company's profile and the lengths to which they will go to find tenants.
- How many potential tenants do they have on their books?
- Do they belong to any of the national letting agents' organisations? Organisations such as ARLA (Association of Residential Letting Agents) or NAEA (National Association of Estate Agents) are able to offer support and guidance should you happen to fall into dispute with one of their member agents. In addition NAEA requires those of its members involved in lettings to hold 'client money protection cover', which guarantees your money up to a certain limit, in the event of the letting agent going out of business.
- Do they have professional indemnity insurance?

Be sure to ask whether there are any 'add-ons' to the commission quoted. A '10% fee' may escalate if the agent charges a separate start-up fee, tenancy agreement fee, inventory fee and check-in fee and you may find a more competitive flat rate fee elsewhere.

PROS AND CONS OF USING A FULL MANAGEMENT SERVICE

Pros

- An agent is experienced in how best to prepare your property for rent and should know how to target the appropriate market directly.
- An agent will have a ready-made database of clients to whom they can market the property and can place adverts in specialist publications on your behalf.
- An agent will undertake all viewings.
- An agent will verify a would-be tenant's references, run a credit check and confirm their employers' details.
- An agent will provide a signed contract from the tenant.
- After your initial gas checks, some agents will ensure that both your appliances are checked at regular intervals at your own cost.
- An agent will arrange all minor repairs and redecoration of the property as and when required, again at your own cost.
- An agent will act as a mediator between the landlord and the tenant.
- An agent will collect the rent from your tenant and ensure that it is paid every month. If a tenant fails to pay, the agent will carry out procedures for eviction, rental recovery and finding a new tenant, although this can take many months.
- An agent will provide support and advice if a dispute arises with a tenant.
- If you ask an agent to manage multiple properties, you may be able to negotiate a reduced fee.
- If you place multiple lets with an agent you will receive a monthly statement with every property listed on it and a consolidated return, which makes life easier when you calculate your cash flow.
- An agent is able to provide specialist insurance policies, which provide extra protection to the landlord at an additional cost: a. Rental guarantee insurance – guarantees part or all of your rent in the event of a disappearing tenant. This usually costs about 3% of the monthly rental income.
  b. Legal costs insurance – covers a legal dispute up to £50,000 for approximately £5 a week.
  c. Emergency repair insurance – protects against large repair bills for approximately £5 a week.

Cons

- Agents cost money.
- Agents can often delay the payment of rental income to the landlord, which can be frustrating and inhibit cash flow.
- Some agents are not sufficiently set up to deal with out-of-hours emergency repairs.
- Just because you are paying for a service doesn't necessarily mean that you will be 100% happy with it.
- Agents may commit the landlord to large repair bills without prior warning or consultation.
- Agents can spring a fee for additional 'extras' on landlords such as rates for advertising. Always check what is included in your fee and never assume services are automatic.
- Some agents offer an inspections service, which is negotiable depending on how many times a year you want them to check the property for deterioration. Don't assume that regular inspections are always part of the package.

Get an impartial expert to draw up a legally binding inventory for you and your tenant

In addition, ask them for a list of their services and fees so you know exactly what you will be getting for your money. Check that the agent is able to provide you with the basics – a signed tenancy agreement, inventory, references, employer's contact details, and at least one month's deposit and one month's rent in advance from a future tenant.

Lastly, insist that the rent is paid by standing order, straight into your bank account.

If you decide to hire a letting agent you will need to organise a valuation. As with selling a property, set up three valuations with different companies. Your gross rent should be at least between 130 and 150% of your monthly loan repayments. Your net rental income should cover both your mortgage costs and your management fees and still leave you with sufficient profit to make the project viable. Remember that this profit will almost certainly be called upon to cover costs of repairs or vacant periods if the property lies unoccupied for any period of time.

SELF-MANAGING A RENTAL PROPERTY
If you manage a property yourself, don't be tempted to let it to people you know. This can complicate the tenant/landlord relationship and contribute to problems, such as late payment of rent. Try to keep on top of repairs, however costly, so that the property does not deteriorate.

If you are tempted to go it alone, I would strongly advise you do all of the following:
- Do some serious research into the rent commanded by similar properties in your area. Look at the property, press, letting agents' websites on the Internet and in local newspapers. Be realistic when deciding on a monthly figure, so that you neither price yourself out of the market nor fall short of the market value.
- Have an Assured Shorthold Tenancy Agreement drawn up (see pages 213–15). This is a legally binding document designed to protect both the landlord and the tenant. You can buy a ready-made contract or ask your solicitor to draft the agreement for you.
- Whether you are letting an unfurnished, part- or fully-furnished property, get an impartial expert to draw up a legally binding inventory for you and your tenant. This will give you, as landlord, the right to hold back part or all of a deposit if any items are damaged during the tenant's stay.
- Build up a contacts database, via personal recommendations, so that you have reliable tradesmen such as a plumber and electrician on file that you can call upon in the event of something going wrong. Don't wait for a crisis to happen.
- Insist your tenants pay you by standing order. These are easy to set up between banks and will minimise the hassle of having to chase rent.
- Keep handy a note of tenants' contact details, for example e-mail, work and mobile telephone numbers.
- Leave a list of useful contact details in the rental property so that tenants can easily contact service providers and the council without calling you first. Remember to include your own details in the list. Your phone number is essential and your tenant should be

able to reach you at all times, even when you are abroad, in case of emergency.

■ Leave instructions for operating such things as the central heating, hot water and electric shower, together with any relevant guarantees.

■ Keep at least two spare sets of keys yourself so that you can lend them out to contractors or to tenants if they mislay theirs or lock themselves out. Make sure you retain the master set as keys cut from copies are never as good as the original.

■ Make appointments to inspect the property every now and then with your tenant. Get someone to fix the little jobs that you notice when you visit, such as wobbly door handles or loose light fittings, so that these problems don't escalate. And have the boiler serviced regularly so that it is less likely to let you down. Remember that your tenant reserves the right to disallow you entry to the property unless you make prior arrangement to visit them and have a verbal confirmation from them that this is convenient.

MANAGING MORE THAN ONE BUY TO LET

Remember, the more properties you own that are let, the more hassle you will have for your money. Think carefully about whether this is really something you want to do and if you are actually motivated enough to make this type of business venture happen. If you decide to manage more than one buy-to-let property at once, you will need to be incredibly organised. When there are double or triple chances of things going wrong there are some ideas to make life easier. My biggest tip would be to adopt a uniform approach to help you be organised, for example:

■ Get all your tenants to pay their rent on the same day each month to make checking up on rents and your cash flow easier.

> If you manage more than one buy-to-let property at once, you will need to be incredibly organised

■ Try to ensure that gas checks are carried out on the same day every year for all your properties. This not only helps you keep up to date but also minimises the cost of employing a plumber (who must be CORGI registered) as you can hire one person to check all the gas appliances on one day rather than on the odd occasion here and there. In addition, getting into the habit of arranging regular checks will avoid potential problems with gas appliances.

Getting a tenancy agreement drawn up is essential to ensure that every aspect of the tenancy is clear for you and your tenants and it offers legal protection for both parties. As a landlord, you would be foolhardy not to get an agreement drawn up as without one it could cost you time and money getting a non-paying tenant out of your property. The example on the following pages illustrates the types of information included.

TENANCY AGREEMENT

(FOR A FURNISHED FLAT OR HOUSE ON AN ASSURED SHORTHOLD TENANCY)

THE PROPERTY

....

....

THE LANDLORD

....

of ....

....

THE TENANT/S

....

....

The **TERM** ....   **months beginning on** ....

The **RENT £**...................... **per week/month***

        payable in advance on the............. of each........ week/month*
                 (*Please delete as appropriate)

The **DEPOSIT £**........................

DATED this .... **day of** ....200_.

SIGNED

....
  (The LANDLORD)   **(The TENANT/S)**

THIS RENTAL AGREEMENT COMPRISES THE PARTICULARS DETAILED ABOVE, THE TERMS AND CONDITIONS ATTACHED AND THE INVENTORY SIGNED BY THE LANDLORD AND TENANT.

IMPORTANT NOTES FOR LANDLORDS

The "LANDLORD's" details on this Agreement must include an address for the Landlord in England or Wales as well as his/her name.
Written Notice to Terminate to the Tenant must be given two clear months before the end of the Term.

(THE FORM REFERRED TO ABOVE: – NOTICE TO TERMINATE IS AVAILABLE ON WWW.LETONTHENET.COM LANDLORD'S ADVICE PAGE.)

Every effort has been taken to make this Agreement as easy to use as possible. There may be situations that make this form inappropriate for use, therefore if you are in any doubt as to your legal rights under this agreement then you should seek professional advice and assistance from a Solicitor, Housing Advice Centre or the CAB. Letonthenet.com cannot be held liable in respect of any loss or damage caused or alleged to be caused directly or indirectly by what is contained or omitted from this document.

Terms and Conditions

(FOR A FURNISHED FLAT OR HOUSE ON AN ASSURED SHORTHOLD TENANCY)

1. This Agreement is intended to create an assured shorthold tenancy as defined in the Housing Act 1988 and the provisions for the recovery of possession by the Landlord in that Act apply accordingly. The Tenant understands that the Landlord will be entitled to recover possession of the Property at the end of the Term

2. The Tenant will:

   2.1   pay the Rent at the times and in the manner aforesaid without any deduction abatement or set-off whatsoever (save for any deduction abatement or set-off allowable in law)

   2.2   pay all charges in respect of any electric, gas, water and telephonic or televisual services used at or supplied to the Property and Council Tax or any similar tax that might be charged in addition to or replacement of it during the Term

   2.3   keep the items on the inventory and the interior of the Property in a good, clean state and condition, and not damage or injure the Property or the items on the Inventory

   2.4   yield up the Property and the items on the Inventory at the end of the Term in the same clean state and condition it/they was/were in at the beginning of the Term (but the Tenant will not be responsible for fair wear and tear caused during normal use of the Property and the items on the Inventory or for any damage covered by and recoverable under the insurance policy effected by the Landlord under clause 3.2)

   2.5   not make any alteration or addition to the property nor without the Landlord's prior written consent do any redecoration or painting of the Property

   2.6   not do or omit to do anything on or at the Property which may be or become a nuisance or annoyance to the Landlord or owners or occupiers of adjoining or nearby premises, is illegal or immoral or which may in any way affect or prejudice the insurance of the Property and the items listed on the Inventory or cause an increase in the premium payable thereof

   2.7   not without the Landlord's prior consent allow or keep any pet or any kind of animal at the Property

   2.8   not use or occupy the Property in any way whatsoever other than as a private residence

   2.9   not assign, sublet, charge or part with or share possession occupation of the Property

   2.10 permit the Landlord or anyone authorised by the Landlord at reasonable hours in the daytime and upon reasonable prior notice (except in emergency) to enter and view the Property for any proper purpose (including the checking of compliance with the Tenant's obligations under this Agreement and during the last month of the Term the showing of the Property to prospective new tenants)

   2.11 pay interest at the rate of 4% above the Base Lending Rate for the time being of the Landlord's bankers upon any Rent or other money due from the Tenant under this agreement which is more than 3 days arrear in respect of the period from when it became due to the date of payment

3. The Landlord will:

   3.1   subject to the Tenant paying the rent and performing his/her obligations under this agreement allow the Tenant peaceably to hold and enjoy the Property during the term without lawful interruption from Landlord or any person rightfully claiming under or in trust for the Landlord

   3.2   insure the property and the items listed on the Inventory and use all reasonable efforts to arrange for any damage caused by an uninsured risk to be remedied without delay

   3.3   keep in repair the structure and exterior of the property (including drains, gutters and external pipes)

   3.4   keep in repair and proper working order the installations at the Property for the supply of water, gas and electricity and for sanitation (including basins, sinks, baths and sanitary conveniences)

3.5 keep in repair and proper working order the installation at the Property for space heating and heating water

But the Landlord will not be required to:

carry out works for which the tenant is responsible by virtue of his/her duty to use the property in a tenant-like manner

rebuild or reinstate the property in case of destruction or damage by fire or by tempest flood or other inevitable accident caused by or due to the Tenant failing to do and for which the insurers refuse to pay out or for which is not covered by the insurance policy effected by the Landlord

4. If at anytime

4.1 any part of the Rent is outstanding for 10 days after becoming due (whether formally demanded or not) and/or

4.2 there is any breach, non-observance or non-performance by the Tenant of any covenant or other term of this Agreement and/or

4.3 any interim receiver is appointed in respect of the Tenant's property or Bankruptcy Orders made in respect of the Tenant or the Tenant makes any arrangement with his creditors or suffers any distress or execution to be levied on his goods and/or

4.4 any of the grounds set out as Grounds 8 or Grounds 10–15 (inclusive) (which relate to breach of any obligation by a Tenant) contained in the Housing Act 1988 Schedule 2 apply

The Landlord may enter the property or any part of the property (and upon such re-entry this agreement shall absolutely determine but without prejudice to any claim which the Landlord may have against the Tenant in respect of any antecedent breach of any covenant or any term of this Agreement)

5. The Deposit has been paid by the Tenant and is held by the Landlord to secure compliance with the Tenant's obligations under this Agreement (without prejudice to the Landlord's other rights and remedies) and if, at any time during the Term, the Landlord is obliged to draw upon it to satisfy any outstanding breaches of such obligations then the Tenant shall forthwith make such additional payment as is necessary to restore the full amount of the Deposit held by the Landlord. As soon as reasonably practicable following termination of this Agreement the Landlord shall return to the Tenant the Deposit or the balance thereof after any deductions properly made

6. The Landlord hereby notifies the Tenant under Section 48 of the Landlord & Tenant Act 1987 that any notice (including notices in proceedings) should be served upon the Landlord at the address stated with the name of the Landlord overleaf

7. In the event of damage to or destruction of the Property by any of the risks insured against by the Landlord the Tenant shall be relieved from payment of the Rent to the extent that the Tenant's use and enjoyment of the Property is thereby prevented and from performance of its obligations as to the state and condition of the Property to the extent of and so long as there prevails such damage or destruction (except to the extent that the insurance is prejudiced by any act or default of the Tenant) the amount in case of dispute to be settled by arbitration

8. Where the context so admits:

8.1 The "Landlord" includes the persons for the time being entitled to the reversion expectant upon this Tenancy

8.2 The "Tenant" includes any persons deriving title under the Tenant

8.3 The "Property" includes any part or parts of the Property and all of the Landlord's fixtures and fittings at or upon the Property

8.4 The "Term" shall mean the period stated in the particulars overleaf or any shorter or longer period in the event of an earlier termination or an extension or holding over respectively

9. All references to the singular shall include the plural and vice versa and any obligations or liabilities of more than one person shall be joint and several and an obligation on the part of a party shall include an obligation not to allow or permit the breach of that obligation

PROS AND CONS OF SELF-MANAGING A PROPERTY

Pros	Cons

Pros

- You will receive all of the rental income minus any costs and your mortgage repayments, rather than handing over 10–17% to a letting agent.
- You will have more control over who rents your property. You can hand-pick your tenants and when you meet possible tenants you can use your own gut reactions as to whom you like and trust.
- You will be at viewings so you can get an idea of why people may not want to rent the property. You may be able to act on their comments and make it more lettable.
- There are a number of basic ready-made forms of the Assured Shorthold Tenancy agreement, which you can purchase from good stationers, to cut down your administration and legal costs.
- You can ensure that many repairs that need to be made to the property can be carried out by contractors whom you trust, at a price you negotiate and to a standard you are happy with.
- You inspect the property yourself so you can be aware of anything that needs to be dealt with before it becomes a crisis.
- Having an independent party conduct an inventory can be costly, but it is essential. At the end of the tenancy, you will need to replenish any broken or damaged items from the inventory using the liable tenant's deposit. For this reason it is wise to remove any items that are more valuable than the sum total of the deposit.
- Marketing your property can be costly and you will need to pay to advertise up-front, before receiving a rental income.
- You will have to show potential tenants your property at their convenience, interview them and trust your judgement. Their references may be the only concrete evidence you can draw upon in the vetting process. It is wise to make a few telephone calls to check their validity.

Cons

- You may find the private letting process slower than using an agent who has more resources at their disposal.
- You will need to tell the tenant to ensure all of the services are transferred into the their name.
- You will have to deal with repairs yourself and swiftly, as soon as things go wrong. This may mean cancelling a weekend away because a boiler has exploded and receiving calls at 10.00pm on a Sunday evening.
- You will be personally responsible for collecting rents and deposits, and handling disputes over when these sums are paid and how.
- You will need to organise for the property to be maintained – this means employing reliable cleaners to vacuum and dust any communal areas, and painters and decorators to freshen up the interior and exterior of the property when necessary.

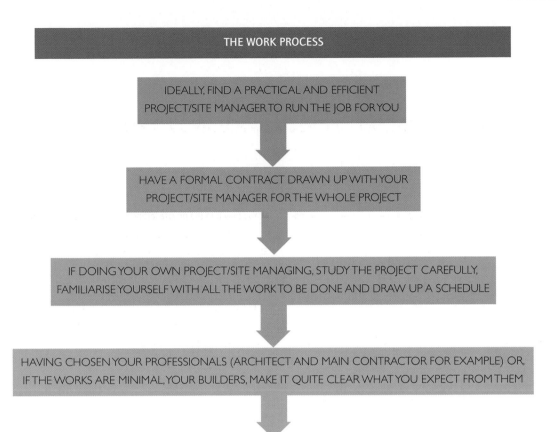

THE WORK PROCESS

IDEALLY, FIND A PRACTICAL AND EFFICIENT PROJECT/SITE MANAGER TO RUN THE JOB FOR YOU

HAVE A FORMAL CONTRACT DRAWN UP WITH YOUR PROJECT/SITE MANAGER FOR THE WHOLE PROJECT

IF DOING YOUR OWN PROJECT/SITE MANAGING, STUDY THE PROJECT CAREFULLY, FAMILIARISE YOURSELF WITH ALL THE WORK TO BE DONE AND DRAW UP A SCHEDULE

HAVING CHOSEN YOUR PROFESSIONALS (ARCHITECT AND MAIN CONTRACTOR FOR EXAMPLE) OR, IF THE WORKS ARE MINIMAL, YOUR BUILDERS, MAKE IT QUITE CLEAR WHAT YOU EXPECT FROM THEM

FIND YOUR BUILDER AND OTHER TRADESPEOPLE

ON THE JOB CHECKLIST

1 Make sure you have an efficient site and project manager. If you are going to do the managing yourself, make sure you understand what's involved and that you have the necessary skills and the time.

2 Draw up a schedule of works so that everything is done in the right order and on time. Keep a chart of the progress of the development.

3 Make sure that whoever is doing the work is experienced and skilled. For electrical, plumbing and gas work it is essential to use a professional.

4 Do your research and find out where to source good quality materials at a good price.

5 Always plan for contingencies. With something as complex as building work, something unforeseen is bound to come up at some stage.

6 When finishing the project, make the décor and furnishings simple. Remember this is not for yourself but for your market. Make the most of period features but don't over-furnish.

7 Don't forget the garden. This is one of the main attractions for many people so tackle it seriously, not just as an afterthought.

8 If you want to let the property, find out all you can about managing a property or emply a good managing agent. Check on the responsibilities you will have as a landlord.

RESOURCES
AND INDEX

RESOURCES

Association of Residential Letting Agents
www.arla.co.uk
0845 345 5752

Centre for Economics Business Research
www.cebr.com
020 7324 2850

Council for Registered Gas Installers (CORGI)
www.corgi-gas.com
01256 372200

Council of Mortgage Lenders
www.cml.org.uk

Department of Trade and Industry (DTI) – *a Guide to the Furniture and Furnishings (Fire) (Safety) Regulations*
www.dti.gov.uk
020 7215 5000

Design Council
www.design-council.org.uk/design
020 7420 5200

DfES School and College Performance Tables
www.dfes.gov.uk/performancetables
0845 933 3111

Electrical Contractors Association Ltd
www.eca.co.uk
020 7313 4800

English Heritage
www.english-heritage.org.uk
0870 333 1181

Environment Agency
www.environment-agency.gov.uk
0845 933 3111

Federation of Master Builders
www.fmb.org.uk
020 7242 7583

Gas Consumer's Council
020 7931 0977

Her Majesty's Land Registry
www.landreg.gov.uk
020 7917 8888

Homecheck: Property advice website
www.homecheck.co.uk

Homesale: Network property website
www.home-sale.co.uk

Hometrack: Prices and market trends
www.hometrack.co.uk

Independent Financial Advisors promotion
www.ifap.org.uk
0800 085 3250

Inland Revenue
www.inlandrevenue.gov.uk
0845 605 5999

Institute of Plumbing
www.plumbers.org.uk
01708 472791

Irish Law Society
www.lawsociety.ie
00 353 1671 0711

Irish Property News: Property information service
www.irishpropertynews.com
00 353 91 565622

The Leasehold Advisory Sevice: Leasehold valuation tribunals
www.lease-advice.org.uk
0845 345 1993

Micropal: Standard & Poors Investment Information
www.funds-sp.com

National Approved Letting Scheme
www.nalscheme.co.uk
01242 581712

National Association of Estate Agents (NAEA)
www.naea.co.uk
01926 496800

National Association of Plumbing Heating and Mechanical Services
www.aphc.co.uk
0800 542 6060

National Federation of Roofing Contractors
www.nfrc.co.uk
020 7435 0387

National House Building Council
www.nhbc.co.uk
01494 735363

National Land Information Services
www.nlis.org.uk
01279 451625

National Rail Enquiries
08457 484950

Office for Standards in Education
www.ofsted.gov.uk
020 7421 6800

Office of the Deputy Prime Minister
www.housing.odpm.gov.uk
020 7944 4400

Online Estate Agents
www.findaproperty.com

Painting and Decorating Federation
020 7608 5093

Rightmove: Property advice website
www.rightmove.co.uk

Royal Institute of Chartered Surveyors
www.nrics.org.uk

Scottish Law Information
www.scottishlaw.org.uk

Scottish Law Society
www.law.scot.org.uk
0131 226 7411

The Heating Ventilation Contractors' Association
www.hvca.org.uk
020 7313 4900

The Historic Buildings Bureau for Scotland
www.historic-scotland.gov.uk
0131 668 8668

The Law Society
www.lawsociety.org.uk
020 7242 1222

The Society of Financial Advisors
www.sofa.org.uk
020 8989 8464

The Victorian Society
www.victorian-society.org.uk
020 8994 1019

Trading Standards Office
www.tradingstandards.gov.uk

Up My Street: Local information website
www.upmystreet.com

INDEX